TIBET PAST AND PRESENT

༄༅། །གངས་རྒྱ་བའི་སྐྱེབས་གནས་ཤིང་ ཀུན་མཁྱེན་རྗེ་འཇང་དཔལ་སྤྲུལ་བཞུགས་ དག་པར་བཞུགས་སོ་ལྷུན་གྲུབ་གནས་མཆོག་ཏུ།།

Tibet Past and Present

Sir Charles Bell

MOTILAL BANARSIDASS PUBLISHERS
PRIVATE LIMITED • DELHI

First Indian Edition: Delhi, 1992
Reprint: Delhi, 1996, 2000

ISBN: 81-208-1048-1

Also available at:

MOTILAL BANARSIDASS

236, 9th Main III Block, Jayanagar, Bangalore 560 011
41 U.A. Bungalow Road, Jawahar Nagar, Delhi 110 007
8 Mahalaxmi Chamber, Warden Road, Mumbai 400 026
120 Royapettah High Road, Mylapore, Chennai 600 004
Sanas Plaza, 1302 Baji Rao Road, Pune 411 002
8 Camac Street, Calcutta 700 017
Ashok Rajpath, Patna 800 004
Chowk, Varanasi 221 001

Printed in India
BY JAINENDRA PRAKASH JAIN AT SHRI JAINENDRA PRESS,
A-45 NARAINA, PHASE-I, NEW DELHI 110 028
AND PUBLISHED BY NARENDRA PRAKASH JAIN FOR
MOTILAL BANARSIDASS PUBLISHERS PRIVATE LIMITED,
BUNGALOW ROAD, DELHI 110 007

DEDICATED BY PERMISSION

TO

HIS HOLINESS THE DALAI LAMA

IN MEMORY OF

A LONG FRIENDSHIP

Author in diplomatic uniform

Author in Tibetan mask of silk and other equipment
for use in the November gales

PREFACE

MY obligations to those to whom this book is indebted have in part been made plain in the text. I would, however, desire to mention individually His Holiness the Dalai Lama —who has accepted the dedication of the work—the past and present Prime Ministers of Tibet, the late Achuk Tsering, a very wise Sikkimese gentleman, and, with especial emphasis, my old friend Pa-lhe-se. But, in addition to these, my debt is great to my friends in all classes—Cabinet Ministers and peasants ; merchants, herdsmen, and mule-teers ; priests and laymen.

The illustrations are in the main from my own photo-graphs. A few have kindly been given by Messrs. Johnston and Hoffmann, Lt.-Col. Kennedy, Mr. Macdonald, Mr. Martin, and Mr. Rosemeyer ; and by Miss Fernie the colour-plate that represents strolling Tibetan players. The colouring of the frontispiece—a photograph of the Dalai Lama which I took in 1910—I owe to the kindness of Gyal-se Ku-sho of Ta-ring, Tibetan squire and artist, elder brother of the Ruler of Sikkim.

The map of Tibet is adapted from the one prepared by the Indian Survey Department. I have added a few places omitted from the latter. All places mentioned in the text, except those whose positions are described in it, will be found in the maps.

NOTE

The Tibetan words used in this book should be pronounced as in English, subject to the following limitations and exceptions :

a as the English *u* in *rub*. But the first *a* in *lama* is long.

e when ending a word or syllable as *é* in French ; e. g. *Rim-po-che, Dre-pung*. Otherwise as in English ; e. g. *Den-sa*.

ö as *eu* in French *peu*.

u as *oo* in *root*.

ü as *u* in French *sur*.

ai as *eye*.

ny as the initial sound in *nuisance*.

ng and *ts* as in English. They are frequently used in Tibetan to begin words. Say *coming in*, eliminating the first four letters *comi*. Similarly, *weights*, eliminating *weigh*.

Hyphens have been freely inserted throughout the book to show where syllables end.

Apart from names I have used Tibetan terms as sparingly as possible. A few explanations will therefore suffice.

Amban denotes the high Chinese official residing in Lhasa. Sometimes also one of similar rank, controlling, or partially controlling, dependent tribes, e. g. the Amban at Sining.

Dzong. A fort, the head-quarters of a Tibetan district. In it reside the *Dzong-pön* or *Dzong-pöns* with their staff.

Dzong-pön, i. e. ' Governor of Fort '. The Tibetan official in charge of a district. In some districts one holds sole charge ; in others two exercise joint control.

Kung. A hereditary title given to the father, or to one brother, of each Dalai Lama, corresponding somewhat to the title of *Duke* in England.

Ku-sho. Honorific form of address applied to the upper classes, especially to officials. Joined to *Cham*—or the higher form *Lha-cham*—it is applied to ladies also.

La = a mountain pass.

Tso or *Nor* = lake. *Tso* is the Tibetan, *Nor* the Mongolian word.

CONTENTS

CONTENTS

APPENDIXES

[1] By the kind permission of John Lane, The Bodley Head.

LIST OF ILLUSTRATIONS

MAPS

Mt. Kinchinjanga in Sikkim

Mt. Chomolhari at the head of the Chumbi Valley

I

INTRODUCTORY

TIBET has ever fascinated the imagination of mankind. High as the country is raised above the ordinary dwelling lands of the human race, higher still are the mountain masses that fence it off from neighbouring nations. To the natural difficulties of entering Tibet and of travelling in its bleak uplands has been added the spirit of seclusion which has moved its Government to keep foreigners out of their sacred Buddhist land.

Standing thus alone, Tibet differs greatly from her neighbours. She differs not only in her physical features, in her flora and her fauna, but also in her Government and her people, in the language, folk-lore, religious customs, recreations, and all that goes to make up the life of a nation. She has lived in the main a life of her own to an extent hardly equalled in any other part of the earth. Till recent years we have known but a fragment of what was happening in this land, seven times the size of Great Britain.

The inaccessibility of Tibet has appealed alike to the explorer, who has found in it a unique opportunity for exploration, and to the Hindu devotee, who finds holy places at the sources of the Indus, Sutlej, Brahmaputra, and other great rivers that rise in Tibet and flow through India. And most of all does it appeal to Buddhist devotees, one-third of the human race, many of whom find their Holy of Holies in some Tibetan shrine. Others are interested in the system of priestly government, which has no counterpart elsewhere in these materialistic days, and which is controlled by the mysterious personality of the Dalai Lama. To others again has come a feeling of sympathy for this isolated country struggling for freedom against the domination of China.

To us of the British race a deep political interest is added, for Tibet stretches for two thousand miles along the northern frontier of India, twice as far as any other border country.

And this frontier, kept peaceful hitherto by a variety of causes, seems certain to demand more attention as time goes on, for those causes are weakening and new conditions are emerging.

In 1900 a succession of illnesses necessitated my transfer from the plains of India—where I had performed the administrative duties that fall to the lot of the Indian Civil Service—to Darjeeling and Kalimpong in the eastern Himalaya. Here I spent three years, devoting in the main such little leisure as I had to the study of the Tibetan language, customs, and ideas.

From 1901 to 1903 I made a land settlement of the Kalimpong district. At this settlement lands were measured and classified, rates of rent were fixed, disputes settled, grazing grounds and fuel reserves arranged, agricultural customs inquired into ; in fine, all the arrangements which belong to a land settlement in India were made. I thus gained a close acquaintance with the lives of the hill people of Kalimpong, who are not Indian, but belong to the same races as those of Nepal, Sikkim, Bhutan, and the nearer portions of Tibet. From March to May 1904, during the British Expedition to Tibet, I was put in charge of a small pioneer party, our duty being to find a route suitable for a railway from India to Tibet. I was fortunate enough to be able to push through Bhutan to Tibet in spite of Bhutanese opposition.

From May to October 1904 the administration of Sikkim was placed in my charge during Mr. Claude White's absence with the Younghusband Expedition in Tibet. From September 1904 to November 1905 I was in charge of the Chumbi Valley, a portion of Tibet. From September 1906 to January 1907 I acted, during Mr. White's absence on leave, as Political Officer in charge of Sikkim and of the political relations of our Government in Tibet and Bhutan. And after Mr. White's departure to England I held the post of Political Officer as above during the ten years 1908–1918.

One of the duties that fell to my lot during these ten years was to suggest a new treaty with Bhutan, and, when my

The British Residency at Gangtok, the capital of Sikkim

Mansion of the Pa-lha family at Dong-tse in southern Tibet

The Potala (the Dalai Lama's Palace at Lhasa)

From the south, with a pillar of record (see App. II) in the middle distance

proposals had been accepted by the British Government, to carry through the necessary negotiations at the Bhutanese capital. In these I was fortunately successful. The effect was to place the foreign relations of this State, about two and a half times the size of Wales, under the British Government. This treaty, concluded in February 1910, brought Bhutan within the British Empire, and effectively barred Chinese penetration into India over two hundred and fifty miles of the frontier.

From 1910 to 1912 I saw a great deal of the Dalai Lama, his Ministers and other officers when these fled to Darjeeling, and had during this period frequent private conversations with His Holiness. 1913-14 found me in Simla and Delhi attending the Conference between Great Britain, China, and Tibet, called to settle the political position of Tibet. Here again the insight gained at first-hand from the Prime Minister of Tibet and other leading Tibetans into the affairs of this large but little-known country was a valuable aid to my work.

In April 1918 I took leave, and retired eleven months later to a Tibetan environment at Darjeeling, where I completed the second edition of a Tibetan Grammar and Tibetan Dictionary, in the hope of rendering the study of the spoken language somewhat more easy for others than I myself had found it. The present work was also taken in hand, to be completed in England. But shortly before I left India, the Government asked me to return to duty for a fresh spell. I returned accordingly in January 1920. Nine months later, in response to repeated invitations from the Dalai Lama and his Government, I was sent in charge of a diplomatic mission to Lhasa, where I remained for nearly a year.

This was to me the most interesting of all my experiences. It was the first occasion on which a British diplomatic Mission —or a Mission from any foreign country—had been invited to Lhasa, and indeed one may say the first occasion on which such a Mission had visited Lhasa at all. Excepting only the few Italian missionaries who stayed in Lhasa some two hundred years ago, and have left but scanty records, no other white man has been so long in the Forbidden City. And, what was even more fortunate for me, where my predecessors had pushed their way into a city and country always aloof and usually hostile, I went as the invited guest and established friend of the Dalai Lama and his Government. All doors were thrown open to me, and conversation with my Tibetan friends, old and new, high and low, was free and unrestrained in this the centre of Tibetan life. My conversations with the Dalai Lama were resumed under auspices happier than those which attended the exile of His Holiness in India.

During my nineteen years in these fascinating lands, two complete winters, and usually some months of each summer, were spent in Tibet. A few tours were made in Bhutan, and the winters were generally spent in Sikkim.

I have set down these biographical details in the hope that they may justify this attempt of mine to write about the history and politics of this land that is so little known. We live in a democratic age. The British electorate and those who lead them have to decide questions of foreign policy. It seems therefore essential that they should have at their disposal—whether to accept or to reject—the facts and opinions put forward by those who have been long connected with foreign relationships.

It would be impossible to live, as I have lived, for many years in Tibet, Bhutan, and Sikkim in friendly relationship with the Dalai Lama and members of the Tibetan Government, with the Tashi Lama and his entourage, with the Rulers and Officers of Sikkim and Bhutan, and with many other Tibetans, Bhutanese, and Sikkimese, without feeling deep interest in and sympathy with them and their countries. I am not versed in the art of writing books, but if, nevertheless, I can pass on a little of this interest and sympathy to my readers, I shall feel that I have not written in vain.

II

BOUNDARIES, AREA, POPULATION

WHAT is Tibet ? Do we mean the lands controlled by the Tibetan Government and the Tibetan tribal authorities, or the lands inhabited by people of Tibetan race? Outlying parts of these vast plains and mountains have been brought under the direct control of China to the east and of the British-Indian Government to the south. Thus political Tibet is considerably smaller than its ethnographic counterpart. While attempting to define the former, let us not neglect the latter, for national sentiment in Tibet, so long in abeyance, is now a growing force. It may be that the Mongol countries at present linked up with the British Government in India may draw back into closer relationship with Tibet or China. The movement for separation is strong in Burma ; it is not unknown in the Himalayan district of Darjeeling. There are indications that it may grow in Bhutan, Sikkim, and those other Himalayan territories which are peopled by men of the Mongol races.

The country under Tibetan rule extends approximately from the 78th to the 103rd degree of east longitude and from the 27th to the 37th degree of north latitude. The frontiers, especially on the north and east, are often ill defined, for the country is large and difficult of access ; the population is sparse, and Governmental control in Tibet and China is loose and shifting.

Again, even in the more settled portions of their country, Tibetans do not necessarily take mountain ranges or rivers as their boundaries. When on a tour of exploration through Bhutan to Tibet in 1904, I found that the boundary between these two countries at the trijunction of Tibet, Bhutan, and Sikkim was what the Tibetans called an ' upland-tree lowland-tree ' [1] boundary. In other words, the pine forests belonged to Tibet and the bamboo forests to Bhutan, which

[1] *Ya-shing Mön-shing* in Tibetan.

means in effect a contour of about 11,500 ft. above sea-level.
A good, practical boundary no doubt, in that it serves the
agricultural and general needs of both countries, for the
Tibetans need the higher lands for grazing their yaks and
upland sheep, while the Bhutanese make great use of the
bamboo. But it is a boundary not easily recognized by
Western people, who look for frontiers along high mountain
ranges, which are easily defended and can be delineated on
maps. And the same type of boundary line may well
account in part for the former Tibetan claim to north Sikkim,
an early source of dispute between Great Britain and Tibet ;
and may possibly have influenced the Tibetans in their claim
to Lingtu which led to the Sikkim Expedition of 1888.

In the north-west the frontier between Tibet and Sinkiang,
or Chinese (Eastern) Turkestan, begins on the Kuenlun
range somewhere north of Lake Lighten, in about 35° 30′
north latitude and 80° 30′ east longitude, and thence
approximately follows the watershed eastward to a point
about 90° 30′ east, where it leaves the Kuenlun range and
strikes in an irregular line northward, west of the Tsai-dam
basin, till it reaches the watershed of the Altyn-tagh. This
it again follows eastward through the intricacies of the
Nan-shan mountains to about 101° east, where it strikes
south, passing just west of Donkyr (Tangar), between Koko-
nor lake and Sining. From somewhere near the northern-
most point of the frontier (94° 30′ east), eastwards the
Koko-nor district marches no longer with Turkestan but
with Kansu, though here again the line of demarcation is
very ill defined. The Tsai-dam and Koko-nor areas are in
dispute between Tibet and China.

From the neighbourhood of Donkyr the boundary runs
generally in a southern or south-eastern direction to near
the 28th parallel, separating Tibet successively from Kansu,
Szechuan, and Yunnan. Der-ge, Cham-do, Tra-ya, and
Mang-kam are under complete Tibetan control ; Am-do,
Go-lok, Nya-rong, Ba-tang, and Li-tang are in dispute.

Turning westward and crossing the Salween river at a
point about 28° 20′ north, the southern boundary, between

The ' Tiger's Lair ' Monastery

(Paro Ta-tsang) in Bhutan

Frozen waterfall at Do-ta in the Chumbi Valley

Tibet and Burma, is at first hardly more clearly defined.[1] Farther west the borders of Tibet are determined by those of Assam as far as where the Dihang or Brahmaputra breaks through the mountains from the north. After this the frontier follows in a general manner the Himalaya range. Here Assam is bounded on the north by a more or less unexplored district inhabited by wild tribes of Mishmis, Abors, &c., which appear to be as free of Tibetan as of British control. Westwards again is Bhutan, lying between the Indian plain and the Himalayan divide, along which the Tibetan frontier here for the most part runs, to stretch south once more down the Chumbi valley between Bhutan and Sikkim. The Sikkim frontier with Tibet is the water-parting of the Teesta, the main river of Sikkim. Farther west the boundary between Tibet and Nepal is almost wholly unexplored; it appears to run mainly along the principal ridge of the Himalayan range, but the water-shed here lies in general farther to the north, and Tibet is known to maintain posts some distance down the southern valleys, particularly in the eastern portion.

The western frontier may be said to begin where the Kumaon district is reached beyond Nepal. Here, in Almora and Garhwal, the boundary continues to follow in general the main divide in a north-westerly direction along the Zaskar ridge. On reaching the Hill States of Tehri and Bashahr it takes a more northerly course, crosses the Sutlej at Shipki, and continues in an irregular northern direction, leaving Dankar in the Spiti district of the Panjab, Karak in Tibet, and Hanle in Kashmir. The frontier crosses the Indus about 25 miles below Demchok (33° north), and cuts the Pangong chain of lakes about midway (79° east), and skirts the basins of the western rivers in a north-easterly direction to the borders of Turkestan.[2]

[1] The boundary from the Isu-Razi Pass to Bhutan was recorded in a map and an exchange of notes between the British and Tibetan plenipotentiaries at Simla, March 24 and 25, 1914.

[2] The above boundaries are taken, in the main, from the Handbook on Tibet prepared a few years ago under the direction of the Historical Section of the Foreign Office.

Sikkim claims to have possessed the Chumbi Valley till the Chinese invasion of Nepal in 1792. But little Sikkim has lost land on all sides, for, as the State Chronicle sadly records, it has been shorn by

> Powerful hordes of elephants from the south,
> Active hordes of monkeys from the west,
> Cunning hordes of foxes from the north.

Whether the causes were good or bad, there is no doubt that the British elephant, the Gurkha monkey, and the Tibetan fox have devoured large slices of Sikkim.

It is noteworthy that Tibet is entirely surrounded by the lands of the British and Chinese Commonwealths. To Britain and China falls naturally the privilege of helping the Tibetan people along the path of progress and self-realization.

Ladakh, a province in the north-east of Kashmir, and the State of Bhutan in the eastern Himalaya are also Tibetan from the ethnographic standpoint. So too the State of Sikkim, originally under Tibetan rule, though three-fourths of its inhabitants are now Nepalese, for its Ruler and most of its leading men are still Tibetan. Along the northern border of Nepal and westwards along the Indo-Tibetan frontier to Kashmir we find many Tibetan settlements on the Indian side, but no Indian settlements on the Tibetan side of the frontier. The British district of Darjeeling was originally in Sikkim and Bhutan, and therefore ethnographically a part of Tibet, but many years of British administration have changed it so completely that it is now inhabited mainly by Nepalese and is a network of British and Indian interests.

The area of ethnographic Tibet is probably between seven and eight hundred thousand square miles, an area seven times the size of England, Scotland, and Ireland combined, and sufficient to cover India, excluding Burma and the territories of the Ruling Princes. The population may be estimated at four or five millions, of whom the majority live in the districts between Lhasa and the Chinese border.

The western half of Tibet supports a population of only about one human being per square mile, for even the plains and valleys lie mostly over 15,000 ft. above sea-level, too high for crops to ripen. The general slope of the country is from west to east. The south-eastern districts descend in places to below 5,000 ft., and here grow not only barley, wheat, and peas, the staple crops of central Tibet, but maize, and occasionally even rice. So it is in eastern and south-eastern Tibet that the population is chiefly found.

The lofty altitude of Tibet and its great size have formed the best possible barrier to India on the north. They have at the same time prevented us from learning much of Tibetan history in days gone by. Very few foreign travellers penetrated the country until comparatively recent years, when the European instinct for exploration asserted itself. The devastating hordes of Mongol conquest, that poured through Asia and reduced the Russian Tsar and half Europe to vassalage, never crossed Tibet, though it lay at their doors and they themselves were denizens of à cold climate. Their robust vigour did indeed enable them successfully to invade India and to impose their will on the softer races of that country, but they came to India only after passing round Tibet through the easier mountains of Afghanistan. Hardly ever have invading forces crossed the vast northern plains of Tibet, where even the hardy Tibetan with difficulty finds the means of subsistence. The Chinese pilgrims who have furnished us with such valuable side-lights on Indian history in the fifth and seventh centuries of our era avoided Tibet, winding round through Chinese Turkestan and the mountain ranges to the north-west of India.

III

PHYSICAL DIVISIONS

TIBET falls naturally into three great physical divisions. Its northern face is covered by the Chang Tang, the ' Northern Plains ', a tangled mass of plains and valleys, lying at an elevation of more than sixteen thousand feet above sea-level, rising several thousand feet higher in its mountain peaks and ridges. Bounded on the north by the Kuen Lun range and the Mongolian steppes of Tsaidam, the Chang Tang falls away in the south to the Tsang-Po, the great river of southern Tibet. The chief rivers rising from its northern limits are the Kiria, which breaks through the Kuen Lun to the north-west, flows past Polu and empties itself into the Takla Makan desert. Three hundred miles further east the Cherchen Daria, rising from the Arka Tagh, flows past Cherchen and loses itself in the marshes of Lob Nor.

Here and there in groups, here and there at longer intervals, the Chang Tang is studded with lakes which are fed by the waters from surrounding mountains and valleys, but have no outlets. The great majority of the streams in the Chang Tang are lost in these lakes, and never find their way to the sea. But their utility is great, for they give fresh water to a country where the lakes are mostly salt. There are no trees, for it is too cold and too high ; the grass, though scanty, is sufficient to maintain large numbers of wild yaks, wild asses, wild sheep, wild goats, antelopes, wolves, and other animals. Here and there herds of yaks and flocks of sheep are tended by the nomads, whose daily allowance of grain is reduced to a quarter of the normal amount, for the barley has to be brought laboriously over the mountains from southern Tibet. Being ground roughly by hand, instead of by water-power, which is plentiful in the settled lands of the south, the barley flour is of poor quality. Radishes are grown, and potatoes on the southern face of the tableland. No grain grows in this country, not even the stunted barley, that is found at an elevation of fifteen thousand feet on the

Herdsman from northern Tibet and his wife

Southern Tibet. Ploughing with yaks at Tse-chen near Gyantse

Southern Tibet. Reaping barley in the Chumbi Valley

plains of southern Tibet. The southern and western ranges of the great plateau form the water-parting of India ; to the east and north of this the rivers of Tibet find their way through Burma Siam, China proper, Mongolia, and Chinese Turkestan.

Fifteen hundred miles from east to west, four or five hundred from north to south, sixteen thousand feet above the sea and almost uninhabited, this inhospitable tableland is the true barrier of India to the north.

The second natural division comprises the valleys of the Indus and Sutlej to the west, and the valley of the Tsang-po, the Brahmaputra of India, to the south and south-east. These three large rivers rise in the same region near the sacred Manasarowar lake. The two former rise on the slopes of the sacred mountain, known to Indians as Kailas, the Paradise of Siva in Sanskrit literature. They cut north-west and then south through the Punjab to the Indian Ocean.

The Tsang-po runs placidly from west to east through the heart of southern Tibet.[1]

The word ' Tsang-po ' in the Tibetan language means the ' Purifier ', and is applied to any large river. The Tibetans have different names for this river on different parts of its course. It is interesting to note that the tributaries as a rule flow in a direction contrary to that of the main river, thus raising the presumption that in earlier times the Tsang-po flowed from east to west. It is very noticeable how these lesser streams now tend to curve backwards towards the course of the Tsang-po.

[1] Tibetan ideas on the geography of the rivers that issue from this mountain, known to themselves as Kang Rim-po-ché, ' The Precious Snow ', are somewhat fanciful. They believe that four great rivers rise here, namely :

From the mouth of a horse, flowing through Tibet, the land of horses:

From the mouth of an elephant, flowing through Nepal, the land of elephants:

From the mouth of a lion, flowing through Ladakh, where men have the strength of lions :

From the mouth of a peacock, flowing through China, the land of beautiful women.

The Tibetan pony is certainly one of the characteristics of the country. Princes and peasants, men and women, all ride ; and children too, from a very early age. And with the mule, the donkey, and the yak, the pony, agile and hardy beyond those of most countries, transports their merchandise and household goods across the plateaux, and up the rough valleys and high passes that connect them.

Down long stretches of the great river go the boats of the country, even during the floods of the rainy season. From Lhatse, near the 88th meridian, to one day's journey below Tse-tang, near the 92nd, a distance of some four hundred miles down its winding course, we have the unique spectacle of a navigable river flowing at more than 12,000 feet above the level of the sea.

The boats, or coracles, are made from the hides of yaks and other cattle, stretched on a framework of withes. These latter are sometimes of willow, but preferably sliced from the tougher wood of the thorny scrub, known in Lhasa as *la*, which grows in profusion along the river banks in the uplands of central Tibet. Often do we see the Tibetan boatman, carrying his coracle ten or twelve miles a day upstream, accompanied by a solitary sheep, which carries his food and other necessaries.

Fragile as they seem for the task before them, and, when empty, drawing only a few inches of water, it is, nevertheless, remarkable what these coracles will carry. At Shi-ga-tse I have seen a large family in its little ' hide-boat '—as the Tibetans call them—after their donkey has clambered in beside them, paddle across the broad river to its northern bank. And down the river that flows by Lhasa—a river as broad as the Thames and twice as long—one may see daily a succession of these coracles carrying not only loads of passengers and light goods, but long, heavy logs of poplar and walnut.

On the banks of the Tsang-po and on the banks of its tributaries lie Lhasa and Shigatse, the two chief towns in Tibet, and Gyantse, also among the largest. Prosperous monasteries minister, more than amply, to the religious needs of the countryside. And hither converge trade routes from Turkestan, Siberia, Mongolia, China, and India. This country is Tibet proper, the seat of the Dalai Lama and his Government. It contains the districts most closely controlled by the Government. The people know it as *Pö* (pronounced like the French word *peu*) in contradistinction to the Chang Tang on the north and the districts of Kham, which embrace what we call eastern Tibet.

Lady travelling with two servants

Trader and his wife on a journey

The word ' Tibet ' is not used by the people themselves. It is possible that it was a corruption of the Tibetan words *Tö Pö* (Upper Tibet) and was first applied to the elevated regions of western Tibet. The earliest mention of the word ' Tibet' is in the Arab Istakhri's works (about 590 A. D.) where it is written ' Tobbat '.[1]

The third great division of Tibet comprises the mountains and valleys of eastern Tibet between the Chang Tang and the frontier of China. On the eastern slopes of these northern plains rise the great rivers of China, Siam, and Burma. The Hwang Ho and the Yangtse flow eastward through China, the Mekong and Salween south through Siam and Burma respectively. In south-eastern Tibet we find the Yangtse, the Mekong, and the Salween, three of the largest rivers in Asia, flowing in deep, parallel troughs close to each other. The Mekong is only twenty-eight miles from the Yangtse on one side, and even less from the Salween on the other.

The Irawadi rises in the tribal territory in the north of Burma between China and the north-eastern corner of Assam.

This third division of Tibet contains many lesser districts and States, some of which acknowledge the Government at Lhasa, while others fall easily under Chinese control, though all respond, in greater or lesser degree, to the religious influence of the Dalai Lama and the Lhasa priesthood. Some States, like Der-gé, are comparatively advanced in civilization ; others live in large measure by highway robbery and brigandage. Others again live chiefly by brigandage during part of the year, and bring salt for sale to southern Tibet at other times ; an arrangement readily tolerated by the Tibetan Government, which is unable to exercise a complete control over its wide and difficult dominion.

Eastern Tibet at all events is a country with a future. The lands on the whole lie at more reasonable elevations. Agriculture is possible on a large scale. Grazing is abundant, and there are extensive forests. Nor is this all. For its mineral wealth—gold, silver, copper, iron, and lead— hitherto almost untouched, may well prove of great value when developed on modern lines.

[1] Rockhill's *Ethnology of Tibet*, p. 669.

It may be noted that the limit of perpetual snow, which is about 17,000 feet in the Sikkim Himalaya, is about 20,000 in central Tibet. This large difference is mainly due to the fact that the southern slopes are exposed to damp winds from the Indian Ocean, which drop much of their moisture before crossing the range. Tibet being exceptionally dry, its snow-line is higher than those of mountains situated in the same latitudes but in other continents. In eastern Tibet the line falls considerably, ranging between 15,000 and 16,000 feet.

The Tibetans do not usually give names to their mountain peaks, unless these are objects of especial worship. Chomolhari, ' The Mountain of The Goddess ', which dominates the plains round Tuna and Phari for fifty miles, is devoutly worshipped, and so are many others. But it does not seem to have been considered worth while to name those peaks of which no use is made. Passes always receive names, for they are used and therefore discussed. The different grazing grounds on mountain slopes are fully named, and the rights in them are zealously safeguarded. When winter covers the plain with a mantle of snow, the Tibetan drives his yaks and sheep up the mountain slopes, which are cleared of snow, at any rate in patches, by the violence of the winds. Here is found the scanty stunted grass, which is far more nutritious than the long, lush growth of the plains and valleys below.

It seems necessary to note that the Tibetan names on our maps are often wofully incorrect, perhaps because the surveyors who recorded them knew Tibetan but imperfectly. Thus Gye-mo Chen, ' The Great Queen ', at the tri-junction point of Tibet, Bhutan, and Sikkim, is recorded as Gipmochi. Cho-mo Yum-mo, ' The Mother of the Goddess ', a lofty snow mountain in the north of Sikkim, figures on our maps as Chumiumo. It is to be hoped that somebody who has the necessary time and experience may correct the map names. But before this is done, an international system of spelling should, if possible, be agreed upon. Confusion results if we spell on one system, while the French, the Russian, and other nationalities have different systems of their own.

IV

LAKES, CLIMATE, TRADE ROUTES

THE rivers of Tibet have been described in the paragraphs above that relate to the three physical divisions of the country. But a little must be said about the lakes, which are studded about the country in great numbers, especially in the Chang Tang and southern Tibet. These lakes have probably been formed in one of the three following ways :

(a) by the damming of a main valley by the material brought down by its tributaries ;

(b) by the rise of a river bed at a rate greater than the rate of erosion of the river, by which a barrier is formed and eventually a dam accumulates across the valley ;

(c) by the filling of a rock-basin previously scooped out by a glacier.[1]

The greater part of the Chang Tang forms a great basin in which rivers flow and empty themselves into lakes, but never reach the sea.

The largest Tibetan lake is that of Koko Nor, to the north-east of the Tibetan plateau and outside the area of the basin. It has an area of 1,630 square miles. The Tengri Nor in the heart of Tibet is about 1,000 square miles in area, and many others are of more than 100 square miles.

These lakes were in past ages much larger than they are now. We can still see salt-covered flats and old beaches on the hill-sides, sometimes several hundred feet higher than the present levels. The mountains of the Himalaya have risen within recent geological ages. They have thus intercepted more and more the rain-currents from India and made Tibet drier and drier. Evaporation from the lakes has increased ; their areas have shrunk and their waters become more saline.

The Ne-sar monastery in the broad valley of the Nyang River, 13,000 feet above the sea, about thirty miles from

[1] *A Sketch of the Geography and Geology of the Himalaya Mountains and Tibet*, by Burrard and Hayden, p. 203.

Shigatse, is reputed to be over 1,200 years old, and is certainly one of the very oldest monasteries in Tibet, as is evidenced by its tiled roof as well as by the reference to it in Tibetan histories. Though now the walls are of sun-dried brick, it was at first built of cypress wood. Even now, the original pillars of cypress are standing, black with age. The priests told me that in the old days there were many cypress trees in Tibet, for the climate was then more moist and more snow used to fall. This tradition is at any rate worthy of mention. Tibetans in general believe that there were more trees and fuller crops in former ages, though, characteristically, they attribute those advantages to greater kindliness and truthfulness among the men and women of olden times.

The suddenness and violence with which storms sweep across the Tibetan lakes have been graphically described by Dr. Sven Hedin after his adventurous journeys through the Chang Tang. In these wide, empty spaces, there is nothing to break their force.

It may well be imagined that Tibet, the highest country in the world, possesses an exceptionally severe climate. And the severity is still further increased by the winds, which blow violently during the greater part of the year, and must be felt to be appreciated. Nothing but good skin and fur keeps them out, and travellers in Tibet in autumn and winter frequently find it advisable to commence marches in the keen frosts of sunrise, in order to escape as far as possible the biting winds of midday and early afternoon.

In the lower lands, those below 12,000 feet, such as the Chumbi Valley, the climate is agreeable and, in spite of the cold, is healthy, for it is dry, bracing, and free from most of the diseases which infest the plains of India. Here Europeans can live and thrive, though a residence of many years is usually found to try the heart, nerves, and digestion, the last-named suffering from the difficulty of cooking food at an altitude at which the boiling-point of water is greatly lowered. One of my young Tibetan friends, returning to Tibet after three or four years in England, expressed to me his appreciation of our English winters, but found the English summers too relaxing.

But in Tibet some Tibetan ladies find the winters trying. ' During winter ', a Tibetan nobleman informed me, ' our ladies do not leave their houses much. They exchange visits with their friends close by, but do not usually go far. They have to think of their complexions, which will turn blue if they go out in the winter winds.'

And this I found to be the case during my year in Lhasa. When going out to visit friends and relatives during the winter—and they are very fond of visits and entertainments —their faces and gorgeous head-dresses are muffled up with meticulous care. And still more is this so, when riding out to visit their estates. To these precautions are due the well-preserved complexions of so many of the ladies of the Tibetan aristocracy.

But when they attend the ceremonies and shows in which all delight, these wrappings are discarded. It matters not that the hour is dawn on an ice-bound winter morning, and that the wind from the north is sweeping over the Lhasa plain. Clad as warmly as may be, each vies with the other in the display of silks, jewellery, and precious stones. Human nature is human nature still.

Each time that one crossed the main axis of the Himalaya into Tibet, one could not fail to be struck by the contrast between the deep, rocky gorges and the moisture-laden air in Sikkim and Bhutan on the one hand ; and the vast plains, the broad valleys, the yellow, round-topped mountains and the dryness of Tibet on the other. Clear as is the air of Sikkim, that of Tibet is far clearer. We travel on our sturdy Tibetan ponies, now cantering, now walking, and now at the favourite Tibetan amble, for mile after mile, but our destination seems to draw but little nearer, as the wind grows stronger and the clouds roll up for the afternoon storm. What seemed four or five miles distant is really fifteen. In 1904, when the British Expedition to Tibet was encamped on the plain of Phari, one of our mountain guns—so it was said —made practice for the edification of the Ruler of Bhutan,

But the distance estimated at a mile proving to be a mile and three-quarters, His Highness had to rely on his well-known tact and courtesy in framing his appreciation of the marvel displayed to him.

Sikkim and Darjeeling have annual rainfalls varying, according to locality, from about eighty to two hundred and fifty inches, but once across the head of the Phari plain, the rainfall averages only eight inches in the year. Four and a half inches was, I think, the lowest and twelve inches the highest annual rainfall recorded at Gyantse during ten or twelve years of observation. The year's fall of twelve inches was enough to cause considerable flood-damage. As one penetrates farther into central Tibet, the rainfall tends to increase. At Lhasa it averages about fourteen inches yearly. Sixty miles north of the capital, judging by the vegetation, it is again slightly heavier, perhaps eighteen to twenty inches.

The Tibetans are keen traders, and we therefore find that Tibet is well supplied with trade-routes, which run to India on the south, to China on the east, and to Mongolia on the north.

From Srinagar, the capital of Kashmir, a route runs to Leh, the capital of Ladakh, and thence through southern Tibet to Shigatse and Lhasa. From Lhasa a much-used route goes to Chamdo. Here it bifurcates. The southern road passes via Batang and Litang to Tachienlu; the northern arrives at the same destination via Kanze and Dango. Tachienlu, the ethnographical boundary between China and Tibet, is the chief entrepôt of trade between the two countries. The wool from the Tibetan sheep is exchanged for the teas of China, which find their way along the rough mountain tracks across the whole length of Tibet, and are found even in the villages of Ladakh. Tibetans aver that the Chinese tea, mixed according to their custom with butter and soda, is more nutritious than the Indian, and suits their constitutions better.

From Lhasa another great trade-route strikes north, past Nag-chu-ka across the Chang Tang to Urga, the capital of Mongolia, and thus connects with the plains of Siberia.

'The clouds roll up for the afternoon storm' (p. 17)

Mules carrying wool in the Chumbi Valley

Cattle with wool for export to India

Once in summer, and again in winter, the caravans assemble near the great lake of Koko Nor, the border-land of Tibet, Mongolia, and China. Thus united for mutual protection against robber bands, the merchants and pilgrims cross north-eastern Tibet and the northern plains, arriving in Lhasa during August or January. Weather-scarred, even in August, were the parties that we met fifty miles north of Lhasa, their religious fervour growing daily as they neared the Holy City. Camels and yaks are used for riding and transport across the northern plateau. The camels are left at Nag-chu-ka, ten days journey north of Lhasa; it is not permitted to bring them nearer the city. From Nag-chu-ka to Lhasa the travellers come in small parties; between these places there is not much danger from brigands.

Simla is the starting-point of an excellent road, which becomes rougher as it nears the Tibetan frontier at Shipki and joins the first route, the road from Leh. Though described grandiloquently as the Hindustan-Tibet road, its trade with the latter country is nevertheless insignificant. The roads from Almora, across various Tibetan passes, carry a considerable traffic. The two main routes through Nepal are one that passes by Kirong Dzong on the upper waters of the Gandak river, and another that crosses near Nya-nam Dzong, on the upper waters of the Arun.

The most important of all the trade-routes between India and Tibet takes off from Kalimpong in the district of Darjeeling, crosses south-eastern Sikkim, and enters the Chumbi Valley by the Jelep [1] La. Thence it proceeds up the Chumbi Valley to Phari. From Phari many of the caravans take a track along the eastern side of the Hram Tso [2] to Lhasa—a line which is shorter and affords better grazing—while a few follow the more circuitous road via Gyantse. Half the entire trade between Tibet and India traverses this Lhasa-Kalimpong route.

The most direct and most natural route from Lhasa to

[1] More properly ' Dzelep ', but the name ' Jelep ' has come into common use.

[2] The ' Bam Tso ' of the maps. The name means ' Otter Lake '.

India is the one which goes via Tse-tang[1] and Tsö-na Dzong [2] to Ta-wang. We may hope much from this route, between Tibet and Assam, in the future, as well as from one which would start from the north-east corner of Assam, run along or near the Lohit valley to the fertile lands of south-eastern Tibet, and connect with China via Ba-tang and Tachienlu— a trunk road from India to China, though a highly mountainous one.

It will be readily understood that the word ' trade-route ' does not connote a well-made road. The tracks, along which the trade passes, are sometimes very rough. But it takes a great deal to daunt the perseverance of the baggage animal, be it yak, donkey, mule, or sheep. The small, stocky Tibetan mule will climb up and down the mountain sides like a cat. I have known one, when carrying its load of a hundred and sixty pounds, drop seven feet through the flooring of a broken bridge, and after being dug out of the rocks and mud at the bottom, resume and complete its journey, none the worse for this trifling misadventure.

The mule is better than the yak on slippery grass, but the latter is unsurpassed in carrying either goods or passengers over apparently impossible rocks and boulders. Though seemingly of clumsy build, it clambers over these with but little difficulty, playfully prodding at man or beast in front with its massive horns.

The muleteers are often to be seen riding on sturdy, shaggy ponies behind their caravans, but dismounting to walk down the steep hills. For the old Tibetan saying tells us,

> If you do not carry him up the hill, you are no pony ;
> If you do not walk down the hill, you are no man.[3]

---

[1] The ' Chethang ' of the maps.
[2] The ' Chona Dzong ' of the maps.
[3] In Tibetan,

> *Kyen-la mi chin-na, ta men :*
> *Tur-la mi pap-na, mi men.*

Image of King Ke-sar, the hero of early Tibetan mythology
In the Ke-sar Temple at Lhasa

King Ke-sar's brother (right) and minister (left)
In the Ke-sar Temple at Lhasa

V

EARLY HISTORY

THE Tibetans anticipated Darwin by claiming descent from a monkey. The latter, who was an incarnation of the Compassionate Spirit,[1] met a she-devil, who addressed him thus : ' By reason of my actions in my former life I have been born in a demon race, but, being in the power of the god of lust, I love you greatly.' After much hesitation and after consulting with his spiritual guide the Compassionate One married her and they had six children. The father fed these on sacred grain, with the result that by degrees the hair on their bodies decreased, and their tails became shorter and finally disappeared. So says the Tibetan chronicle.[2] Another chronicle [3] adds, ' Those who took after their father were full of faith, diligence, love, and piety, and were eloquent and meek ; those who took after their mother were full of sin, contention, and jealousy, and were greedy and mischievous. But all possessed strong bodies and courage.' The above traits, good and bad, have thus come to the Tibetans as an inheritance from their first ancestors.

Thus far their own tradition. Western science places the Tibetan race among the Mongolian family of nations, which, with their allied Turkish tribes, inhabited high Asia from time immemorial. It is generally believed that the Tibetans came partly from the north-east, and later from Assam and Burma in the south-east. Philologically the Tibetans belong to the same linguistic family as the Burmese. And, so far as appearance goes, it is even now difficult to distinguish a Tibetan from a Mongol, until he speaks. The early Tibetans would appear to have led an entirely pastoral life. It is among the shepherds and the yak-herdsmen that we still find the purest type of the race.

---

[1] *Avalokitesvara* in Sanskrit ; *Chenrezi* in Tibetan.
[2] Pu-tön Rim-po-che's Chö-chung, fol. 110.
[3] Third volume of Pa-wo Tsuk-lak-re Chö-chung.

The early history of Tibet is obscure. The number of historical works written by Tibetans is not small. I have received from my Tibetan friends most of those that are held in good repute. They deal chiefly with religious happenings, many of which seem trivial to us. They abound in myths and miracles, in dreams and religious discussions. For Buddhists, like Hindus, lack the historical sense, as the latter is understood by Europeans, Chinese, and Mahomedans. It is noteworthy that, even at the present time, Tibetan monks are not allowed to read histories. ' Otherwise ', as I was informed in Lhasa, ' they would be constantly reading them, and neglecting works on religion and philosophy which are more difficult and less attractive subjects.' It must not, however, be assumed that Tibetan histories are valueless. They give much information on the growth of Tibetan Buddhism and some also on the general life of the people. But lack of space will permit only a limited reference to them here.

Tibet did not escape the notice of the Father of History. Writing some two thousand four hundred years ago, Herodotus tells us of a rumour about a race of enormous ants that delved for gold in a country to the north-west of India. From time to time travellers attempted to steal the gold and to ride away with it, but the ants gave chase and killed them if they caught them. An explanation, which has found credence with some, is furnished by the gold diggings at Thok Jalung in western Tibet. The intense cold of this lofty tableland, aggravated by the violent winds that sweep unceasingly over it, compel the Tibetan workmen to dig hunched up in their black yak-hair blankets. They are accompanied by their watchdogs. These too are usually black ; ferocious and swift, they would certainly pursue and attack the robbers after the manner described by Herodotus.[1]

The ' Blue Record ',[2] one of the best Tibetan histories, referring to the visits to Tibet of an Indian saint, who had acquired the power of living a very long time, mentions

[1] *Herodotus*, Book III, chapters 102–105.
[2] *Tep-ter Ngön-po* in Tibetan.

a tradition, which says, ' The first time that he came, he saw
Tibet under water. The second visit showed the water
receding, patches of brushwood, and a few deer roaming
about.' [1] It brings to notice also ' a tradition, which says
that Tibet at first consisted of a group of twelve States, but,
as they were insignificant and none of their rulers served the
Faith, their history ends there.' History, unless it centres
on religion, does not appeal to the Tibetan mind.

Passing by the legendary kings, who lived between the
first century B.C. and the seventh century A.D., and during
whose reigns charcoal was made, reservoirs and irrigation
introduced, mules imported and mining further developed,
we come in the seventh century to King Song-tsen Gam-po
and the dawn of Tibetan civilization. Buddhism had
entered Tibet some two hundred years earlier, but obtained
only a scanty hold on the country. The new king acceded to
the throne at the age of thirteen and reigned for many years.
His armies conquered Upper Burma and Western China.
The Emperor of China was forced to yield a princess in
marriage to the conqueror, who also took to wife a princess
from Nepal. The two queens, being Buddhists, converted
the young king to their faith, and he used all his influence
to spread Buddhism in Tibet. A portion of the Buddhist
Scriptures was brought from India. Tibetan had hitherto
been an oral language only, but, in order that the sacred
books might be translated, a written character was invented.
This was based on the Indian alphabet as then used in
Kashmir.[2] Considerable opposition was aroused, but the
work was pushed on, and Buddhist monasteries were erected.
For the Chinese queen had discovered by astrology that
Tibet was ' like a female demon lying on her back '.[3] So
the monasteries were built in those parts of Tibet which
corresponded with the arms and hands, and with the legs
and feet of the demon, whose power was thereby lessened.
We are told of this king that he retired into seclusion for four
years, to learn reading and writing.[4]

[1] Fol. 18.
[2] Pu-tön Rim-po-che's Chö-chung, fol. 111.
[3] Op. cit., fol. 112.
[4] Pu-tön Rim-po-che's Chö-chung, fol. 111.

We are also told that ' he established laws for the punishment of murder, robbery, and adultery. He encouraged
learning and the practice of the sixteen righteous duties. He
founded the priesthood, ordaining a few priests as a beginning. And in other ways also he gave a strong religious
impulse to the whole of Tibet.' [1]

Another account [2] refers to the order introducing the new
laws as follows : ' The high should be pressed down by law,
the poor should be governed according to a reasonable
system. Establish measures, cultivate land and teach the
people to read and write. Establish good manners. Fine
those who quarrel ; compensate for murder ; make thieves
pay ninefold the amount of the stolen property. Banish one
who commits rape to another country and cut off one of his
limbs. Cut out the tongue of the liar, make the people to
worship God, to respect and repay the kindness of their
parents, the loving mother, the old father and the uncle.

' Return good for good. Do not fight with gentle people.
Read the scriptures and understand them. Believe in
Karma,[3] forsake everything that is irreligious, help your
neighbour. Drink in moderation. Be modest. Pay your
debts promptly and do not use false measures. Do not
listen to your friend's wife. If there be a " yea " and a
" nay ", take the gods as witnesses.'

The law was introduced with song and dance. Sixteen
girls sang and offered flowers. The people held races and
sports, and hoisted flags on trees. It is recorded that the
sacred doctrine spread over the whole land as the sun and
moon cover the earth.

The form of Buddhism which prevailed in the neighbouring
hill-country of Nepal was adopted as the State religion. We
may assume that it was strongly mingled with nature-
worship, as is the Hinduism of Nepal at the present day.
And in any case the Pön religion, which then prevailed

---

[1] Tep⁴ter Ngön-po, vol. i, fol. 20.
[2] Gye-rap Salwe Melong, fol. 43.
[3] The doctrine which explains the good and bad events of each life as
the result of good and bad deeds committed in previous existences. ' As
a man sows so shall he reap ' in this and future existences.

throughout the country and was itself largely animistic, was too powerful to be ousted altogether by the new doctrines.

The Buddhist missionaries, who came mainly from Nepal, Kashmir, and China, introduced arts and customs from India and China. The Chinese queen introduced butter, cheese, and barley-beer, and the people were taught how to make pottery works and water-mills. The king himself built a palace by Lhasa, on the ' Red Hill ', where the Dalai Lama's palace, known as the Potala, now stands. By his successive conquests he extended his influence over Nepal, as well as over Upper Burma and western China. As a conqueror, a law-giver and a religious and educational reformer, Song-tsen Gam-po has established an undying name in Tibetan annals. To this day his chapel in the great Temple in Lhasa is thronged with worshippers, who sing songs of prayer and praise, and bring huge jugs of barley-beer as offerings to the great king. And in his first palace, three or four miles outside Lhasa, religious services are still held whenever there is danger of war.

His grandson introduced tea from China, and this in time became, and still is, the national beverage. The well-to-do Tibetan of modern times drinks thirty to seventy cups of tea in a day.

In the years that followed, several works on astronomy, astrology, and medicine were translated from Sanskrit and Chinese. We may in fact say that the present civilization of Tibet was taken mainly from China, and only in a lesser degree from India. The religion was brought partly from India and partly from Nepal and Kashmir, but developed by the Tibetans according to their own lights. In this connexion it must be mentioned that the population of Nepal is Mongolian, and has thus always formed a suitable channel of communication between India and Tibet. Moreover it is not impossible that Buddha, who was born in what is now Nepalese territory, was, partly or wholly, of Mongolian origin. The general appliances of civilization apart from religion—and in a lesser degree religion also—have come from China. It is noteworthy that in the early days of Tibetan

Buddhism the Indian influence was considerable, while during the last six or seven centuries it has been but slight, that of China and Mongolia predominating. The common kinship—partial though not complete—of Chinese, Mongolians, and Tibetans asserted itself against outside influence.

During the latter half of the eighth century another famous king, Ti-song De-tsen, ruled over Tibet. He summoned the Tantrik Buddhist, Padma Sambhava, from Udyayana in north-western India. Padma Sambhava suppressed demons, performed miracles, and established Buddhism firmly. Among other monasteries which he built was the great monastery at Sam-yé, fifty miles south-east of Lhasa. It is the oldest of the large monasteries in Tibet, and is still a flourishing institution. Padma Sambhava is one of the patron saints of Tibet, and the chief saint of the Red Hat sect, the followers of the original Buddhism of Tibet. Among the Red Hats his image occupies the place of honour on Tibetan altars as often as that of Gotama Buddha himself. For the people say that Buddha would be helpless without the priests who spread his doctrines and the books in which those doctrines are expounded.

The historian of this period emphasizes the difficulty which the monarch encountered in summoning teachers from the south, for the ministers urged the dangers of sorcery, remarking that the Indians and Nepalese were noted for their knowledge of the black arts.[1] By this period the original teaching of Buddha had been wellnigh discarded in India and replaced by the Tantrik doctrines with their charms and mystic meanings. It was this later phase of Buddhism that penetrated Tibet. We are further told that many sacred books were translated from Chinese, as well as from Nepalese, into Tibetan, and thus the religion was made as clear as daylight to the people.

King Ti-song De-tsen also instituted codes of civil and criminal justice. He was a wise and powerful monarch, one of the landmarks in early Tibetan history.

The Tibetans have several democratic traits in their

---

[1] Pu-tön Rim-po-che's Chö-chung, fol. 113.

character. One of these was exemplified in the next king, Mu-ni Tsem-po, who ordained that all men should share equally in the wealth of the country. An equal division was made, but the equality soon disappeared. Yet twice again all were made to share and share alike. But the inequalities became worse than before, for it was found that the poor, who had become indolent during their time of ease, became poorer than ever. After the third attempt the king was poisoned by his mother.

In the Western world the doctrine of ' equal opportunities for all ', whether in educational or other advantages, is held by many. But the hundreds of millions who follow the Hindu or Buddhist religions cannot reconcile such a doctrine with their creeds. For both believe in transmigration of the soul, or mind, through successive worldly existences. And the Law of *Karma*, one of the chief foundations of their religion, could never permit that all should start equal in this life, however good or bad their previous lives had been. Thus it was that the Tibetan priesthood ascribed the failure of the scheme to the deeds, good and bad, of previous lives working out their inevitable results.

During the reign of Ral-pa-chan, in the latter half of the ninth century, standard weights and measures were introduced from India.[1] The priesthood was organized and increased, temples built, and Buddhism zealously extended throughout the country. Many Indian teachers came to the country and translated religious books.[2]

Tibetan priests also went to India to study the religion there, halting on the way in Nepal to learn the Indian languages. Some of these passed on to India, though their death-roll was heavy. Out of a party of eight or ten, not more than two or three would return to Tibet. It is not without reason that the Tibetan fears the Indian climate.

Of Ral-pa-chan we read that ' Fastening to his clotted hair a sheet of silk, he made the priests sit on it. He allotted seven lay households to the support of each of the priests, and paid great homage to the priesthood.' The zeal of the king

[1] Gye-rap Sal-we Me-long, fol. 126. [2] Op. cit., fol. 126.

appears to have been too much for his people, for when only forty-eight years old, he was assassinated at the instigation of his brother, Lang-dar-ma, who was at the head of the anti-Buddhist party. As soon as the latter succeeded to the throne, he did what he could to destroy Buddhism in Tibet. ' The religious law broke like a rotten rope. The peace of Tibet became as a lamp without oil. Evil arose like a storm ; the good intentions were forgotten as a dream. The monks, finding none to serve them, returned to their homes ; the evil ministers gained the power. These appointed as king, Lang-dar-ma, an incarnate fiend.' [1]

From the time of Song-tsen Gam-po to that of Ral-pa-chan, Tibet and China were constantly at war, with varying fortune. Tibetan tradition records that after the death of Song-tsen Gam-po, which occurred about A. D. 650, the Chinese captured Lhasa. During the reign of Ti-song De-tsen, Tibet was at the zenith of her power, and was indeed one of the great military powers of Asia. Her empire touched those of the Arabs and Turks across the Pamirs. Turkestan and Nepal seem to have been subject to her, and her victorious armies had overrun the western parts of China. The terrified Chinese paid tribute to Tibet to save their capital, Changan. But when, with the advent of a new Emperor, they failed to pay this tribute, the Tibetans attacked again, and in A.D. 763 or thereabouts captured the Chinese capital.

It was probably during the reign of this king that the Tibetans and Nepalese invaded India. This event occurred after the death of Harsha, who was king of northern India during the visit of the Chinese pilgrim Hiuen Tsiang in the seventh century of our era. One of the histories of western Tibet records of Ti-song De-tsen's reign, ' All the countries on the four frontiers were subdued. China in the east, India in the south, Baltistan and Gilgit in the west, and Kashgar in the north were brought under his power.' [2]

Another chronicle describes the extent of the Tibetan kingdom during the reign of Ral-pa-chan thus :

' During the time of King Ral-pa-chan, the Lord of

[1] Op. cit., fol. 131.   [2] Ladakh Gye-rap, fol. 19.

A mounted soldier, old style

A foot soldier, old style

Power, the frontiers held with the Kings of the four borders were as follow : The range of the Sro-long-shen [1] mountains, resembling a curtain of white silk, was the frontier with the Chinese King of Astrology ; near the great river, Ganges, there was an iron pillar, which was the frontier with the Indian King of Religion : the gate of Pa-ta Sha-dung was the frontier with the Persian King of Wealth ; and the ridge of sand, which looks like the back of Nya-mang-ma, was the frontier with the King of Be-ta.'

Twenty years later, Tibetan armies again overran western China. A treaty was concluded by which the Koko Nor lake was fixed as the north-eastern boundary of Tibet. The Tibetan king abandoned his conquests in China, but retained the mountainous lands, the homes of his race. Tibetans have ever dreaded the hot countries. The fear of disease must often have saved India from the incursions of their hardy neighbours on the north.

The Bhutanese, living in a somewhat warmer climate, have frequently raided Bengal and Assam. They would carry men, women, and goods back to their mountain fastnesses, a former Raja of Kuch Bihar having been one of their victims. It was not until the establishment of British power in north-eastern India that the Bengalis and Assamese could feel secure from raids.

The remarkable conquests of the Tibetan kings and their treaties with China are made known to us, partly by the Chinese and Tibetan histories, and partly by two stone pillars at Lhasa. The writing on these has been obliterated in parts, both by the passage of time and by the Chinese during their subsequent occupation of Lhasa. But enough remains, when read with the references in the Tibetan and Chinese books, to give us an outline of what happened.[2]

Song-tsen Gam-po, Ti-song De-tsen, and Ral-pa-chan are the outstanding figures, both in war and peace, among the kings of Tibet. They are known to Tibetans as 'The Three Religious Kings, Men of Power.' The development of Buddhism, which forbids the taking of life and preaches peace and

---

[1] A district in Gya-rong, a province in eastern Tibet, but for many years past in the occupation of China.

[2] See Appendixes I and II.

renunciation, checked, if it did not sap, the martial ardour of a race akin to the conquering and devastating hordes of Jenghiz Khan. It is noteworthy that, when in recent years the Russians re-introduced the arts of war into Mongolia, the Mongols frequently proved themselves more than a match for the Chinese troops So too with the Tibetans. Ill-trained, but possessing a few thousand modern rifles with only twenty or thirty rounds per rifle, they have expelled the regular forces of China from large areas of their country. The fighting spirit is not yet dead in Mongol or Tibetan.

Lang-dar-ma was himself killed after a reign of only three years by a lama. Smearing his white pony with charcoal— so the tradition runs—the priest donned a black robe with white lining and rode into Lhasa. He found the king examining the inscription on one of the stone pillars mentioned above. Dancing a fantastic dance, which he had invented for the occasion, he came gradually closer to the royal presence. Lang-dar-ma called him to come near and show the dance. While making the threefold prostration which the occasion demanded, the lama drew a bow and arrow from his broad-sleeved robe and shot the king. Then mounting his steed he galloped off. The crossing of a river washed the charcoal from his pony. He himself turned his robe inside out and, thus transformed, escaped into safety.

This dance, now known as ' The Black Hat Dance ', is still celebrated throughout Tibet in commemoration of the avenger's exploit. But the set-back to Buddhism continued for seventy years.

With Lang-dar-ma the long line of Tibetan kings comes to an end. The country became full of petty chiefs, who built forts on hills and ridges overlooking their subjects on the plains below. Thus came into use the Tibetan saying :

> The fort on the hill,
> The fields on the plain.

The fort protected the villages below and the villages fed the fort.

When a chief died, his widow or daughter would sometimes seize the reins of government and rule the little kingdom with vigour and wisdom. There are records of several of these chieftainesses in old times, and to this day are pointed out the forts in which they held sway. For the position of women in Tibet has always been a good one ; they too have shared in the control of their country's destiny.

Indian pandits, the chief of whom was Atisha, continued to visit Tibet, promoted the religion and were well-received. The cave where Atisha lived, sixteen miles east of Lhasa, is still preserved. High up on the sunny mountainside, surrounded by stunted junipers and bushes of wild currant and wild rose, it seemed a fitting home for a religious reformer in this land of ice and snow.

We have an interesting glimpse of Tibetan life at this time, the period of the Norman conquest of England, in the autobiography of the Tibetan poet-saint, Milarepa. We read how he lived in caves, as Tibetan hermits do at the present day ; how he was ill-treated by robbers, who were subsequently caught by the prefect of the district and had their eyes put out ; and how shells were then the accepted currency of the country. To aid him in his meditation he resorted to bending and breathing exercises. Life in Tibet does not appear to have altered very greatly during the last eight hundred years.

During the twelfth and thirteenth centuries the priests of the new religion, Buddhism in its Lamaïstic form, were steadily extending their influence among a people always prone to believe in spirits and mysticism. The grandson of Jenghiz invited the High Priest of the large Tibetan monastery at Sakya to his Court. In A. D. 1270 Khublai Khan, the first Mongol Emperor of China, having similarly invited the Sakya Hierarch of the period, became a convert to Lamaïsm, and gave the sovereignty of Tibet to his visitor. Thus began in Tibet the rule of the priest-kings. This first instalment of it lasted for seventy-five years, from about 1270 to 1345. During this period many Indian priests found their way to Tibet, and the religion in its Tantrik form obtained a firmer hold.[1] It is recorded also of the chief of these Hierarchs that he ' was very liberal as regards religious opinions. He encouraged every one to do his best and to be earnest in his creed, whatever it might be.' [2]

The power of Sakya was broken by King Chang-chub Gyal-tsen, who brought nearly all Tibet under his sway and inaugurated the Second Monarchy of Tibet. He continued to promote the religion, but discarded many of the Chinese and Mongolian innovations introduced by the Sakya priest-kings. But the martial vigour of the Tibetans was not what it had been. Chinese and Mongolian influence continued to be felt in Tibet. The Sakya Hierarchs had depended on the Mongol Emperors. The new dynasty, which is known as the Sitya, was, in some measure at any rate, dependent on China.

The Sitya dynasty ruled in Tibet for three hundred years, till 1635, when the king of the Tsang province of Central Tibet ousted it, but was himself a few years later subdued by Gushi Khan, the chief of the Oelöt Mongols. It was on the whole a time of peace and prosperity.

It was natural that Mongolia should adopt the religion of her Tibetan cousins, for the affinity between the two races has always remained strong. Even at the present day the Tibetan Government regards the two countries as bound together by a close understanding, if not by an actual alliance. But the advent of Buddhism has centred the thoughts of both on religion, so that the two nations, even if allied, would be infinitely less powerful for the purposes of war than either standing alone before Buddhism obtained a hold.

[1] Tep-ter Ngön-po, vol. iv, fol. 7.   [2] Ibid.

Ganden Monastery

Mausoleum of Tsong Kapa in dark building (right centre)

VI

THE RULE OF THE PRIEST-KINGS

THE Buddhism of Tibet, having entered the country mainly between the seventh and the ninth centuries, was derived from the later and weaker phases of Indian Buddhism with a strong admixture of the nature worship prevailing in Tibet and the border countries. Neither the doctrines of the religion thus evolved, nor the condition of the priesthood, satisfied the more ardent minds in the country. Reform came from within. Tsong Kapa, ' The Man from the Land of Onions ', was the reformer. He was born in 1358 in the province of Amdo in north-eastern Tibet. His disciples, known as the Yellow Hats in contradistinction to the Red Hats of the existing priesthood, were forbidden to marry or to drink wine, and a stricter code of morals was instituted. He founded the large lamaseries at Ganden and Sera, which with the Drepung monastery are now the three most powerful religious bodies in the country. They are known collectively as ' The Three Pillars of the State '.[1]

Tsong Kapa's successor was Ganden Truppa,[2] who founded the monastery of Tashi-lhünpo which in the seventeenth century became the residence of the Tashi Lama, the second Grand Lama of the Yellow Church. After Ganden Truppa's death in 1474 his spirit was held to have passed into an infant born two years later. This child became his successor, and this system of reincarnation rapidly became popular and spread throughout the country. There are nowadays five hundred to a thousand incarnate Lamas, of greater or lesser merit, distributed over the different sects of the Tibetan priesthood.

It was during this period, in 1533, that Mirza Haidar, a Chagatai Mongol in the service of the Mongols—or Moghuls

---

[1] *Den-sa Sum* in Tibetan.

[2] This is how the present Dalai Lama and Lhasa Tibetans pronounce this name, which is spelt *Gedundub* and *Geden-tub-pa* by other writers.

—who then ruled in Turkestan, attempted an invasion of Tibet through Ladakh. But it failed completely, as has indeed been the fate of all invasions by Mahomedans and Hindus, except those by the Nepalese, the great majority of whom are akin to the Tibetans in race, and some in religion also.

The following incarnation, Sönam Gyatso, spread the new faith not only in Tibet, but through Mongolia also. From the Mongol chieftain, Altan Khan, he received the title of *Dalai Lama Vajradhara*, ' The All-embracing Lama ; the Holder of the Thunderbolt '.

In the Tibetan biography of Sö-nam Gyatso, known as ' The Chariot of the Ocean of Wisdom ', there is a reference to a custom—similar to that of *sati* in India—by which widows were burnt on the funeral pyre with their deceased husbands. It is interesting to note that the Dalai Lama forbade the practice in Mongolia, as in later years the British forbade it in India. Preaching before a large assembly of Mongols, headed by the Chief, the Dalai said : ' In the past when a Mongol died, his wife, servants, horses, and cattle were burnt alive. Henceforth ye shall not sacrifice lives . . .' And the edict continues : ' If you kill a man, as you have done in the past, your life shall be separated from your body. If you kill horses or cattle, your property shall be confiscated. If you assault a priest, your house shall be destroyed. Hitherto ye have sacrificed horses and cattle, monthly and annually to Ong-kö, the image of the dead. Now you must burn Ong-kö in fire. If you do not, your house will be destroyed. In place of Ong-kö you must keep an image of six-handed Buddha, the Protector, and worship it with milk, butter, and curds only, not with flesh and blood.' We may notice here the practice which was frequently adopted by the leaders of both Buddhism and Hinduism towards their converts. When a deity of the old religion was dethroned, the gap was not left unfilled. A divinity of the new religion took its place. The feeling of loss was thus averted, and the change more easily accepted.

And again : ' You must not commit robbery, but you must do as is done in U and Tsang.'[1]   Thus many laws were introduced.[2]

A word as to the method by which these biographies of Dalai Lamas have been composed seems necessary here. The Dalai Lama writes notes of important events at the time of their occurrence, or dictates them to an official. When the Lama is a minor, one of his tutors[3] writes these notes, which are rolled up into bundles. Ten or fifteen years later they are transcribed into books, block prints of these being made. Occurrences throughout the whole of Tibet are thus recorded. Similar records are kept for the Tashi Lamas, but they relate mainly to Tashi-lhünpo and surrounding districts.

From now onwards Buddhism took firm root in Mongolia and the title of Dalai Lama was held in turn by each Head of the Yellow Church. The connexion with Mongolia was further cemented by some of the subsequent Dalai Lamas who were born in princely Mongol families.

The fifth in the succession was Lob-sang Gyatso, the son —so the present Dalai Lama informed me—of a poor man at Chung-gye, two days' journey to the south-east of Lhasa. He called on the Oelöt Mongols to help him in his struggles against the older Church. The Oelöts accordingly came to his assistance in 1641, subdued the Red Hats and gave the Dalai Lama the sovereignty of Tibet. The Lama then commenced the erection of the great Potala Palace, the residence of all his successors. The Palace and fort built by King Song-tsen Gam-po had been destroyed during the wars that followed. The Lama's old teacher was made the Grand Lama of Tashi-lhünpo and declared to be an incarnation of Amitabha,[4] ' The Boundless Light '. The Dalai Lama himself was regarded as an incarnation of Avalokitesvara,[5] ' The Lord of Mercy '. Amitabha being the spiritual guide of Avalokitesvara, it is held by many Tibetans that

---

[1] The provinces in which Lhasa and Shigatse are situated.
[2] Biography of Sö-nam Gyatso, fol. 95.
[3] *Yong-dzin* in Tibetan.   [4] *Ö-pa me* in Tibetan.
[5] *Chen-re-zi* in Tibetan.

the Tashi Lama is spiritually higher than the Dalai. But his power in worldly affairs is small.

This Dalai Lama visited Peking. During one of my talks with the present Dalai Lama he gave me some details of the visit, as recorded in the Tibetan histories. The Emperor met him one day's journey from the capital. Arrangements were made by which the Lama passed over the city walls instead of under the usual archway, for the city walls carry traffic, and it is unfitting that any should pass over His Holiness's head. When receiving the Dalai in the Imperial Palace, the Emperor came down from his throne, and advanced eighteen yards to meet him, a point of etiquette that will be appreciated by all who have lived in Eastern countries. In fact, he was treated as an independent Sovereign, for the Emperor wished to secure his alliance in order to establish Manchu rule among the people of Mongolia. The Manchus had recently succeeded the Mings on the throne of China.

The Mongol invasions left a deep impression on Tibet. They are one of the reasons assigned for the ruined houses that one sees everywhere in the southern parts of the country. In one of the outlying chapels of ' The Happy Hermitage ', an interesting monastery near Gyantse, there is a picture of one of the old kings of Gyantse, reputed to be the last and most powerful of them all. It is noticeable that his clothes were Mongolian, not Tibetan.

It was during the early years of the fifth Dalai Lama, about 1626, that the first European entered Tibet. This was a Portuguese, the Jesuit Father Antonio de Andrada. He does not appear to have penetrated very far into the country, though he claims to have done so, and he certainly did not reach Lhasa or Shigatse. The claim made on behalf of Friar Odoric of Pordenone, who lived three hundred years earlier, cannot, I think, be substantiated. And Marco Polo crossed the Pamirs, but never entered Tibet.

The first Europeans to enter Lhasa were Johann Grueber, an Austrian Jesuit, and Albert d'Orville, a Belgian. They started from Peking in June 1661, travelled by way of the

A Priest of the Yellow Hat sect

In front of him from right to left are his Dor-je, bell, cup made from
a skull, and drum made from two skulls

A religious service in progress in a monastery

The officiating priest is on a raised seat at the back (left centre)

Koko Nor lake through northern Tibet to Lhasa, stayed there a month, and then came to Katmandu in Nepal. At Lhasa they witnessed the rule of the fifth Dalai Lama, whom the Jesuit Grueber styles the ' devilish God-the-Father who puts to death such as refuse to adore him '.

But nothing succeeds like success. To the modern Tibetan the fifth Dalai is a national hero. While each other Dalai Lama, with the occasional exception of the seventh, is known simply by his number or his name, Lob-sang Gyatso is known as ' The Great Fifth '. His Holiness did not himself exercise the secular power for many years, but retired, as was usual, to the higher sphere of things religious, leaving mundane affairs in the hands of his Chief Minister, Sang-gye Gyatso, a man of remarkable talents. The ' Great Prayer ' festival was established on its present basis. This, the largest and most striking festival of the year in Lhasa, lasts for twenty-one days during February and March, trebling or quadrupling the population of the capital.

The government of the country was centralized in Lhasa and made more orderly, so that many of the old forts were disused and gradually fell into ruin. The Potala was completed in its present form by Sang-gye Gyatso a few years after the fifth Dalai Lama's death.

There is no doubt that this Dalai and his Chief Minister were men of exceptional ability. But the increased power of Buddhism had lessened the martial ardour of the Tibetans. From now onwards the influence of Tibet in the councils of neighbouring nations was religious rather than military. The Chinese under the able rule of the early Manchu Emperors sought the goodwill of the Dalai Lama, the Head of the Buddhist Church, to aid them in controlling the Mongols and their other Buddhist subjects.[1] Lob-sang Gyatso was a powerful aid to the Chinese Government by lending the weight of his great name to their policy in Mongolia.

In 1680 the fifth Dalai Lama died. The minister, Sang-gye

[1] For a fuller history of this period the reader is referred to *The Dalai Lamas of Lhasa and their relations with the Manchu Emperors of China*, by W. W. Rockhill (T'oung-Pao, Series III, vol. i, No. 1).

Gyatso concealed his death for some time, and the Chinese Government, though subsequently affecting indignation, appear to have abetted the concealment. The former wished to rule in the Lama's name : the latter were enabled to continue quoting his authority in support of their dealings with their neighbours in the north. But in due course a successor, who had received the name of Tsang-yang Gyatso, was installed in the Pontifical Chair.

The new Dalai was unorthodox. Instead of devoting himself to religious matters, he led a life of pleasure, beautifying his palace and grounds, resorting to the drinking bowl and the society of women. Withal he was a youth of high intelligence. The songs which he composed, and which are still popular among all classes of Tibetan society, reflect the pathos of his misplaced life. A few verses, which I have roughly translated, may serve as examples :

> Last year the crop was young and green
>   'Tis now but withered strands ;
> And youth, grown old, is dried and bent
>   Like bows from southern lands.[1]

> Dear Love, to whom my heart goes out,
>   If we could but be wed,
> Then had I gained the choicest gem
>   From Ocean's deepest bed.

> I chanced to pass my sweetheart fair
>   Upon the road one day ;
> A turquoise found of clearest blue,
>   Found—to be thrown away.

> High on the peach tree out of reach
>   The ripened fruit is there ;
> So too the maid of noble birth,
>   Though full of life and fair.

> My heart 's far off : the nights pass by
>   In sleeplessness and strife ;
> E'en day brings not my heart's desire,
>   For lifeless is my life.

.   .   .   .   .   .

[1] The bamboos, from which bows are made, grow in Bhutan and other countries to the south of Tibet.

> I dwell apart in Potala,
>   A god on earth am I ;
> But in the town the chief of rogues
>   And boisterous revelry.
>
> .   .   .   .
>
> It is not far that I shall roam,
>   Lend me your wings, white crane ;
> I go no farther than Li-tang,
>   And thence return again.[1]

The mode of life followed by Tsang-yang Gyatso caused many Tibetans and Mongols to doubt whether he could be a true incarnation. Dissension arose, and the Chinese were able to strengthen their hold on Tibet. In 1700 Tachienlu, a strategic point on the high road from Lhasa to the Szechuan province of western China, was occupied, and a portion of eastern Tibet was at the same time annexed to the Chinese Empire. In 1706 the Chinese and Mongols removed the Dalai and put him to death, thereby arousing deep resentment throughout Tibet. The Chinese announced that Tsang-yang was not a true incarnation. A Lama, twenty-five years old, was produced as the real incarnation of the fifth Dalai and installed in the Potala. But the Tibetans refused to recognize him. Reports reached Lhasa that Tsang-yang had reincarnated at Li-tang, and the Tibetans recalled with joy the verse (the last of those quoted above) in which he had announced his return from Li-tang. These words were held to be prophetic of his death and reincarnation. With the help of another body of Oelöts, who pushed through to Lhasa, the Tibetans gained their end. But during these dissensions the Chinese succeeded in strengthening still further their hold on the country.

One of Tsang-yang Gyatso's verses foretells that his sweetheart will be found in Chung-gye, the birthplace of his immediate predecessor. Tibetans believe that if the Dalai Lama had married her, his descendants would have proved too powerful for the Chinese, and therefore the latter removed him before this could happen.

[1] Each stanza consists of four lines of blank verse ; each line of six syllables. But Tibetan is so highly condensed that it can hardly be translated into English within similar limits.

The Chinese Emperor, Kang-hsi, found that nearly all the Mongol tribes were in favour of the Tibetan choice, and regarded his own selection for the post of Dalai Lama as an impostor. He feared a Mongol-Tibetan combination against China, resulting perhaps in the foundation of a new Mongol Empire. He decided accordingly to gain control over Tibet.

His first army, dispatched in 1718, was defeated by the Oelöts and Tibetans. Recognizing the difficulty of his position, he abandoned his own nominee for the Dalai Lamaship and adopted the boy chosen by the Tibetans. He then dispatched another and larger army to Lhasa, saying that it was coming to enthrone the latter. Tibetan opposition was thus removed, and the Chinese army, after ejecting the Oelöts, was able to make its entry into Lhasa.[1] A Mongol garrison of 2,000 men was left in the capital, and the road between Tachienlu and Lhasa was kept open by detachments of troops. The Jesuit Father Desideri was a witness of these events. So also no doubt were the Capuchin Friars, who resided at Lhasa from 1708 to 1733 and eventually quitted the city because they were not supplied with funds from home, rather than from Tibetan opposition.

In 1750 the Chinese Residents, known as Ambans, murdered the Tibetan Regent. The people in their turn massacred the Chinese at Lhasa. The Emperor Chienlung dispatched an army, restored Chinese ascendancy, and strengthened the power of the Ambans.

In 1779 Pal-den Ye-she, the Tashi Lama, a man greatly venerated throughout Tibet and Mongolia, visited Peking at the invitation of the Emperor. The latter desired to gain his influence to support the political projects of China ; the Lama hoped to gain a greater measure of autonomy for Tibet and the Yellow Church. His death by small-pox in Peking the following year caused universal lamentation, and prevented any great results following from his mission. Tibetans have always been especially liable to small-pox,

[1] For a full account of this period see *The Dalai Lamas of Lhasa*, by W. W. Rockhill (reprinted from the T'oung Pao, Series III, vol. i, No. 1), pp. 37–42.

severe outbreaks of which have frequently occurred in
their country. Vaccination, however, is now gradually
extending, as its benefits are coming more and more to
be recognized.

A few years earlier the Bhutanese had, as was their wont,
raided Bengal. But the growing power of the British in
this province could not tolerate raids. Accordingly Warren
Hastings, then Governor of Bengal, exacted due retribution
from Bhutan. The Dalai Lama was a minor, and the
Tashi Lama on his behalf wrote to Warren Hastings to
intercede in favour of his erring vassal. Hastings with his
usual insight seized the opportunity. In 1774 he dispatched
George Bogle, a young writer of the East India Company,
not only to Bhutan but also to Tashi-lhünpo, to improve
the intercourse, commercial and otherwise, between Bengal
and Tibet. After some opposition Bogle was permitted to
enter Tibet. He stayed several months at Tashi-lhünpo,
where he gained the friendship of the Tashi Lama, the one
who died a few years later of small-pox at Peking. Thus
commenced the connexion between Tibet and the British.
It was renewed, with but partial success, by the dispatch
of Samuel Turner to Tashi-lhünpo in 1783, and was then
discontinued for many years. Manning, the eccentric
Englishman who visited Lhasa in 1811, cannot be said to
have strengthened the connexion.

Among the several petty kingdoms which occupied Nepal
during the first half of the eighteenth century was one
known as Gorkha, to the north-west of Katmandu. In
1769 the Ruler of Gorkha gained the ascendancy throughout
Nepal. It was not long before this warlike people turned
their attention to Tibet. In 1774 they attacked Sikkim,
then a tributary of the Tibetan Government. In 1788, on
various pretexts, they occupied some Tibetan districts near
the Nepal frontier, but were bought off by a secret arrangement promising to pay them an annual tribute. The failure
to pay this brought them back in force in 1791, when they
captured Shigatse, the large town half a mile from Tashi-
lhünpo. But an epidemic, attributed by the Tibetans to

a divine curse, broke out among the troops of the Gurkhas
—for such the Gorkhalis, i. e. people of Gorkha, are called
in English—many of whom returned with their officers to
their own country. The Chinese Government, hitherto kept
by its representatives in ignorance of the previous aggression,
dispatched an army composed partly of Chinese and partly
of Tibetans, which marched through Tibet in the heart of
winter, defeated the remaining Gurkhas in several engagements during the spring of 1792, and finally dictated peace
within a few miles of their capital. Among other terms the
Gurkhas agreed to send a tribute Mission every five years
to Peking.

The stone pillar erected by the Chinese in Lhasa in
commemoration of their victory was a familiar object to
me during my year in Lhasa. The inscription on it is in
Chinese, Tibetan, and Manchu, and was written—as itself
records—' on an upper date (i. e. between the first and the
middle of the month) in the first month of winter in the fifty-
seventh year of the reign of the Heavenly Protector (i. e.
the Emperor Chien-lung).' It states that the troops were
composed of men from Solon and Szechuan. Now Solon—
also called Solong, Solongchen and Sorong—is a district in
the Tibetan province of Gyarong. Thus it is clear that there
were Tibetan soldiers in the Chinese army.

The inscription, which is in the usual grandiose Chinese
style, goes on to record that the Sino-Tibetan army, after
crossing ' mountains as though they were level plains and
rivers with great waves and narrow gorges as though they
were mere streams, fought seven battles and gained seven
victories. The thieves were panic-stricken '.[1]

European histories, derived presumably from Chinese
sources, make no mention of Tibetan soldiers in the Chinese
army, which they put at seventy thousand men. The Lhasa
pillar does not mention the number. But Tibetans, who are
in a position to know the facts, estimate that there were
only some three or four thousand Chinese and some five or
six thousand Tibetan soldiers in the army. I found the

[1] For a translation of this inscription see Appendix III.

The defeat of the Gurkhas is recorded on the pillar seen within
this building.   Below the Potala

The granary at Palha (right).   Note the ventilation holes at the
base of the wall

same great difference between Chinese and Tibetan estimates
in the numbers of troops employed in Mongol invasions.
' The Chinese on such occasions ', Tibetans used to say to
me, ' always multiply the actual figure many times over.'
Perhaps one might put the strength of the Sino-Tibetan
army in the Gurkha campaign at or about twelve thousand
men, of whom a large number, at any rate, were Tibetans.
Whatever be the total, it was a large one, for the old men
of Lhasa recount that when they were boys they were told
that even milch cows were employed among the other kinds
of transport.

There seems no doubt that the army was under Chinese
generalship. And though the number of troops on both
sides has been exaggerated, yet, in view of the bravery of
their opponents and the difficulties of the terrain, the
achievement will always remain a memorable one. Even
now, one hundred and thirty years later, it serves to
inspire the Gurkhas with a lingering dread of China.

Surprise has naturally been expressed in European books
that so large a force as seventy thousand men could feed
themselves on the scanty resources of Tibet. I think the
explanation is twofold. Firstly, the extent of this army
has been vastly exaggerated, as pointed out above.
Secondly, the Government of Tibet, Tibetan landowners,
and in a lesser degree the peasants also, keep stocks of grain
in their storehouses. These accumulate during years of
prosperity, and, except in periods of prolonged shortage of
crops, assume very large dimensions. In the cold, dry climate
of Tibet barley grain keeps good for at least fifty years—
perhaps one might safely say for a hundred years. The
granary at Palha, near Gyantse, which I found by measure-
ment to be capable of holding over ten thousand cubic feet of
grain, was only one of several belonging to the Palha family.
And it must be noted that the Tibetan Government take
more revenue in grain than in cash, and store this grain, for
future as well as for present payments, in granaries throughout the country. When, in 1910, the Tibetan Government
refused supplies to the Chinese troops who were advancing

against Lhasa, the Amban pointed out to them that they had given supplies to the army that invaded Nepal.

The Palha granary was full of grain until destroyed in the Expedition of 1904. The overflow was stored in rooms in the mansion itself. The floor was of crushed stone, dry and hard. Ventilation was secured by holes in the floor as well as in the outer and inner walls. Grain was thrown in loose from the top, and extracted, when required, through the holes at the foot of the walls.

The barley and wheat, taken from the numerous granaries, were no doubt supplemented, in the case of the soldiers from southern China, by rice imported from Bhutan, then as now the chief exporter of rice to Tibet. For the men from Szechuan and the neighbouring southern provinces require a substantial proportion of rice in their diet. The soldiers from northern China and the Tibetans themselves would be fed from Tibet itself.

After rescuing Shigatse and other districts of Tibet from the Gurkhas, the Chinese Government felt themselves not only entitled, but also strong enough, to control more closely the general administration of Tibet. The Tibetan officials, both lay and ecclesiastical, were ordered to submit all important matters to the Ambans. Even the Dalai and Tashi Lamas were instructed to prefer their requests to the Ambans; they were prohibited from communicating direct with the Emperor. Chinese officials were posted at Shigatse, at Ting-ri on the Nepal border, and at Cham-do and Tra-ya in eastern Tibet.

Until this time, according to tradition prevalent in Sikkim, the Chumbi Valley and Phari were part of Sikkim. The latter country was ordered to send a representative to join China and Tibet in the discussions with the Gurkhas. As no representative appeared, Phari and the Chumbi Valley were brought under direct Tibetan rule.

The Ambans were also to aid in the selection of the Dalai, the Tashi, and other high incarnate Lamas. A golden urn was sent from China. When any of the great Lamas was reincarnated, a selection was to be made among the children reported as likely to be the re-embodiment. ' The name, the day, the month, and the year of birth of each shall be written on a slip, and this slip shall be placed in the urn. The Dalai Lama shall then hold a religious service, after which he, assisted by the Amban, shall, in the presence of all the people, take a slip from the urn and hold it up so that all may see, and this shall be the re-embodiment.' So runs the Chinese order. In the case of Mongol dignitaries of the Church, a somewhat similar procedure was to be followed at the Peking Lamasery, known as the Yung-ho-kung. All these high Lamas, both Tibetan and Mongol, were to receive patents of investiture from the Chinese Government.

Allowance must be made for the fact that the orders of the Chinese Government in their distant dependencies are not usually executed in full. Only twelve years after these strict orders, the Tibetans chose a Dalai Lama without conforming to the Chinese rules, and the Government of China found it wise to condone the irregularity. Still there is no doubt that at this time China exercised, as she was indeed entitled to do, a considerable measure of control over the Tibetan administration.

The Chinese also conceived the idea that the British in India had assisted the Gurkhas in their campaign. They accordingly promoted a policy of exclusion. The door, which Warren Hastings had succeeded in opening a little, was closed more firmly than ever, until the British military Expedition of 1904 established direct and formal relations between the Governments of India and Tibet.

During this time of Chinese ascendancy and until the birth of the present Dalai in 1876 the Dalai Lamas always died young. The ninth, born in 1804, died when eleven, the tenth at twenty-three, the eleventh at seventeen, and the twelfth at twenty years of age. It is possible that not only the Regents and Ministers of the time, who wished to retain their power, but also some of the Ambans were concerned in these early deaths, since the latter could impose their wills much more easily on a Regent than on a God-king, whose

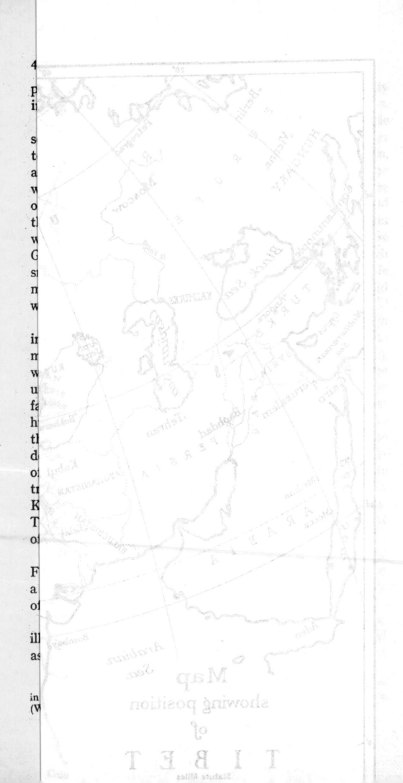

Map
showing position
of
TIBET

Statute Miles

to establish an Agency at Lhasa, an annual subsidy of ten thousand rupees, the right of free trade in Tibet, and extra-territorial rights. In return for these concessions the Gurkha Government undertook to assist Tibet if invaded by foreign foes. A treaty was concluded on the above lines.[1]

A quarrel between Der-gé and Nya-rong, two States in eastern Tibet, broke out in 1863. Nya-rong invaded Der-gé, but the Lhasa Government came to the assistance of the latter and drove out the invaders. They occupied Nya-rong and brought it under regular Lhasan administration. While these disturbances were in progress, the Chinese invaded Gya-rong, the country of the eighteen clans of Gya-rong-wa in eastern Tibet, and annexed it to China.

[1] See Appendix IV.

VII

THE DALAI LAMAS

I SHALL perhaps be pardoned if I digress at this stage to describe from a more personal standpoint the lives of the priest-kings or god-kings, whose rule-period has formed the subject of the preceding chapter. The Dalai Lama is regarded by Tibetans as a Bodhisatwa, i. e. one who has attained the right to Nirvana, but consents to be reborn for the spiritual benefit of his fellow-creatures. In almost every Asiatic country which has had a spiritual ruler, the latter has been the object of veneration, but has not been allowed to exercise power and has been frequently kept more or less as a prisoner in his palace. The actual power has been wielded by a Minister, and has frequently been hereditary in the Minister's family. Even in Bhutan, a country adjoining Tibet and inhabited by men of Tibetan stock, the spiritual ruler, or Shab-tung Rim-po-ché, known to Europeans and Indians as the Dharma Raja, did not govern. The duty of government was deputed to the Desi or Deb Raja, who was also a priest, and who in latter years had himself ceased to govern. The real power has lain for at least fifty or sixty years with the Penlop (Chief) of the Tongsa district, which covers the eastern half of Bhutan. The present Penlop has assumed the hereditary title of Regent of Bhutan and the Desi has retired. Thus in a country akin to Tibet in race, religion, and language, the actual power lay for many years not even with the second, but with the third man in the kingdom.

But Tibet has at times proved an exception to this almost universal rule. Since the time of the fifth Dalai Lama, i. e. from 1641, the Dalais, when they succeeded in attaining their majority, have at times ruled in fact as well as in name. A notable instance of this was the great fifth Dalai Lama, who himself conducted the administration for several years before placing it in the capable hands of his chief Minister, Sang-gye Gyatso. But the most striking example of all is the present God-king, who for the last twenty or thirty years, while introducing salutary reforms on the religious side, has also controlled the multifarious details of the secular government. How numerous and how varied the duties of Buddha's Vice-regent are, even I can in some measure realize after being in close contact with him for two years in India, and even more after eleven months' close personal intercourse in Lhasa.

When a Dalai Lama himself rules—and probably when a clever Minister rules in his name—his authority is unrivalled. Even though the Council and Parliament are united in opposition to his proposals, he can enforce them, and has not infrequently done so. Backed as he is by the veneration of a people who regard him as more than Pope, as in fact a Divinity ruling on earth, there can be no direct opposition to His Holiness's orders. The Nepalese have a characteristic proverb, which says :

There's no answer to an order ;
There's no medicine for death.

Things are not indeed as strict as this in the Lama's domains, for the great wastes of Tibet cannot be controlled as easily as the fertile little lands of Nepal, and the Tibetan nomad wandering over his mountains is not so susceptible to discipline as the Nepalese peasant tied to his farm.

In practice also the Dalai's power is limited through his being kept in ignorance of events by monasteries, officials, and others. His position precludes him from touring frequently and seeing things for himself. Governmental proposals and important events come to him from the Council, through the Lord Chamberlain or the Chief Secretary, both of whom thus exercise great influence. But the Dalai has his private and semi-private employees, who bring him news and enable him to sift, in some degree, the official sources of information. In districts far from Lhasa, the natural independence—one might perhaps say the democratic tendency—of the Tibetan character asserts itself, and unpalatable orders are apt to be regarded but lightly.

A few of the earlier Dalai Lamas were born in aristocratic families. Among these was Yön-ten Gyatso, the fourth, the son of a Mongoi prince. But the ' Great Fifth ' was apparently the son of a peasant at Chung-gye, two days' journey south-east of Lhasa. And in the later incarnations the Dalai Lama has almost invariably been chosen from a family of humble position. If he be selected from one of the leading families of the country, several of which are descended from the brothers of previous Dalai Lamas, that family is likely to become inconveniently powerful. Public appointments too are not usually given to members of his family during his lifetime. But these may hold, and usually do hold, private posts about his person, which carry great, though unacknowledged, influence.

Dalai Lamas do not drink wine or spirits, but they may and do eat meat, a necessary article of diet in Tibet, where the climate is cold and fruit and vegetables are scarce, often indeed unobtainable. As, however, the taking of life, even for food, is to Buddhists a sin, a religious ceremony is performed on behalf of the animals so killed, and this is held to insure their rebirth in a higher state of existence. Thus the loss of their lives means a gain to them. Dalai Lamas do not marry, but keep altogether apart from women.

The method of appointing a successor is unique. For the following description of it I am indebted to His Holiness the present Dalai Lama, to the late Prime Minister, and to other high Tibetan authorities.

Some Dalai Lamas are more believed in, some less. One of the former class, before he dies, or—as the Tibetans say —before he ' retires to the heavenly fields ', will usually tell those round him where he will reincarnate. He may give particulars as to the house in which the small boy will be found, the stream, if any, near it, the shape of the mountains round it, &c., &c. His entourage are themselves afraid to ask for these particulars, when they see their divinity ill, for they fear that they may thereby make him more eager to go.

Three or four years after the Dalai Lama has ' departed ',

the Tashi Lama, if of age, and fifteen or twenty other great lamas, e. g. the abbots of Sera, Drepung, and Ganden—the three huge monasteries near Lhasa—the State Oracle at Lhasa, known as the Nechung, and the Oracle at Sam-ye, one of the most famous monasteries in Tibet, decide as to the tract of country in which the new Dalai Lama will be found, the year of birth of his father, his mother, and himself, the kinds of trees growing near his house, and so forth.

Inquiries in the district indicated are then set on foot, and lead usually to the tracing of three or four boys whose birth has been heralded by heavenly manifestations. For instance, a rainbow has appeared over his house from a clear sky when he was born, and his parents have had heavenly visions concerning him. Particulars of these miraculous births are laid before the Oracles and lamas referred to above, and these decide which is the new Dalai Lama. The latter, a boy of three or four, has to recognize the sacred thunder-bolt,[1] the bell and other religious implements of his prede-cessor—or rather, as one should say, of himself in his previous life.

The young boy will be found to carry on his person some of the marks that distinguish the incarnation of the four-handed Chenrezi from ordinary mortals. Among such signs are :

(a) Marks as of a tiger-skin on his legs.
(b) Eyes and eyebrows that curve upwards on the outside and are rather long.
(c) Large ears.
(d) Two pieces of flesh near the shoulder-blades indicating the two other hands of Chenrezi.
(e) An imprint like a conch-shell on one of the palms of his hands.

The present Dalai Lama bears the last three signs. An unearthly light is believed to issue from his countenance when he blesses pilgrims, so that even his ministers and immediate attendants find it hard to look him in the face.

---

[1] *Dor-je* in Tibetan.

The names of the different candidates had, however, usually to be placed in the golden urn, presented in 1793 by the Chinese Emperor Chienlung. One was picked out with a pair of chopsticks, and opened by a Tibetan Grand Secretary.[1] This contained the name of the new Dalai Lama. The Prime Minister asserted to me that this has always hitherto been the same as the name favoured by the Oracles. In the case of the present Pontiff the Tibetan Government represented to the Chinese Emperor that there was no doubt about the identity of the new Dalai Lama, and therefore no need for the Amban to perform the ceremony of picking out a name. The ceremony was accordingly remitted, an event which appears also to indicate that the Chinese suzerainty was then merely nominal.

By presenting the urn and arranging for the Amban to assist at the choice of each new Dalai Lama and other high Incarnations, the Chinese Government no doubt hoped to gain some hold over the personage who influences not only Tibet but Mongolia, and is revered by many millions in Asia, and even by some in European Russia. For the Lama, owing his accession in some measure to their representative, might naturally feel bound to repay his debt by subservience to their requests. According to Chinese accounts they had good grounds for their innovation, for at the time the choice of a high Incarnation was often made corruptly. A ruler of Ladakh had many relatives who were chosen among the highest of the Incarnations. A Tashi Lama chose a Dalai Lama from a prominent family in the Tsang province ; the latter in turn made his first cousin Tashi Lama when the former Tashi Lama died. But the climax was reached when the Ne-chung Oracle of Lhasa declared that the reincarnation of the Grand Lama of Urga would be the child that the wife of the reigning prince of the Tushot Mongols was expected to bring forth. For the child was born, but proved to be a girl.[2]

Lönchen Shatra,[3] the late Prime Minister—whose early

[1] *Trung-yik Chem-po* in Tibetan.
[2] Rockhill's *The Dalai Lamas of Lhasa*, pp. 54, 55.
[3] Pronounced *Shutter*.

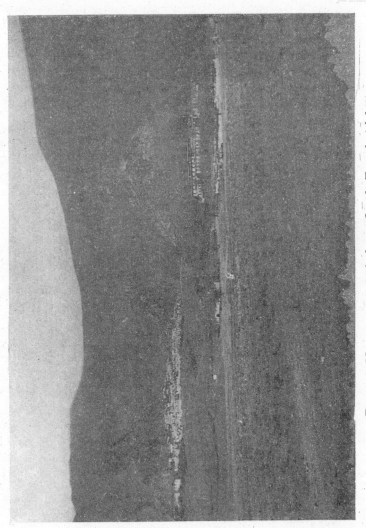

Drepung Monastery and Nechung Oracle Temple (right)

leath was a very heavy loss to his country—told me the story of the finding of the present Dalai Lama, then a boy of two or three years old, in words somewhat as follows :

' The Ne-chung Oracle gave certain particulars, showing the names of the father and mother, the approximate whereabouts of his house, the kind of country round it, and so on. The Oracle of Sam-ye also gave some particulars; e.g. that a mountain by the house was " shaped like an elephant ".

' After this, a leading lama, with a number of doctors of divinity[1] in attendance, was instructed to go to a lake named " Mu-li-ting " in Sanskrit-Tibetan and " Chö-kor Gyal-ki Nam-tso " in popular Tibetan. Here he was to see an image of the Dalai Lama's house and surrounding country. The lama went accordingly, but found the lake frozen and under snow, so wondered how he could see as directed. But soon afterwards a strong wind got up and blew off the snow, making the ice clear to the lama, who was looking at it from a neighbouring hill. Then, so the story goes, the lake rose up on end and the lama looked into it as into a glass. And in it he saw the image as foretold.

' Later on in a dream the lama saw the baby Dalai in his mother's arms. When he arrived at the house, he found the baby in the arms of his mother, and the face of the boy corresponded with the face in the dream.

' A deputation of priests and officials waited on the boy, who picked out property of the late Dalai Lama from among a large number of articles. And in spite of his tender years he was able to indicate occurrences that had happened in the lifetimes of previous Dalai Lamas. Among other cases he indicated that of a Chief[2] of Li-tang,[3] to whom a former Dalai Lama had given an image of Buddha. For fear of losing this, the Chief had encased it in a golden urn, and hidden it in a beam in his house, unknown to anybody. The young Dalai Lama told people that the Chief of Li-tang had done this.

' Dalai Lamas cease identifying property and telling of such occurrences, when they grow older.

' If there is no doubt as to the true Dalai Lama, the names are not put into the golden urn. The names of the 9th Dalai Lama, Lung-tok Gyatso,[4] and of the present one were not put into it.'

---

[1] *Ge-she* in Tibetan.   [2] *Depa* in Tibetan.
[3] A town in eastern Tibet.   [4] Born in 1804.

The Prime Minister, who narrated this account to me, was a man of exceptional intelligence and strong common sense. As Tibetan Plenipotentiary at the diplomatic Conference in 1913–14, he proved himself to be more than a match for his Chinese colleague. But in matters of religion Tibetan faith is strong and deep.

The father of a Dalai receives the rank of Kung, the highest rank held by a layman in Tibet. He receives also the insignia of the Ruby Button and the Double-Eyed Peacock Feather. There are very few Kungs; they are descended from the fathers of recent Dalai and Tashi Lamas.

The abandonment by China of the use of the golden urn in the choice of the present Pontiff is a measure of the growing impatience felt by Tibet towards the Chinese suzerainty, and of the steady decline of the latter. This decline is further evidenced by the attainment to his majority of the present Dalai. The four immediately preceding him all died before they could take up the reins of government. Thus for nearly a hundred years Tibet was administered by Regents. As pointed out in Chapter V, this enabled the Chinese to enjoy greater power in Tibet than would have been likely under the administration of the Dalai Lamas themselves.

When seven years old, or even earlier, the Dalai is brought to Lhasa, and takes up his residence in his palace, known as the Potala. At the age of eighteen he is entitled to receive his full powers. The present Dalai Lama was taken from his mother when about three years old and brought to Lhasa. His father and mother thereafter saw him only at occasional visits. 'The Master of the Bed Chamber',[1] so the Lord Chamberlain informed me, ' took his mother's place, fondling him in his arms, and looking after him in every way. He also gave him his early education, and it is largely owing to him that the Dalai Lama has become so learned and wise.'

The title Dalai Lama (or more properly Ta-le Lama), being of Mongolian origin, is used mainly by Chinese and

[1] *Simpön Chempo* in Tibetan.

Mongols. The Tibetans know him rather as *Kyam-gön Rim-po-che*, ' The Precious Protector '; *Gye-wa Rim-po-che*, ' The Precious Sovereign '; *Buk*, ' The Inmost One '; *Kyam-gön Buk*, ' The Inmost Protector '; *Lama Pön-po*, ' The Priest Officer '; sometimes also as ' The All-Knowing Presence ', and often just simply as ' The Presence ', *Kün-dün*.

The Dalai Lama informed me that he had five chief seals of office. ' The Golden Seal of the Rainbow and of the Earth ' [1] bears on it the name of the Emperor of China, who ruled at the time of the fifth Dalai Lama. It is a red seal, about one inch square. It is supposed to be kept in the personal custody of the Lama himself, and is one of the chief symbols of his authority. It is not stamped on documents nowadays, but is found on some of the more ancient title-deeds of the old families of Tibet. Another seal of primary importance, known as ' The Inmost Seal ',[2] bears on it the words ' Gan-den Po-trang ', ' The Blissful Palace ', and ' Dalai Lama '. It is red, square, and a little larger than the first seal. It is applied to title-deeds of large properties, and to other documents issued by the Lama himself. A large photograph of His Holiness, which I took for him, and which he presented to me, shows him seated on his throne, and arrayed in the robes in which he blesses the pilgrims and others in his Palace at Lhasa.[3] This he signed himself and sealed with the Inmost Seal. The signature runs, ' In accordance with the Precepts of the Lord Buddha the Great Dalai Lama, Unchangeable, Holder of the Thunderbolt, the Thirteenth in the line of Victory and Power.'

In foreign affairs the Dalai Lama is expected to act in conjunction with the two Councils, the Greater and the Lesser, and with the National Assembly. Until the expulsion in 1912 of the Chinese Amban and his troops from Lhasa, it was the custom, when the matter was one of great importance, that their decision should be communicated to the Amban, who in his turn submitted it to the Chinese Government. The Tibetan report was known as ' The

---

[1] *Ja-sa Se-tam* in Tibetan. [2] *Buk-tam* in Tibetan.
[3] See frontispiece.

Request for Power ',[1] and the Amban's communication as
' The Golden Ears '.[2] After sending their report, the Tibetan
authorities considered themselves at liberty to act according
to thei⁻ decision, without awaiting the Emperor's reply,
which was not received in less than three months, even in
urgent cases. By this practical method they gained their
own way, while satisfying the dictates of Oriental courtesy.

It is indeed clear that, for many years prior to 1904, China
had very little control over Tibetan foreign policy. Nor indeed was Tibet in the habit of acknowledging her authority,
except when desirous of avoiding foreign pressure. In such
cases the Tibetan Government was able to plead the Chinese
relationship, and the consequent impossibility of taking
action until a report had been submitted to the Emperor
and a reply obtained from him, a plea by which several
months' delay could always be assured. Among other
instances in which the Tibetans availed themselves of the
Chinese relationship may be mentioned the Dalai Lama's
refusal to reply to the two letters that the Viceroy of India
wrote to him in 1900 and 1901. As regards the first letter
he wrote, ' The Ambans, when they first came here, made
an arrangement forbidding us to correspond direct with
your Government '. Lord Curzon's second letter to the
Dalai Lama was returned unopened.

Per contra their disavowal of the Chinese suzerainty is
evidenced by their refusal to acknowledge the Anglo-
Chinese Convention of 1890 as binding on Tibet, when
Colonel Younghusband in 1903 pressed for its observance.
Similarly by their refusal to permit the Amban to go to meet
the Expedition of 1904. And once again, by their refusal to
acknowledge the deposition of the Dalai Lama by the Chinese
Emperor after this Expedition. The Emperor's proclama-
tion was mutilated and bespattered with filth, and the
Tibetan Government continued to submit matters for the
orders of the Lama, though His Holiness was absent in
Mongolia.

In the internal administration also a Dalai Lama is

---

[1] *Wang-shu* in Tibetan.   [2] *Ser-nyen* in Tibetan.

supreme. An appeal lies to him against the decision of the Council in cases of exceptional importance. If, for instance, the dispute is between persons of high rank, or if a large landed property is involved, the party aggrieved by the decision of the Council may apply for the intervention of the ' Precious Sovereign '. Such appeals are known as ' The Placing of the Names of the King and Ministers ' ; [1] and are so called from the fact that the petition is addressed in the names of the Dalai Lama and Council. In every murder case also the decision of the Court used to be submitted to the Dalai Lama for confirmation. But the present Dalai Lama gives his Prime Minister full control in criminal cases, for it is held to be unfitting for His Holiness to touch things of this kind.

Although in Tibet, as elsewhere, rank and position are shown by the height of the seat above the floor of the room, yet a Dalai Lama, the Supreme Head of Tibet, will frequently sit on a lower seat than a learned Lama, when taking lessons in religion from the latter. This happens especially when the Dalai Lama is a youth. But even when His Holiness was 36 years old, at the time of his flight to India, there were in Tibet two learned Lamas, who were privileged to sit equal with the Dalai Lama himself. Such is the respect paid to learning by the Buddhists of Tibet, where it is regarded as the highest of all moral attainments. To the Christian, Love is the greatest virtue ; to the Tibetan Buddhist, Learning. In India the man or woman who desires to please, will address you as ' Protector of the Poor ' or ' Incarnation of Justice ', but in Tibet as ' Learned Sir '.

The two leading officers in the Dalai Lama's household are the Lord Chamberlain [2] and the Chief Secretary.[3] The former is the head of all the ecclesiastical officials in Tibet. The recent incumbent was a clever doctor, and, as such, always attended His Holiness in addition to his ordinary duties, which include, among other charges, the control of the parks round Lhasa.

---

[1] *Gyal-lön tsen-kö* in Tibetan.   [2] *Chi-kyap Kem-po* in Tibetan.
[3] *Dro-nyer Chem-po* in Tibetan.

The Chief Secretary is the main medium of communication between His Holiness and the outside world. As such, he has many enemies, but his power is very great. For, when the Dalai Lama, dissatisfied by the Council's handling of some important issue, takes the direct control in his own hands—as happened once during my year in Lhasa—the Chief Secretary for the time supersedes the Prime Minister and the Council.

The Chief Secretary has ten assistants who combine the duties of secretaries and aide-de-camps. One of these was attached to my Mission in Lhasa; his alertness, political acumen, and knowledge of his own national concerns, would have made him a man of mark in any country.

The Master of the Bedchamber, the Court Chaplain, and the Chief Butler wield considerable power indirectly, because they have access to His Holiness, and can put in a word on this side or that. The four orderlies are men of great stature: when we were in Lhasa, all were well over six feet and one was just seven feet in height. They and the soldiers of the Bodyguard are patient with crowds, but are not to be lightly disregarded.

VIII

BRITISH MILITARY EXPEDITIONS

WE now come to the period of recent history, and to the reopening with Tibet of those British relations which had been broken since the time of Warren Hastings about a hundred years previously.

In 1885 Colman Macaulay, a Secretary of the Government of Bengal, obtained Chinese assent to conduct a Mission to Lhasa. But Macaulay, who had interviewed Tibetan officers of low position and devoid of authority, meeting them on the Sikkim-Tibetan frontier, had not gained the consent of the Tibetan Government. The latter would have nothing to do with the idea, which was accordingly abandoned in return for a concession in the newly-annexed province of Upper Burma. Chinese power in Tibet was by this time at a low ebb, and the Tibetans were opposed to closer inter-course with India. The persistence of foreigners in exploring their country, so long secluded, had made them suspicious. In particular, the secret explorations of the Bengali, Sarat Chandra Das, carried out under the auspices of the Indian Government, filled them with distrust of the Power that ruled India. In a conversation which took place in 1910 the late Prime Minister of Tibet informed me that Sarat's clandestine entry and his surreptitious inquiries constituted —together with the Sikkim Expedition of 1888—the chief causes which led Tibetans to suspect British intentions with regard to their country. Officials who had been on duty at the barrier-gates through which Sarat had passed, and those who had shown him hospitality, were severely punished. The property of some was confiscated, others were thrown into prison. Some were even executed, including a high Incarnate Lama, the high priest of the Dong-tse monastery, thirteen miles north-west of Gyantse. This was a most unusual, perhaps unprecedented, occurrence in Tibet. The Chinese told the Tibetan authorities that, if the latter permitted foreigners to enter the country, these would subvert their religion and introduce Christianity in its place. Designs on the Tibetan gold mines were also suspected. The Government and people of Tibet were seriously alarmed. It is well to realize this in view of what followed.

After the abandonment of the Macaulay Mission, the Tibetans proceeded to occupy Ling-tu, a mountain near Gnatong and some eighteen miles within the Sikkim frontier. They were instigated to do this by the Ne-chung Oracle at Lhasa, which declared that its magic influence inside the fort would disarm any troops that the British sent against it, while the occupation would give them a commanding position in any negotiations that took place for the delimitation of the boundary between Tibet and Sikkim. It was this Oracle that had declared in favour of the Dalai Lama when the latter was a young boy, and had refused to countenance any rival candidates. It had then great influence, though nowadays very little. For the Dalai Lama has dismissed the last two seers, the former after the Younghusband Expedition for false prophecies, the latter about 1915 on account of disorderliness among his monks.

No doubt our abandonment of the Macaulay Mission was attributed to weakness. For the Tibetans, secluded in their mountain fastnesses, had as yet but a limited idea of British power. At this time also we find the anti-foreign movement strong at Ba-tang in eastern Tibet, whence the Roman Catholic missionaries were expelled, their mission-house burnt, and some of their converts massacred.

The British Government demanded the withdrawal of the invaders. The communication addressed to the Chinese was fruitless; the subsequent threat addressed to the Tibetans was equally so. More than a year having elapsed, in March 1888 General Graham attacked the fort, defeated the Tibetans in three engagements, and advanced twelve miles across the frontier into the Chumbi Valley. But, in order to avoid offending Chinese susceptibilities, our troops were recalled immediately to Gnatong within Sikkim territory.

This display of force brought the Chinese Amban to India.

The Indian Government desired that a British Protectorate over Sikkim should be recognized, the Tibet-Sikkim frontier delimited, and Indo-Tibetan trade promoted. A year's negotiation having followed without result, the Chinese were informed that the British Government had decided to close the incident, as far as China was concerned, without insisting upon a specific agreement.

But, as often happens with the Chinese, when you drop, or appear to drop, a matter, they themselves become uneasy, and, fearing that you have a trump-card up your sleeve, grow anxious to take the matter up again. So it was in this case, and in March 1890 the Treaty was signed.[1] It recognized a British Protectorate over Sikkim, and stipulated that the water-parting of the Teesta river should form the boundary between Sikkim and Tibet. A Trade Treaty followed in December 1893,[2] the chief provision of which established a trade mart at Yatung, eight miles on the Tibetan side of the frontier. The mart was on an altogether unsuitable site, in a narrow side-valley running down from Sikkim towards the Chumbi Valley. A few yards farther down this little valley a wall was built from side to side and manned by soldiers to prevent British traders and travellers from going any farther into Tibetan territory.

When the time came to carry out these treaties, it was found that the Tibetans, not having signed them, refused to recognize them. The Chinese control over Tibet was purely nominal. The war between China and Japan showed the Tibetans that Chinese power was not sufficient to protect them against strong nations. Attempts to develop Yatung were frustrated by Tibetan obstructiveness. Tibetan officers refused to countenance the delimitation of the Sikkim-Tibet frontier : when boundary pillars were erected, they were mutilated or destroyed. The trade through Yatung continued to increase in spite of restrictions, for the Tibetans are keen traders. But the Tibetan Government desired at all costs to keep us at arm's length, for they feared

[1] For a full copy of this treaty see Appendix V.
[2] For a full copy see Appendix VI.

us and distrusted us. To them we were a pushful people, forcing ourselves in where we were not wanted, and harbouring ulterior designs on their country and their religion.

The powerlessness of the Chinese suzerainty, and the consequent futility of attempting to deal with the Amban in Tibetan matters, were now recognized by all the British authorities. In 1899 Lord Curzon, then Viceroy of India, gained permission from the British Government to communicate direct with the Tibetans. The idea was to obtain Phari as a trade mart instead of Yatung, in return for a concession to Tibet as regards the Sikkim-Tibet frontier. In Kalimpong there lived a somewhat remarkable man, by name U-gyen, whose position among his neighbours was recognized throughout the district by the courtesy title of Kazi. He was a native of Bhutan and the intermediary between his country and the British authorities. Kazi U-gyen was employed to write to the Dalai Lama, suggesting that a high Tibetan official should be deputed to discuss frontier and trade questions. His letter met with an unfavourable response. Captain Kennion, the British Political Officer on the Kashmir-Tibet frontier, sent to the Governor of Western Tibet a letter from the Viceroy to the Dalai Lama, asking that it might be forwarded. Six months later it was returned with the intimation that it could not be forwarded in view of the regulations against the intrusion of foreigners into Tibet. Kazi U-gyen was then himself dispatched to Lhasa with another letter from the Viceroy to the Dalai Lama. The Dalai Lama refused to receive this letter, which was brought back unopened.

Casting about for a method of frustrating the British advances, the Dalai Lama now turned to Russia. That Power was indeed far away, but its prestige stood higher in Tibet and Mongolia than that of any other country. Dorjieff, the Dalai's agent, was a native of the Buriat tribe, which, though of Mongolian origin, is included in the Siberian territory of Russia. To Tibetans he is known as Tse-nyi Kem-po, which indicates that he is a professor of metaphysics. He had been one of the tutors of the young

' A wall was built from side to side and manned by soldiers ' (p. 61)

Dorjieff

Dalai Lama, and had always been recognized as a man of ability.

Kashmir and the countries surrounding it were once Buddhist, but are now Mahomedan. There is an old Tibetan prophecy to the effect that the Mahomedan power will spread until in due course a Buddhist king arises in a country to the north of Kashmir. The country will be known as North Shambala and its king will break the Mahomedan power and restore Buddhism.

Dorjieff had left Tibet when the Dalai attained his majority, but returned soon afterwards and appears to have spread the story that North Shambala was Russia and the Tsar was the king who would restore Buddhism. He is said even to have written a pamphlet to prove this.[1] He urged on his master and on the leading men of Tibet the desirability of seeking the friendship of the great northern Power. The Dalai and others were told that, since their annexation of Mongolia, more and more Russians were adopting the Tibetan religion and the Tsar himself was likely to embrace it. With a common religion—the one thing that really mattered —and with unlimited resources, Russia was, of all the Powers, the one most likely to aid Tibet.

To Dorjieff then was entrusted a Mission from the Dalai Lama to the Tsar of Russia. The Russian *Messager Officiel* in July 1901 announced that His Majesty the Emperor had received the Envoy Extraordinary from the Dalai Lama of Tibet. The Envoy and his suite paid visits to the Russian Foreign and Finance Ministers. The Russian Press welcomed the Envoy as showing that the Dalai Lama regarded Russia as ' the only Power able to frustrate the intrigues of Great Britain'. The Russian Foreign Minister assured the British Ambassador that the Mission was of a purely religious character. But in the East religion and politics are closely interwoven with each other. And the British Government was faced with the fact that the Dalai Lama, while refusing to receive a letter from a British Viceroy, had not only written a letter, but dispatched an

[1] Kawaguchi, *Three Years in Tibet*, p. 499.

Envoy to the Russian Tsar. Among the goods brought by
the Mission to Lhasa on their return from Russia was a consignment of Russian arms and ammunition. There came
also a magnificent set of Russian Episcopal robes, a present
from the Tsar of all the Russias to the God-King of Tibet.

The Dalai Lama's chief assistant in his pro-Russian policy
was the Prime Minister Shatra, with whom, after his flight
to Darjeeling in 1910, I was fortunate enough to gain a close
friendship. A man of great ability and patriotism, he was
already one of the leading forces in the political life of the
country. The pro-Russian attitude of the Lama and his
Minister was natural enough, for they were genuinely dis-
trustful of British designs and, in their inexperience, thought
that this would be a good way to check them.

In 1902 reports which appeared in the Chinese Press
alleged the existence of a secret agreement between Russia
and China. The former was to use its great power to
guarantee the integrity of China, which in return was to
transfer to Russia its entire interest in Tibet. In Lhasa
the leading men were telling each other in confidence that
Russia was making a new Treaty with China, by which she
would help China, if the latter were in trouble. If Tibet
needed assistance, both Russia and China would supply it,
for both countries followed the religion which looked on the
Dalai Lama as its Head and on Lhasa as its Holy of Holies.
The rumours in the Chinese Press were officially denied by
the Chinese Government. But, taken in conjunction with
the Dalai Lama's dealings with the Tsar, they added to the
apprehensions felt by the Government of India.

The establishment of Russian influence in Tibet and
Lhasa, with the connivance of China, would undoubtedly
have constituted a serious menace to India. It will be
remembered that Russia had not yet suffered her defeat at
the hands of Japan. She was still fulfilling what she believed
to be her destiny in moving forward in Asia. The Anglo-
Russian Agreement had not yet been made ; she was free to
follow her ambitions.

Let us not exaggerate the situation. A Chinese army,

reinforced by Tibetans, might cross Tibet and invade Nepal. But a Russian army could not have crossed Tibet and invaded India. India would not have welcomed such an adventure ; and the combined Indo-British resources would have sufficed to frustrate it. But Tibet, the chief bulwark of India's northern frontier, would have been crossed. If Russia and China remained in sympathy, we might expect trouble also in Burma, formerly under Chinese overlordship, connected by race and religion with Tibet, but recently annexed by force to the British dominions. And so, from Kashmir to Siam—over two-thirds of the long land-frontier of India—the former security would have been replaced by constant unrest.

The Government of Nepal was already indeed disturbed by the mere report of the Agreement. Bhutan would have followed suit in due course, so also the tribes on the frontiers of Assam and Burma. And in time Burma itself with Sikkim and Darjeeling might well have been infected. It would have been necessary for the Indian Government to station several thousand extra troops, British and Indian, in the malarial districts of north-eastern India.

Accordingly, in January 1903 Lord Curzon proposed to dispatch a Mission with an armed escort to Lhasa, to deal direct with the Dalai Lama, to discuss the entire question of British relations, commercial and otherwise, with Tibet, and to establish a permanent British Representative at Lhasa.[1] Three months later, however, Lord Lansdowne, then Foreign Minister, received a clear assurance from the Russian Government [2] that Russia had ' no Convention about Tibet, either with Tibet itself or with China, or with any one else, nor had the Russian Government any Agents in that country or any intention of sending Agents or Missions there.' The Russian Foreign Minister expressed astonishment that the reports of such Conventions should have been believed by the British Government. The Ambassador went on to say that, although the Russian Government had no designs whatever upon Tibet, they could not remain indifferent to any serious

---

[1] Tibet Blue Book, p. 155.   [2] Ibid., p. 187.

disturbance of the *status quo* in that country.   Such a disturbance might render it necessary for them to safeguard their interests in Asia, not that, even in this case, they would desire to interfere in the affairs of Tibet, as their policy ' ne viserait le Thibet en aucun cas ', but they might be obliged to take measures elsewhere.   This significant warning materialized, after the return of the British Expedition from Lhasa, in the forward movement of Russia in Mongolia.

In spite, however, of the Russian assurances, Lord Curzon .continued to press for the dispatch of a Mission to Tibet, in order to discuss the entire question of our relations with that country, commercial and other.   The Home Government agreed to the Mission proceeding as far as Kampa Dzong, a small station a few miles across the Sikkim-Tibet frontier.   It was provided with an armed escort and was under the leadership of Colonel Younghusband, an officer of experience in trans-frontier politics.   With him were associated Mr. White, the Political Officer in Sikkim, as Joint Commissioner, and Captain O'Connor, a young Artillery officer, whose knowledge of the Tibetan language and politics was especially valuable, as Intelligence Officer, and subsequently as Secretary.   The Mission remained at Kampa Dzong from July to November 1903 without result. The Tibetans refused to negotiate, and urged its return to Sikkim territory.   The Chinese professed friendliness, but pleaded that Tibetan obstruction prevented them from taking action.

An advance was then made towards Gyantse through the Chumbi Valley.   The Tibetans resisting, more troops were sent up, and the Mission, which had now become a military expedition, halted at Tuna, some thirty miles beyond the head of the Chumbi Valley, till the end of March 1904. Those Tibetan Ministers who advised coming to terms with the British were incarcerated in Norpu Lingka, the park, near Lhasa, in which the Dalai Lama's country palace stands.

Throughout the expedition not only Nepal, but also the

Phari Dzong, at the head of the Chumbi Valley, captured and dismantled by the British expedition

View of the surrounding plain from Gyantse Dzong

Tongsa Penlop, the leading Chief in Bhutan, showed great friendliness to our side. This was due in the first instance to Mr. Paul, an officer in the Indian Civil Service, who was for a long time connected with frontier affairs, as Deputy Commissioner of Darjeeling, Political Officer in Sikkim, and British Representative in the negotiations that supervened on the Sikkim Expedition of 1888. Mr. Paul's good work with Bhutan was continued by Mr. White, who succeeded him as Political Officer in Sikkim. And thus it came about that, while the Tibet Expedition was at Tuna, Mr. Walsh of the Indian Civil Service, who had been appointed Political Officer in the Chumbi Valley, was enabled to gain what might have proved a valuable concession from the Tongsa Penlop. This was that we should be permitted to make a road through Bhutan to the Chumbi Valley, and thus avoid the high passes between the Chumbi Valley and Sikkim.

I was summoned from a district on the Bhutan frontier, where I had recently gone as Deputy Commissioner, to conduct the survey for this road. In spite of the hostility of the Paro Penlop, a semi-independent chief through whose territory the road was to run, I was successful, with the assistance of a dozen Gurkhas and of Kazi U-gyen, who accompanied us part of the way, in pushing through Bhutan from the plains of India to the Chumbi Valley, rendering it possible for Mr. Stevens, a young engineer of the Public Works Department, to make the preliminary survey. The project was subsequently abandoned on the score of expense, but the incident served to show the friendly feelings that animated the most influential Chief in Bhutan.

From Tuna the Younghusband Expedition fought its way to Gyantse and eventually to Lhasa. The bravery of the Tibetans came as a surprise to their opponents, but they had no military training and were in the main armed with antiquated muzzle-loaders locally made. Neither these, nor the swords that they carried, were of any use against modern firearms. The British-Indian forces were, however, fighting far from their base, in an unknown country, intensely cold

and almost destitute of supplies. The chief difficulty therefore lay in providing the transport for the carriage of supplies
from India, four hundred miles away, over the high passes
and the wind-swept plains of the Tibetan tableland. The
Mission was at length recognized as a military expedition by
the Indian Government, who issued a war medal for it with
clasps for the principal actions.

The Dalai Lama and his entourage fled to Urga, the
chief town of Mongolia. Urga is comparatively near the
Russian frontier, and contains the residence of a Grand Lama,
who may be said to rank next after the Dalai and Tashi
Lamas in the Mongol-Tibetan hierarchy.

The Chinese Government took the opportunity of issuing a
proclamation deposing the Dalai Lama. This the Tibetans
entirely declined to recognize. They bespattered the proclamation with dirt and, throughout the long exile of His
Holiness, continued to refer to him all important questions
affecting the welfare of the country.

At Lhasa a Convention was negotiated between British
and Tibetans with the assistance of the Amban, the Nepalese
Representative, and the Tongsa Penlop.[1] This Treaty drew
the bonds between the British and Tibetan Governments
much closer. Its leading provisions were :

1. Two fresh trade marts were opened, namely at
Gyantse and at Gartok, the latter name presumably refer-
ring to a small trade centre in western Tibet, known as
Gar Günsa.

2. The Tibetans abolished all dues on trade to and from
India.

3. An indemnity of half a million pounds was to be paid
by the Tibetan Government in seventy-five annual instalments. The Chumbi Valley to remain in British occupation
until the payment was completed.

4. Without British consent, no Tibetan territory to be
ceded, leased, &c. to any Foreign Power, no concession for
roads, mines, &c., to be given, and no Tibetan revenues to be

[1] A full account of the Expedition is given in Younghusband's *India
and Tibet* (John Murray).

pledged to a Foreign Power or to any of its subjects. No such Power to be permitted to intervene in Tibetan affairs, or to send Agents to Tibet.[1]

The Convention was not final, for the assent of China, whose suzerainty over Tibet we had recognized, was not gained. The necessary negotiations with that Power had to be undertaken after the return of the Expedition to British territory.

The British Government were of opinion that the indemnity terms were too severe. The amount was accordingly reduced to twenty-five lakhs of rupees (£166,000), and the evacuation of the Chumbi Valley rendered possible after three years, provided that three lakhs of the indemnity were meanwhile paid and the Convention observed in other respects.

Colonel Younghusband also obtained from the Tibetans an Agreement by which the new British Agent at Gyantse might visit Lhasa in order to settle such commercial matters as could not be settled at Gyantse. The Home Government vetoed this Agreement as it had vetoed the Indian Government's earlier proposal for an Agent at Lhasa.

It may be fairly claimed that the general conduct of the expedition and the behaviour of our troops left a favourable impression on the Tibetans. The latter were surprised at being paid for supplies, and greatly surprised at being paid at liberal rates. Our treatment of their wounded seemed to them an unusual way of doing things. The British officers did not desecrate the monasteries or interfere unnecessarily with the Tibetan administration, in both of which respects this expedition compared favourably with the subsequent Chinese invasion.

The British expedition was compared to a frog, the Chinese to a scorpion. The frog is classed by Tibetans as one of the fiercer animals from its habit of jumping and its general aspect, but not as approaching the scorpion in

---

[1] For the full text of this Convention see Appendix VII

ferocity. They recalled the old proverb, ' When one has seen a scorpion, one looks on the frog as divine.' [1]

The high prices at which supplies were paid for by the British Expedition and the presents of money made by them aroused Tibetan satire against their own officials, reflected in the following skit :

> At first, they speak of ' Foes of our true Faith ' ;
> And next the cry is ' Foreign Devildom ' ;
> But when they see the foreign money bags,
> We hear of ' Honourable Englishmen '.

It is a remarkable fact that this invasion, which penetrated into the heart of Tibet, captured the sacred city, and drove the Dalai Lama to flight across the cold wastes of northern Tibet, yet left the Tibetans less unfriendly towards us than did the petty Expedition of 1888, when we pushed only a few miles into the country and immediately retired. They saw that, though we had the power, we did not seize the country to the extent we might have done, or to the extent that the Chinese did when they invaded it a few years later. The heavy indemnity and other provisions of the Lhasa Treaty did indeed cause fear that we might use them as a pretext for pushing farther in at a later date. But our retirement from Lhasa in the hour of victory showed them that we coveted their country less than they had hitherto believed.

One of my Tibetan friends put the Tibetan point of view as follows :

' The story that Russia had concluded a treaty with China about Tibet was, I think, incorrect. But Dorjieff misled the Dalai Lama by telling him that many Russians were Buddhists and had great religious faith in him, and that the Tsar of Russia was very friendly towards Buddhists. And all Tibetans then believed that Russia was far more powerful than · Britain, and that Britain, having taken Darjeeling and Sikkim, coveted Tibet also.

' The Tibetans did not think that the British could reach Lhasa. By showing that they could fight their way to Lhasa ; by withdrawing their troops from Tibet and thus

[1] In Tibetan, *Dik-pa tong-na be-pa lha-la ngön.*

'Lion and dog do not fight!'

Tibetan picture symbolizing the oppression of the weak by the strong.
Though its drooping tail shows its fear, the dog turns to bite the lion

showing moderation in the hour of victory ; most of all, by
treating the Dalai Lama—their former enemy—well, when
he fled to India some five years later ; and lastly, by the
help which they have subsequently given to Tibet, the
British have made a great and favourable impression on us
Tibetans.

' I am a Tibetan, and I know well that Tibetans would
not have treated a former enemy like that. We Tibetans
looked on the British Expedition as an act of oppression—
" the large insect eating the small insect", as our saying
runs—but subsequent events have turned out in such a way
that the British have now a unique name in Tibet.

' When the Dalai Lama and his Government were in
India in 1910, they wanted a British Protectorate over
Tibet. The fact that the British Government would not
agree to this showed us all that Britain had enough territory
of her own and did not covet ours.'

Whether the Expedition of 1904 was justifiable or not on
moral grounds or on grounds of political expediency, it may
be thought that having gone to Lhasa the British Government ought to have stationed a permanent Agent there.
By going in and then coming out again, we knocked the
Tibetans down and left them for the first comer to kick.
We created a political vacuum, which is always a danger.
China came in and filled it, destroying Tibetan freedom,
for she feared that if we came again we should keep the
country. And Russia, in conformity with her warning,
advanced into Mongolia, without any intention of retiring
as we had retired from Lhasa.

And yet the British Government, in my opinion, did
right in retiring. The Tibetans were still suspicious of our
motives. The Chinese still held the confidence of the country
to the extent of being able to increase Tibetan suspicion of
our designs. Later on, China invaded Tibet, seized a great
part of the administration, desecrated monasteries, and
oppressed the people. The Dalai Lama and his Government
fled to India. We afforded them sanctuary ; we showed
them consideration and kind treatment. It was then that
Tibetan opinion veered round to the British side, that closer
connexion with the British was desired. But at the time

of the Lhasa Treaty, following on military operations, there was no such wish.

Even now, with the improved relationship, it is permissible to doubt whether it is advisable to station a permanent British Representative at Lhasa, unless necessity compels the acceptance of a Chinese Representative also. Though temporary deputations may be necessary in times of stress, our strength lies in our moderation. Let us help the Tibetans as far as we can, but in the main leave them alone to live their own life, for this is what above all they desire.

IX

ADMINISTERING THE CHUMBI VALLEY

In May 1904 I was posted to Sikkim, to take charge of affairs in that country during the absence of Mr. Claude White, the permanent Political Officer, with the Expedition to Lhasa. A few months later I was put in charge of the Chumbi Valley as Mr. White's assistant, and here I remained until November 1905.

For the time being the valley, with an area of seven hundred square miles but a small population, was in British occupation. It was necessary to organize its administration. A simple organization was evolved which differed from the Chinese and Tibetan systems as little as was consistent with freedom from oppressiveness. The Government was left mainly in the hands of the village headmen, for Tibet is in many respects a democratic country. The practice of forced labour without payment, one of the weak spots in the Tibetan administration, as in that of so many Oriental countries, was abolished. A yearly sum, substantial but reasonable, was fixed as the taxation for each of the five divisions of the valley, and the headmen took the responsibility for realizing this. They also received powers in petty matters of justice and police. The two officials of the Central Government of Tibet were necessarily barred from sharing in our administration, but were permitted to remain in their official residences in the Phari Dzong. They interviewed me on the subject of the changes. They denied the right of the Indian Government to administer their charge, and hinted that the Tibetan Government might behead them if they gave way to us. ' Now, if we were bachelors,' said one of them, ' that would not matter much, but we have wives and families to support. How can they be supported, for our estates will certainly be confiscated ? ' I turned a deaf ear to these agonized appeals, and it is perhaps unnecessary to add that nothing untoward happened to these gentlemen.

The four companies of Indian infantry, left behind by the Expedition, were amply sufficient as a garrison. Only a dozen or so of policemen were employed, the rest of the policing being done by the villagers themselves.

These arrangements were accepted by the Indian Government, and I think I may say that they worked well. In November 1905 I was transferred to an Indian district, and a junior officer was sent in my place. Two years later, the indemnity of twenty-five lakhs of rupees for the Younghusband Expedition having been paid in full by the Chinese Government, the valley was restored to Tibet.

It may be of interest to add here a few details regarding the people who live in this area known to Europeans as the Chumbi Valley, a wedge of territory that cuts between Bhutan and Sikkim to within twenty-five miles of the plains of Bengal. To the people themselves the valley is known as Tro-mo, and the people as Tro-mowa. In addition to Tro-mo we took over the Phari plain at the head of the valley. This extends for fifteen miles in length by two or three in breadth to the Tang La (' Clear Pass '), and includes the large village of Phari (' Hog Hill '), a considerable trade centre ; and Chu-kya (' Frozen Stream '), a hamlet lying in all its bleakness at the foot of the great snow mountain Chomo-lhari. The district centring on Chu-kya is known as Perri. We took over also the Kampu Valley, which, coming down from the north, joins the Chumbi Valley at Shasima, where the British Political Officer resided. These three, Phari, Chu-kya, and Kampu, together with Upper Tromo and Lower Tromo, comprised five separate communities, each with their own headmen and local councils. Of the five, Upper and Lower Tromo have the largest population and are also the most prosperous.

The two small settlements of Perri and Kampu were peopled originally from eastern Tibet ; Lower Tromo from the district of Ha in Bhutan, a district well known for the vigour of its people and their love of highway robbery. But nowadays the Tromowas are peaceful and prosperous folk, and before our occupation were suffering greatly from Bhutanese depredations.

The Chumbi Valley near Pipitang

Under Tibetan rule the administration of the entire tract lay in the hands of the two Dzongpöns of Phari, but lesser matters were settled by the local councils of village elders. In spite of their two military garrisons, one in the valley and a smaller detachment at Phari, the Chinese had but little share in the control of affairs, except during the trial of a case in which a Chinaman was concerned. If a Chinaman and a Tibetan were concerned in a case, the magistrates of both nationalities sat together for its decision. When those who were convicted of offences were men of substance, fines were usually inflicted ; but the poor might expect to be flogged with considerable severity. For the Tibetan proverb which says ' The sheep has wool, so fleece it ' advocates a different treatment for ' the hairless fish '.

The Chinese civil official, known to the Tibetans as Popön (' The Paymaster '), had very little to do and took no great interest in his surroundings. During a conversation at his official residence in Pipitang, a village three miles down the valley from Shasima, he admitted complete ignorance of the whereabouts of the Bhutan frontier, though this was but five or six miles away. Chinese officers, both civil and military, regarding the Tibetans as a vastly inferior race, refused to learn their language. Even when there is racial affinity, the sympathy that is born of knowledge can hardly thrive in these conditions. Some indeed, who lived in Tibet a long time, undoubtedly acquired a fair knowledge of Tibetan through their temporary Tibetan wives and other sources, but these concealed their knowledge as something to be ashamed of, and would not speak Tibetan to outsiders.

The Chinese military officer known as Tungling had 140 soldiers on his roll and drew pay regularly for these. It is however a common practice for Tunglings to keep their numbers far below the strength, and to appropriate for their own use the pay of the vacant posts.

Among criminal offences theft was the commonest. The village headmen were empowered to inflict punishment up to twenty strokes with a rod, or, with the sanction of higher authority, up to one hundred strokes. They kept whatever was on the person of the thief ; his money, dagger, earrings, &c. Earrings are generally worn in Tibet by all classes ; there is a widespread belief that he or she whose ear-lobes are not pierced will be reborn in the next life as a donkey. The headmen in the Upper Valley held office for three years, those in the Lower Valley for one year.

Medical science on Western lines was, and still remains, in its infancy in the Chumbi Valley, and indeed throughout Tibet. When a Tromowa fell ill, a priest or a wizard was summoned to decide the cause of the illness, and usually laid the responsibility on some evil spirit. He himself conducted the religious service and offered the sacrifice necessary to appease the demon or drive it away. In such cases the patient was forbidden to take medicine, and feared to do so lest the evil spirit should be turned to anger. If the illness became serious, the wizard might announce that the evil spirit had been exorcised. The patient was then free to consult a doctor, but by that time it was often too late for medicine to be of any use.

The practice among Tibetans at Phari and in central Tibet generally was similar, except that they did not sacrifice animals to the same extent as did the Tromowas, whose religion is even now strongly tinged by the pre-Buddhist beliefs of Tibet, known as Pön and based largely on nature-worship. Buddhism came to Tibet eleven centuries ago in a form already differing greatly from the tenets of its Founder, and had to submit still further to change, for it gained and kept its hold only by adopting many of the Pön beliefs and practices.

Partly as a result of its proximity to Sikkim and the British district of Darjeeling, and still more as a result of our occupation, which brought British and Indian doctors into the Chumbi Valley, the belief that illness is caused by evil spirits has grown less there in recent years. Doctors both of Tibetan and of other nationalities now find plenty to do. Lack of space prevents any detailed mention here of the methods, sometimes peculiar, of Tibetan doctors.

It remains only to note that many Tibetan herbs have a

widespread reputation as drugs in China and India and other lands. It is said that the late Tsar of Russia for some time employed a Tibetan herbalist. This man's treatment was indeed harmful, but so it was meant to be by those who introduced him into the Imperial Household. It was believed that he was able to weaken the Tsar's will-power by the herbal decoctions that he gave him.

A brief reference must also be made to the hot springs at Kampu village near the head of the Kampu Valley, which have a high reputation among the numerous medicinal springs in Tibet, and are visited from far and near. There were ten springs in all, of which six had sheds of stone built over them, comprising a stone platform round the spring, and sufficient space in addition to accommodate the patients for a few days. The landlady in charge of the springs received a fee of one *tre*, i. e. about two pounds of barley meal, from each party of visitors, whether the party was large or small, and their stay long or short. She was expected to keep the sheds in repair, though some wealthy individual, whether a patient or not, would often repair a shed as an act of spiritual merit.

Each spring was considered effective for particular ailments. But patients often made the round of all the springs, for it was held that the spring which cured the disease under treatment brought into action other diseases, which had hitherto lain dormant. Thus the stay would vary as a rule from one to three weeks.

The traveller from India is struck at once by the superiority of the houses and standard of living in the Chumbi Valley to those of Indian village communities. The houses of many of the richer Tromowas are equipped with private chapels, in which are carvings, pictures, and images worth several hundreds of pounds. Some will be found with the Buddhist Bible (*Kan-gyur*) complete in one hundred and eight volumes, each wrapped in a silk cover. In other houses there are good paintings on the walls. Nearly all have pictures, images, and chapel ornaments. The ground floors of the houses form, as a rule, part of the courtyard, and are given up to ponies,

mules, cattle, &c. Many houses have two storeys above the
ground floor ; the windows and wooden balconies of these,
simply but effectively carved, remind one of Swiss chalets.

Thirty years ago the good people of Tromo were far less
prosperous than now. It is the opening of the trade route to
India through their valley that has worked the change. The
Tromowas control the trade between Phari, at the head of the
valley, and Kalimpong, ninety-five miles away to the south-
west across Sikkim and the Indian frontier. They buy at
one end and sell at the other, whether it be the wool that
pours down unendingly over the passes into India, or the
cotton goods, silks, indigo, vessels of enamelled iron and of
aluminium, matches, soap, and other miscellanea, that find
their way into the Grand Lama's dominions. To the Tromowas also belong the mules, ponies, donkeys, and yaks that
transport the goods along the difficult mountain tracks
between the two trade centres. Through the Chumbi Valley,
as through the neck of a bottle, is poured half of the entire
trade between India and Tibet. For the trade of all other
routes, west and east from Kashmir to Assam, a distance of
nearly two thousand miles, totals barely as much as that
which passes along this one road. Thus it comes that the
Tromowas are prosperous.

The inhabitants of Phari are in poorer circumstances ;
those in Chu-kya and Kampu are the poorest of all. At
Phari, 14,300 feet above sea level, and at Chu-kya, a little
higher, no crop ripens; but barley is sown every year, and the
straw with its half-formed grain is sold at good prices as
fodder for the animals passing along the trade routes.

Slavery was not unknown in the Chumbi Valley during
our occupation, but proximity to British India had greatly
lessened the numbers of the slaves, so that only a dozen
or two remained. Across the frontier in Bhutan there were
a great many.

Slaves were sometimes stolen, when small children, from
their parents. Or the father and mother, being too poor to
support their child, would sell it to a man, who paid them
sho-ring, ' price of mother's milk ', brought up the child and

kept it, or sold it, as a slave. These children come mostly from south-eastern Tibet and the territories of the wild tribes who dwell between Tibet and Assam.

Two slaves whom I saw both appeared to have come from this tribal territory. They had been stolen from their parents when five years old, and sold in Lhasa for about seven pounds each. Of their country they remembered but little save that it was isolated, and outsiders who entered it were killed.

Slaves received food and clothing from their masters on the same scale as servants, but no pay. Every year a servant received a woollen robe and a cotton robe jointly worth seventeen shillings ; a pair of excellent cloth boots (I often wore similar ones myself) reaching nearly to the knees and costing four shillings ; and a fresh pair of soles for these boots every month, each pair of soles costing fivepence. The clothes of a maidservant, two gowns, underclothing, apron, and boots, were even cheaper, but the clothes of both men and women were warm and efficient. Menservants received pay at the rate of ten shillings a month ; women at the rate of seven shillings.

The slavery in the Chumbi Valley was of a very mild type. If a slave was not well treated, it was easy for him to escape into Sikkim and British India.

Though, as keen traders, the Tromowas travel through other countries, they remain devoted to the religion of their own. It is mainly in Upper Tromo that the Pön religion maintains its hold, though modified by the Buddhism around it. During one of my subsequent visits to the valley, after the Dalai Lama's return from India to Tibet, two of the headmen complained to me—though of course it was no concern of mine—that an Oracle from Lhasa had established himself in a monastery, and by his divination and prophecies was perverting the followers of the Pön faith.

' He has enticed away eighty families from our Pön monastery,' said one headman. ' He tells the people that the Pön religion is no more the true religion than are those of foreign nations. During the last twelve months of this quarrel between the Buddhists and ourselves, eight of the leading men of this neighbourhood, including four headmen, have died. There is no peace since this Oracle came into our country.'

I duly expressed my regret at the disagreement, and he continued : ' This Oracle is indeed possessed by a supernatural power, but it is a demon, not a good spirit. Please put several things secretly into a box and ask the Oracle what is in the box. If he can answer correctly, it is indeed a god and there is no more to be said. But if he fails, as he will fail, please write and inform the Precious Protector (i. e. the Dalai Lama) that this Oracle is false, for we know that you are on terms of friendship with His Holiness.'

' But Tibetan officials do not interfere in the religious concerns of British or Indians, when they come to India. Similarly, I do not interfere in the religious affairs of Tibetans when I come to Tibet.'

' That is an excellent principle ', he replied, ' for ordinary use. But this is not an ordinary matter of religion. Surely you will not allow a demon to masquerade as a god.'

High above all the villages, on the crest of the mountain range that separates the Chumbi Valley from Bhutan, is the Pang-kar Bi-tsi chö-ten, a strong, square building, made of stones laid one on top of the other without mortar or mud. It is fifty feet in length and breadth, forty feet in height, and roofed with flat, slate-like stones. Grey and sinister it stands, defying the gales that beat against it. Inside is a chö-ten, or stupa, and inside this is a copper urn. When the building was under construction, many years ago, blood was poured into this urn, and in it were placed the corpses of a boy and girl, each eight years old, who had been slain for the purpose. The bodies were placed head downwards, the feet pointing towards the roof. It is a boundary mark between Bhutan and Tromo, fixed after many disputes and bloody conflicts.

Scenting the corpses and the blood, a demon took possession of the chö-ten. From the spot can be seen the hills skirting the Tromo villages, but away to the east the villages of Bhutan lie hidden. The chö-ten lies south-east from Upper Tromo, an inauspicious direction. Thus it comes that,

My old friend, the lama from Sikkim (right), and his disciple

while Bhutan goes unharmed, the devil grievously afflicts the Chumbi Valley.

It is some twelve hundred years since Buddhism came to Tibet, but the fierce beliefs and savage practices that preceded it still speak to the people. This chapter may fittingly conclude with an example of the newer and truer spirit, the spirit of Buddha himself.

Down below, a few hundred feet above the sunny fields in the valley, yet secluded from these, is a large cave. But a devil lives in the precipice on the opposite side of the valley, and breaks in on the meditation of any hermit who dwells in the cave to mortify the flesh and exalt the spirit. Few therefore were able to remain for more than a week.

Visiting the cave one day, I found there the disciple of an old Sikkimese friend of mine. It was with surprise that I learned that the young priest had been there in meditation for three months. I asked whether the devil had not interfered with him.

' Yes,' was the reply. ' At first he often entered the cave during the evening in the form of a monk, and sought to disturb my meditation. But I felt nothing but pity towards him ; and so, after some days, he left without doing me any harm.'

X

A VISIT TO THE TASHI LAMA

IN the autumn of 1904 Captain O'Connor visited Shigatse from Gyantse and made the acquaintance of the Tashi Lama, thus renewing in person the friendship which had been interrupted since the time of Warren Hastings, more than a hundred years before. In the winter of 1905 the Tashi Lama, with the Tongsa Penlop of Bhutan and the Maharaja of Sikkim, came to India. He was received by the Prince of Wales, witnessed a review of 70,000 troops at Rawal Pindi, and visited the sacred places of Buddhism.

Mr. White went to England for four months in September 1906, and I was then recalled from my Indian district to take up his work during his absence. This now included Tibet and Bhutan in addition to Sikkim.

The Tashi Lama sent me a warm invitation to visit him at his seat at Tashi-lhünpo, and the Indian Government permitted me to accept this. Mr. Dover, the State Engineer in Sikkim, accompanied me. Shigatse, the second town in Tibet, is situated only half a mile from Tashi-lhünpo, a monastery containing four thousand monks. Our way from Gyantse lay down the broad valley of the Nyang Chu past the Dong-tse monastery, where a high Incarnate Lama was done to death, in the old unfriendly days, for sheltering Sarat Chandra Das ; then past Nor-bu Kyung-tse and other prosperous villages till we came to the valley of the Tsang-po. My welcome at Shigatse was hearty in the extreme. It commenced thirteen miles outside the town with the arrival of high officials bringing silk scarves of welcome. Farther on, officers invited me to a large tent erected by the roadside, where Tibetan tea and other light refreshments were provided. By the time we reached Shigatse our cavalcade was large and picturesque, for in the wonderful clearness of the Tibetan atmosphere the coloured silks and brocades of the Tibetan nobility show to great advantage. I was lodged in the villa belonging to the Kung of Shigatse, the Tashi Lama's brother. Here further presentations took place. Bags of rice were brought for myself and my servants, barley and peas for my ponies and mules, and scarves of welcome multiplied more and more. A guard of Tibetan police, holding whips with short stocks and long, workmanlike thongs, kept off the curious.

My visit lasted for a week. There is no need to describe it here in detail. The main point is that the Tashi Lama and his people, whose friendship Captain O'Connor had already gained, showed the utmost friendliness to myself as the agent of the Indian Government.

On the day following our arrival I called on His Holiness. Mr. Dover and I were ushered through successive rooms, up dark, steep staircases, worn and slippery from the feet of countless pilgrims. Very impressive was the reception by the enthroned Incarnation of ' The Buddha of Boundless Light ' in the dim, pillared hall. After giving our scarves of greeting we were led to seats on his right hand, while his Ministers stood on his left, and farther off priests intoned solemn chants suitable to the occasion.

But though the official calls of greeting and farewell were of interest and showed the friendliness prevailing, my two private calls showed this still more clearly. These took place in a beautiful, secluded pavilion, surrounded with water, and standing in the park of the Lama's country seat on the outskirts of the town. Here no curious ear could listen to what passed between us, and the conversation ranged over many subjects.

The Lama is fond of animals, and has a creditable menagerie in his park. He is interested in most novelties. Producing a modern rifle with telescopic sights, he asked me to explain its mechanism. But his interest centred chiefly on the political situation. He had accepted the Indian Government's invitation to visit India, depending on their support if his acceptance should subsequently lead him into trouble. The Chinese were regaining power in Tibet, and he feared their reprisals. Would our Government come to his aid if necessary ? I gave him such comfort as my instructions allowed, and it is probable that my visit to Shigatse helped in some degree to preserve him from untoward consequences. He feared also the Tibetan Government at Lhasa. Our Government had fought with Lhasa, but showed friendliness to Tashi-lhünpo, and the enmity of his own Central Government was, therefore, inevitable. The latter suspected that Tashi-lhünpo aimed at soliciting the help of Britain to obtain independence from their rule, and thus to divide and weaken Tibet as a whole.

As regards China, our Government was saved by the subsequent outbreak of the Chinese revolution. As regards Lhasa, the cordial relations with the Central Government, which were afterwards established, enabled me to tender advice in the right quarter, thus helping to prevent reprisals and to promote the unity of Tibet.

Truly the Tashi Lama has a wonderful personality. Somewhat short in stature, with a fair and healthy complexion, the smile with which he regards you is touched with the quiet saintliness of one who prays and works for all mankind, but it is at the same time the smile of a friend who takes a personal and sympathetic interest in your own concerns. It is not surprising that he should be loved by his people. It is good that there is such a man in Tibet ; it is good that there are such men in the world.

It would not, however, be correct to assume that, while the Dalai Lama takes a large share in politics, His Holiness of Tashi-lhünpo is entirely engrossed in things spiritual. For he too has his worldly dominion, though it is far smaller than that of the Dalai and is under the Dalai's overlordship. The Tashi Lama has temporal power over three districts, of which Shigatse is not one, for the Central Government see the advantage of having their own officers there to watch events at Tashi-lhünpo. When the occasion seemed to demand it, the Tashi Lama has made diplomatic moves, unknown even to his Chief Minister, by acting through an aide-de-camp or other personal attendant.

Between Lhasa and Tashi-lhünpo. as mentioned above,

The Tashi Lama

The Tashi Lama's mother, who was deaf and dumb

In front, left to right, bowl of barley flour, jade teacup, and prayer
wheel, worked by hand, in its case

The Tashi-lhünpo monastery. The fort at Shigatse (p. 86) in the distance on the right

there is a deep and abiding jealousy, but Tibetans will tell
you that the Grand Lamas themselves are untouched by
feelings of antagonism, which are kept alive by the subordinates on both sides. In common with most Orientals,
Tibetans have indeed the habit of blaming ministers rather
than rulers when things go wrong. But it does seem to me
also that the rivalry is stronger among the subordinates.
The Grand Lamas, being deeply imbued with religion, are
able to rise to some extent above feelings of personal jealousy.
And the Tashi Lama, with his lesser worldly interests, is able
to devote himself almost entirely to his spiritual duties.
'As to my part,' wrote a former Tashi Lama to Warren
Hastings a hundred and fifty years ago, 'I am but a religious
devotee, and it is the custom of our sect, with the rosary in
our hands, to pray for the welfare of all mankind, and for
the peace and happiness of the inhabitants of this country.'
So it is in the main at this time also. And the Tashi Lama
reaps his reward in the love and reverence with which his
people regard him. When he came back from India, men
as well as women literally wept with joy at his safe return,
though the Tibetan does not weep easily.

The monastery of Tashi-lhünpo with its four thousand
monks is a town in itself, surrounded by a wall. Built on the
slope of a rocky spur, its tall houses rise one above another,
facing south across the plain. Through them runs a line of
five strong, impressive buildings, each like the other, and
surmounted by gilded roofs of Chinese design, which dazzle
your eyes in the morning sun. These are the mausolea of the
five departed Tashi Lamas, the present Lama being the sixth.
While the exteriors of these mausolea are dazzling, their
interiors also are surprisingly beautiful, that of the first
Lama being especially fine. Even after the lapse of so many
years a vision still remains with me of altars, fully but taste-
fully equipped with cups of solid gold and silver, of corals,
turquoises, and other precious stones, some of these even let
into the floor, and behind the altar in each case a pyramid,
some twenty-five feet high, adorned with gold, silver, and
precious stones. On the top of the pyramid is an effigy of

the deceased Lama. Vases of old porcelain and cloisonné complete the picture. No garishness is here, but a beautiful, harmonious design.

A visit to the Tashi Lama's metal factory found only some thirty artisans at work. They were engaged in turning out five hundred images of the god, Tse-pa-me, ' Eternal Life ', for distribution to various monasteries throughout Tibet. Another day I went over the monastery with its printing establishment at Na tang, seven miles out of Shigatse, along the road to Sakya. Thirty-three monks are employed in the printing establishment, which is said to be the largest in Tibet. The letters are carved on heavy rectangular blocks of wood, which are arranged on high racks in the rooms assigned to them, and numbered alphabetically. The printing is done rapidly. Three monks work together, one taking the impressions, another handing the paper, and the third looking after the blocks. The paper is manufactured from the bark of one of the species of *Daphne* plant (*Edgeworthia Gardneri*), and comes mostly from Bhutan. During my visit three copies were being made of the Teng-gyur, the great Commentary on the Lamaïst Scriptures. It consists of some two hundred and twenty volumes ; the Scriptures themselves, known as the Kang-gyur, being contained in preferably one hundred and eight volumes, though often in about one hundred only. The number one hundred and eight is sacred to Tibetans, and happy is the man who lives to be a hundred and eight years old, attaining the perfection of old age ! The memory of a Tibetan friend of mine, who is said to have died at this age, will long be treasured among his descendants and their neighbours.

The Tashi-lhünpo monastery has its own printing place, but it is on a much smaller scale than the one at Na-tang. The other chief printing place is at Der-gé in eastern Tibet. There the blocks are of metal, and the impressions are said to be clearer than those at Na-tang.

The fort at Shigatse is of especial interest, for it is said to have been built by the celebrated king of Tsang, who defeated the last king of the Sitya Dynasty in 1635, but was himself subdued a few years later by Gushi Khan, the Mongol, who installed the fifth Dalai Lama on the Tibetan throne. The people of Shigatse claim that the present form of the famous Potala, the Dalai Lama's Palace at Lhasa, was copied by the Chief Minister of the fifth Dalai Lama from the Shigatse fort. Tradition ascribed the power of this king of Tsang to the fact that his mother was a demon, and many are the stories told of the cleverness and trickery which enabled him, a young groom in the stables, to rise to supreme power in the Tsang province.

It was during this visit to Shigatse that I was introduced to a curious Tibetan custom. Letters from the Tashi Lama would be brought by his servants, who would bring at the same time a verbal message from His Holiness. The latter was invariably the most important part of the communication and frequently modified the terms of the letter. Later on I found this custom to be common among high Tibetan officials. Fear that the letter may be seen by the Chinese or other unfriendly persons has given rise to the practice. Sometimes Europeans travelling in Tibet have been shown letters issued by those in authority to Tibetan officials, enjoining the latter to help the traveller. But difficulties appear and the instructions in the letter do not seem to be obeyed, in the spirit at any rate. The reason is that instructions of a very different nature have been conveyed verbally.

Another way of sending secret messages is to write them on wooden tablets. These are dispatched by a trustworthy servant, who can erase them immediately in the event of danger. The Tibetan tablets consist of five or six thin and narrow strips of wood bound together in an outer cover.

On the 6th November 1906 I paid my farewell call on the Tashi Lama, and at his request went round to see him privately afterwards. He gave me a photograph of himself, coloured by a Tibetan artist. At its foot he wrote his name and titles in golden letters and affixed his seal. As a rule he makes one of his officers write his signature, for he considers his own handwriting to be inferior. A neat handwriting is ranked as a matter of the highest importance in Tibet.

XI

CHINESE ASCENDANCY

AFTER the Expedition of 1904 returned to India, attempts were made to gain Chinese adhesion to the treaty with which it had concluded. But the Expedition had thoroughly alarmed the Chinese Government, who were determined to work for the restoration of Chinese power in Tibet. In April 1906 a Convention was concluded between Great Britain and China at Peking.[1] This modified the Lhasa Convention by providing that the preservation of Tibet's integrity should rest with China, and that China, but no other Power, should have the right to concessions in Tibet. The old mistake of concluding a treaty with China about Tibet without consulting the Tibetan Government was repeated. It afforded the Tibetan Government a ground for complaint, of which they availed themselves when they came into touch with us after the flight of the Dalai Lama to India in 1910, and at the Simla Conference in 1914. And the complaint was reasonable, for the effect was to deliver Tibet into the power of China. While ourselves engaging not to interfere in the internal administration of Tibet, we ought to have obtained a similar engagement from China, limiting her strictly to such suzerainty as she actually enjoyed before the Lhasa Expedition.

The Chinese Government were not slow to take advantage of the altered circumstances. Mr. Chang Yin Tang was appointed High Commissioner for Tibet. He arrived in Tibet via India in the autumn of 1906, and proceeded to Gyantse and Lhasa. Here he worked to gain control over the Tibetan administration, enfeebled as it was by the 1904 Expedition and the absence of the Dalai Lama. He worked also to lessen British influence in Tibet, a policy in which he was aided by the Peking Convention and the unwillingness of the British Government of the day to take any part in

For a full copy see Appendix VIII.

Tibetan affairs. For the Chinese Government are quick to note the temper of the Governments with which they have to deal. Mr. Chang's especial efforts were devoted to preventing direct dealings between the British and Tibetan officials. For instance, the supplies for our Trade Agents and their escorts had to be obtained through Chinese intermediaries and at prices fixed by the latter.

The reduced indemnity of twenty-five lakhs of rupees was paid by China in three instalments. On the 8th February 1908, after payment of the third instalment, the Chumbi Valley was evacuated.

While at Lhasa, Mr. Chang endeavoured to assert Chinese suzerainty over Nepal and Bhutan, an early sign of the danger that threatened India if China obtained a firm hold over Tibet. He attempted also to secure the withdrawal of the fifty Indian sepoys from Gyantse, on the ground that China would establish a police force to protect foreigners. But those who knew the weakness of the Central Government in China were well aware that Peking could not afford efficient protection in countries so far away as Tibet.

The High Commissioner's reforms were unpalatable to most of the Lhasa officials, who had to work hard and on unaccustomed lines. With the Tibetans as a whole he was at first popular, for he stood in their eyes as the barrier against British aggression, and he initiated measures for the development of the country. As his schemes did not bear much fruit and he interfered with old established customs, his popularity to some extent declined. But many Tibetans still cherish a friendly regard for the ' Overseas Amban ', as he is called, since he came by sea to Calcutta instead of by the overland route through Eastern Tibet.

My personal relations with Mr. Chang, official and social, were uniformly excellent. Though some of his methods were not such as to commend themselves to the British mind, one had to recognize that our presence in the country was distasteful to him. He worked, as he believed, in the best interests of his country, and the policy of our Government, right or wrong, gave him the means of promoting those interests.

In 1907 Great Britain and Russia made a comprehensive Agreement designed to prevent collisions between the two Powers in Asia. It included agreements concerning Persia, Afghanistan, and Tibet. As regards the last-named, while recognizing Great Britain's ' special interest in the maintenance of the *status quo* in the external relations of Tibet ', it bound both Powers

(*a*) to abstain from interference in the internal administration of Tibet ;

(*b*) to enter into negotiations with Tibet only through the intermediary of China, except on matters arising out of the Lhasa Convention ;

(*c*) not to send Representatives to Lhasa ;

(*d*) not to seek or obtain concessions for roads, mines, &c. ;

(*e*) not to appropriate any part of the revenue of Tibet.[1]

The Agreement as a whole was admirable, for it laid the foundation of that co-operation between Russia and Britain that freed each from the menace of the other, secured India from attack, and did so much to win the Great War. But by the provision which bound both Powers to negotiate on Tibetan matters—with a few exceptions—through China alone, as well as in other ways, it placed Tibet still further in the grip of China. It thereby rendered possible a Chinese menace, not so much of brute force as of insidious penetration, on the north-eastern frontier of India. Had it been necessary to open the door for a Chinese advance in order to stave off the Russian menace, the position might have been accepted as the lesser of two evils. But from the speeches of British statesmen at the time, as well as from the light of subsequent events, it seems clear that we need not have withdrawn from Tibet as fully as we did, in order to obtain Russia's signature to the Agreement.

China felt that her dignity had been wounded deeply inasmuch as she was not consulted, though several of the provisions of the Agreement concerned her. She had ' lost face '. And this rendered her more obdurate than ever towards us.

---

[1] For the portion of the Agreement relating to Tibet see Appendix IX.

Neither was Tibet consulted; she too felt a sense of injury.

Meanwhile Mr. Chang and a British Representative were engaged in discussing new Trade Regulations for Tibet, rendered necessary by the opening of the new marts at Gyantse and Gartok. In April 1908 these were signed.[1] A Tibetan delegate, who was admitted to the negotiations only as Mr. Chang's subordinate, appended his signature also.

The general effect of these Regulations was still further to push British and Indians out of Tibet. I will not weary the reader with details. As an example, I may note that by the ninth Regulation our Government agreed that 'British officers and subjects' (including Indians) should be barred from travelling in Tibet beyond Gyantse. No such restriction had ever been accepted by us during the whole course of Tibetan history. Indian pilgrims were accustomed to visit the sites sacred to Hindus at Manasarowar and elsewhere. Such pilgrimages now became illegal. The objection to the travel of Europeans had become much less than before. This therefore was not the time to prevent British travellers, while making no regulation against the travel of Russians, Japanese, or others.

And the Tibetans were not pleased. For matters which they regarded as within their own control were placed under the control of Chinese officers. In one way and another they were placed under Chinese domination, and the British Government were primarily responsible for putting them there, first by the Lhasa Expedition and next by the treaties which followed it up.

The Chinese now held all the cards in their hands. Tibet, disheartened and unarmed, lay at their mercy. Britain had divested herself of all power to help the weaker party. There was in fact every element of instability in the position. And yet the future of Tibet was of great importance to India and the British Commonwealth, for, as civilization advances, India and Tibet are bound to be drawn into closer relationship. And no Indian frontier is so long, or nearly so long, as that which separates India from Tibet.

[1] For a full copy see Appendix X.

Such was the position when in April 1908 Mr. White left the Agency for good, and I was summoned from the charge of a district in Bihar to succeed him. Mr. White had been twenty years in Sikkim, where he was regarded with affection and respect by all classes of the population. The first Political Officer to be posted there, he had developed the resources of this little State out of all recognition.

I had been recently on a year's leave, part of which I had spent in attempting to learn something of Tibetan literature, and part in studying matters, Chinese and Tibetan, in China. At Peking Sir John Jordan, the British Minister, and his Secretaries, with characteristic kindness gave me a valuable insight into Chinese politics and their bearing on the Tibetan question.

It soon became evident that our position in Tibet was precarious. Chinese troops were still pushing in from the east through Tachienlu. Our treaty rights were infringed in various ways. The Lhasa Convention forbade the levy of dues, yet the old duties were reimposed at Phari in the Chumbi Valley, and in western Tibet. The same Convention forbade restrictions on trade by existing routes, yet the Sikkim traders, who from time immemorial had gone to Kampa Dzong, were stopped. A monopoly in wool and hides was inaugurated in contravention of the Trade Regulations of 1908. A consignment of Indian silver to Tibet was stopped by the Chinese at the frontier. The Tibetan officers at Gyantse were unable even to accept invitations to lunch from British officers there, without first obtaining permission from their Chinese masters. The power of China was recognized in Sikkim, where people said openly that the Chinaman was the equal of the Englishman. I was told by more than one good authority, that the Maharaja and Maharani of Sikkim would prefer to be under China rather than under Great Britain, if this were possible. And Mr. Chang was already stretching out his hand towards Nepal, whose Representative he informed that Tibet and Nepal, ' being united like brothers, under the auspices of China, should work in harmony for the mutual good '—a tentative assumption of Chinese suzerainty

Books and bookseller in the streets of Lhasa

Tibetan literature

over Nepal, to be pressed or disavowed later by Mr. Chang's Government, according as circumstances might suggest.

The absence of the Dalai Lama from Lhasa [1] and the payment by China of the Younghusband indemnity strengthened the Chinese position. All Chinamen who entered Tibet preached to the Tibetans that China was now run on modern lines, that it had modern guns and up-to-date troops which could hold their own against any country, statements which Tibetans, living like hermits in their own country, had no adequate means of testing. 'Everything therefore ', said these messengers from the outside world, ' must be done through us. You Tibetans can of yourselves do nothing.' Many Tibetans who had lost faith in the power of China, now began to look again to that country to protect them.

It may be freely conceded that China's work in Tibet had its own good points. The Chinese officials of the modern school, who came in now, lessened the bribes taken by the Tibetan officials from the poorer classes, and in ordinary non-political cases gave straighter justice than that dealt out by the Tibetan magistracy. There was no doubt some foundation for the Amban's claim that the poorer classes in Tibet were in favour of China.

But in spite of these alleviations Tibetans were contrasting British methods with Chinese, saying that the former did not interfere with the old customs, but the latter were trying to uproot them. This most conservative of peoples was unwilling to abandon its national costume in favour of Chinese dress, or indeed to change any of its customs at foreign dictation.

Great though the Chinese power might be, one could see that it stood on an insecure basis. Tibet was seething everywhere. Even at Batang, comparatively near the Chinese border, and elsewhere, the Christian missionaries, British, French, American, &c., were in danger, for the Chinese troops were unable to afford adequate protection to Batang and the surrounding country. When the Dalai Lama and his Government were in India and his troops in the ascendant,

[1] See p. 96.

I impressed on him the desirability on all grounds of seeing that these missionaries were not harmed by the Tibetans during the fighting that from time to time took place. His Holiness was fully alive to this necessity, and thus it came about that the missionaries in the distant towns of eastern Tibet were henceforth able to escape molestation. Hitherto, they and their converts had been not only molested, but even massacred from time to time by fanatical Tibetans.

The Chinese Power in Tibet was great and steadily growing. We British officers on the spot could do little but work, quietly and unfalteringly, to promote the good will of the Tibetans towards us. And this we did. Major O'Connor, Captains Campbell, Bailey, Kennedy, and Weir, and Mr. Gould gave the Tibetans an idea of British justice, sympathy, and geniality, and helped to establish more and more a good understanding between British and Tibetans.

With the same object in view I obtained the services of Mr. Macdonald to fill the post of British Agent at Yatung in the Chumbi Valley, one of the most important posts under my control in Tibet, for almost all travellers between central Tibet and India pass through this valley. Mr. Macdonald is partly of Lepcha extraction—a race akin to the Tibetans—was educated at the Tibetan school in Darjeeling as a Buddhist, though subsequently converted to Christianity, was married to an Anglo-Nepalese Christian, and had been to Lhasa with the Expedition of 1904. Writing and speaking Tibetan as one of themselves, thinking along Tibetan lines, and endowed with a patient and kindly temperament, he never failed to gain the good will of Tibetans of all classes.

My predecessor's confidential clerk having left, I took in his place A-chuk Tse-ring, who had worked with me in Kalimpong and Sikkim and was now to be associated with me for many years in Tibetan work. Trustworthy and industrious was A-chuk Tse-ring, and to a high level of general intelligence he added a deep political insight into Tibetan affairs. His death in Lhasa, during the early days of my visit there twelve years later, was a heavy blow to us all.

As my personal guide, philosopher, and friend, I had Ku-sho Pa-lhe-se, a scion of one of the older families in the

Ku-sho Pa-lhe-se

Chinese troops in Tibet with modern rifles

Tibetan soldiers armed with flintlocks. Prongs made of antelope horns
are used to support the guns in aiming

Tibetan nobility, the only one of his kind who has ever been induced to live in British territory. I had come into touch with him through the medium of a Tibetan friend, and had attached him to my private service before I ever entered Tibet. In him I found the best possible teacher of the Tibetan language, manners, and customs, and especially of everything connected with the Government and politics of the country. For Tibet is still in the feudal stage, and the nobility, side by side with the leading priests, rule the land. For seven successive generations Pa-lhe-se's ancestors had been on the Grand Council of Tibet, the highest honour to which a layman could attain. The break came in the time of his father, who would probably have gained the same distinction, had he not, in the kindness of his heart, aided an Indian who subsequently proved to have been engaged in the secret exploration of Tibet. Pa-lhe-se subsequently entered the service of Government in my Agency, but left ten years later when I did, for he used always to inform me, ' If you give up your Government post to-day, I give up mine to-morrow.' When I returned to work, he too came back. I owed much to this son of the Pa-lha house.

Our perseverance in cultivating Tibetan friendship, following on the perseverance of those who had been before us, was a matter of some difficulty, in view of the efforts of the powerful Chinese to keep us apart. But it was rewarded in the end. For when the Chinese hand became too heavy and the Dalai Lama fled, it was to us that Tibet turned.

What in the meanwhile was happening to eastern Tibet and to the Dalai Lama ? When the Expedition of 1904 quitted the country, the Chinese resolved to lose no time in regaining hold of it. Chinese troops were pushed through Tachienlu, on the border between Tibet and western China. Control was steadily obtained over some of the nearest districts in eastern Tibet. Disturbances followed, but no organized opposition. In August 1905 Chao Erh Feng, who was appointed to control the operations, was able to advance. By the end of 1906, Ba-tang was overpowered. Within the next three years Der-gé, Tra-ya, and Cham-do, important centres in eastern Tibet, were occupied by Chinese troops.

The Dalai Lama had fled from Lhasa in 1904 on the approach of the Younghusband Expedition. He went first to Urga, in North Mongolia, near the Siberian frontier. The Chinese Emperor issued a proclamation deposing him, but the Tibetans treated it with contumely, and continued to refer to him for orders as far as his absence permitted. In the next year he went to Sining, in the Kansu province of China, and in 1908 to Peking. Here he was received by the Emperor and had to render homage. Not for him the reception accorded to the fifth Dalai, who visited the Chinese Emperor as one independent Ruler visits another. An additional title was conferred upon him, and this too showed that the Chinese Government were determined to keep him in strict subordination. ' The Great, Good, Self-Existent Buddha of Heaven ' became ' The Loyally Submissive Viceregent, the Great, Good, Self-Existent Buddha of Heaven '.

In Peking the Lama gave an interview to Sir John Jordan and expressed a desire for friendly relations with the Indian Government. Leaving his Chinese hosts in December 1908, he travelled to Tibet by the northern route through Kansu, but it was not till October of the following year that he arrived at Nagchuka. Here his wanderings through the cold deserts of the Chang Tang ended. He had reached a northern outpost of central Tibet, ten days' march from Lhasa, and in close touch with central and eastern Tibet.

The news that greeted him must have filled him with dismay. We find him writing for help to the foreign Ministers in Peking, British, French, Russian, and Japanese. To the British Trade Agent at Gyantse he sends telegrams for dispatch to ' Great Britain and all the Ministers of Europe '. In these he asks that the invading Chinese troops may be compelled to withdraw from Tibet, for—most serious charge of all—they wish to abolish the religion of the Tibetans. Again he telegraphs : ' Large insects are eating and secretly injuring small insects,' a common Tibetan saying, that illustrates the oppression of the weak by the strong. To his Chinese overlords in Peking he telegraphs the same saying and adds : ' We have acted frankly and now they steal our hearts.'

At the end of 1909 the Chinese Government asked for

permission to send troops to Tibet through Indian territory, but permission was naturally refused.

It was at the end of December 1909 that His Holiness entered Lhasa. And in truth he had good reason to be alarmed. Eastern Tibet was in the hands of the Chinese, who were trying to force it to become a province of China. They were endeavouring to change the habits of this most conservative nation and—most heinous crime of all—they had trampled on the religion, its dearest possession. Tibetan officers, talking to me subsequently of Chinese oppression, could never forget that, when the Chinese destroyed the great monastery and temple at Ba-tang, they used the Buddhist Scriptures there for soling their boots. More even than the killing of noblemen and priests, this excited their horror and disgust.

Throughout the Chinese advance into Tibet the Tibetan Government had abstained from ordering its troops to fight. Chao Erh Feng had therefore to meet only sporadic and unauthorized risings of tribesmen. Even when the Chinese troops were in possession of Chamdo and threatening an advance to Lhasa, and the Tibetan soldiery were drawn up only half a mile from them, the Dalai Lama forbade the latter to fight. For he wished to avoid a quarrel with China, whom Tibet, without resources or organization, was unable effectually to oppose.

The Junior Chinese Amban at Lhasa appears to have promised the Tibetan Ministers that not more than one thousand Chinese troops should come to Lhasa, and that on their arrival their distribution along the frontiers would be considered. However, two days later, on the 12th February 1910, two thousand Chinese troops arrived within two marches of Lhasa, and the same day forty Chinese cavalry and two hundred infantry entered the city, fired on the populace, killing a few of them, and endeavoured to seize the Tibetan Ministers.

The latter feared that they would be put to death and that the Dalai Lama would be deprived of power and kept as a State prisoner. Accordingly in the middle of the following night His Holiness, the Ministers and other leading officials, accompanied by two hundred soldiers, fled towards India, taking their seals of office with them. Twelve hours later, at Chak-sam, they reached the Tsangpo, the great river forty miles from Lhasa. On the further side they left the soldiers to hold back the pursuing Chinese soldiery as long as possible. The Tibetans did so, killing a good many of the pursuers, and then dispersed across the country.

Nine days after leaving Lhasa, the Dalai Lama and his following rode into safety across the Sikkim frontier. The distance travelled was two hundred and seventy miles, with three high passes and a broad river to cross. A few days later he arrived in Darjeeling. For the Lama himself and his elder Ministers, accustomed to travel in leisurely luxury, it was a remarkable achievement.

In defence of their proceedings the Chinese Foreign Office pointed out that the Indian Government had blamed them in the past for failing to make the Tibetan Government observe treaty engagements and had in consequence, in 1904, dispatched the Expedition to Lhasa. The Government of China had accordingly sent their troops to secure the observance of treaty obligations, to protect the trade marts, and to maintain peace and order. The Expedition which Lord Curzon and the British Government dispatched and withdrew in 1904 was clearly the cause of the Chinese advance. But it was hard on Tibet, and subsequently disastrous to the Chinese themselves, that the latter should have carried it forward in such a tactless and savage manner. It is curious that one Asiatic race should not know how to treat another, allied to it more or less by the strong ties of race and religion. But the history of all Asia abounds in such instances. Perhaps the explanation, partly at any rate, is that Asiatic Governments have not yet learnt and inwardly digested the value of tolerance as an art of Government—of tolerance, that is, in the things that really matter. And thus it has fallen out that the white foreigner has spread over Asia, giving to her people something that they cannot give to each other.

On the Dalai Lama's route to India.   Travellers halting on the Tang La above Phari

XII

NEGOTIATING A TREATY WITH BHUTAN

THE personal views of Their Highnesses of Sikkim, referred to in the last chapter, were not of much consequence, for they did not yet understand what was happening in eastern Tibet. Moreover, the Maharaja was advanced in years and the old order was passing away. But in Bhutan there was real danger.

Shortly before his departure, my predecessor had advocated closer relations with Bhutan, fearing Chinese intervention in that State. Our Treaty of 1865 provides that disputes between Bhutan on the one side and Sikkim or Kuch Behar (a small Indian State near the southern frontier of Bhutan) on the other shall be referred for the decision of the British Government. Mr. White proposed to ask Bhutan to agree to refer disputes with all neighbouring States, and to increase her subsidy for so agreeing. The Government asked me to advise.

Bhutan has a population of only a few hundred thousand, but an area equal to two and a half times the area of Wales ; it marches with the Indian frontier for two hundred and fifty miles and with the Tibetan frontier for somewhat less. It had long ago shaken off the shadowy suzerainty of China, as was proved by the events of the last hundred years. When we made war on Bhutan in 1865, the Chinese did not come to their assistance. We had made the Treaty after that war direct with Bhutan ; China had no part or lot in it. In 1885 the Ambans at Lhasa demanded of the two leading Chiefs in Bhutan, the Penlops of the Tong-sa and Pa-ro districts, that they should restore a Bhutanese Chief, whom the Penlops had expelled, but the demand was disregarded and abandoned. In the Sikkim Expedition of 1888 the Tibetans had asked the Bhutanese to help them, but the latter had refused. Shortly afterwards, a Tibetan Minister had asked the Bhutanese Chiefs to come to Phari in order to concert measures for counteracting British penetration. Again a refusal. And in our dealings with Bhutan for several decades we had dealt with her alone. To Lhasa indeed yearly remittances were sent, but these, claimed by some Tibetans as tribute, were acknowledged by the Bhutanese Government only as religious offerings to the Dalai Lama, the Head of the Faith. It was in fact a completely independent State, neither under China nor under Britain.

Possessed of a temperate climate and a fertile soil, less than a quarter of which was occupied by the Bhutanese themselves, it offered a tempting field for Chinese penetration. Not immediately, but later on and by degrees, Chinese colonists might well have followed, for the climate and soil would have been appreciated no less by the southern Chinaman than the plains of Mongolia are by the Chinese of the north.

It would have been natural for China to have sought this relief for her overflowing population. For she appears to regard the Mongolian peoples that border on her own and the Tibetan frontiers, Nepal, Sikkim, Bhutan, and even Burma, as within her natural sphere. And with Bhutan, inhabited by people of Tibetan stock and revering the Dalai Lama as their spiritual head, past centuries had given her a connexion which might well have been magnified into a suzerainty of the shadowy Chinese type, though any such claim at the present day would be unwelcome to the Bhutanese. And Bhutan, garrisoned by Chinese troops, peopled more and more by Chinese colonists, and overhanging the tea gardens of Assam and Jalpaiguri, would have been a new and very disturbing factor on the Indian frontier. The disorganization of the labour supply, resulting in a heavy loss to this great industry, would have been only a small part of our troubles.

These were no imaginary perils. Two months earlier the Chinese Amban at Lhasa had addressed the Chiefs in Bhutan in somewhat the following words : ' The Bhutanese are the subjects of the Emperor of China, who is the Lord of Heaven.

You, Deb Raja and two Penlops, think you are great, but you cannot continue without paying attention to the orders of your Ruler. Bhutan is the gate on the south which prevents entry (by the British). The Popön[1] will inspect your climate, crops, &c. The Deb Raja should endeavour to improve the trade of the country and the condition of the peasants. If you want any assistance, let me know.'

It was at this time that the Chinese official at Gyantse, a capable diplomatist and administrator, visited Pa-ro, the capital of western Bhutan. Here he met the Pa-ro Penlop and the Timbu Dzongpön, who, after the Ruler himself, wield the greatest power in the country, and in many respects hold semi-independent positions. There was indeed at this time strong evidence of Chinese propaganda in Bhutan.

When therefore I joined my post in April 1908, and the Indian Government asked for my advice about Bhutan, I placed these considerations before them. It appeared to me that Mr. White's proposals would not counter the Chinese advance. For we should have the right to intervene only in the case of *disputes*. If Bhutan, at any time in the future, *agreed* to Chinese intervention in her affairs, e. g. by receiving Chinese Agents in Bhutan, we could have done nothing.

Accordingly I advised that we should endeavour to persuade Bhutan to place her foreign relations under the British Government, while the latter should agree to abstain from interference in the internal administration of the country. The latter proviso appeared to me of prime importance, for my residence on the frontier had already convinced me of both the justice and the expediency of Home Rule, wherever such was possible. Ardent administrators, usually with the best of motives, introduce changes in the government of what are—perhaps somewhat arrogantly—termed backward races. But such changes, unless desired by the people themselves, do more harm than good in the long run. In any case, they promote resentment, and

---

[1] The Chinese magistrate in the Chumbi Valley.

we want no resentment against things British on this vulnerable section of our frontier.

My proposals were accepted by Mr. (now Sir Harcourt) Butler, who was then the head of the Foreign Department in Simla. In due course the Indian Government agreed : but Lord Morley, the Secretary of State, was not to be hurried. Some ten months elapsed before we received his sanction. The delay was dangerous, for Chinese intrigue continued active. A Chinese newspaper, which had been started in Lhasa, after vilifying the British, exhorted the Tibetans to combine with the Nepalese and Bhutanese— a people of the same race and religion as themselves— against us.

The consent of the Home Government having been given, I received instructions to negotiate with Bhutan in respect of the new treaty provisions, and to make such increase in the yearly subsidy as might be necessary. I lost no time, but determined that I would not go to Bhutan until I had made sure of my ground. With Kazi U-gyen, the exceptionally able Agent of the Bhutan Government, I had made friends in previous years. I gained his co-operation, and he brought the Maharaja, the subordinate Chiefs who formed the Council, and the Representative of the monasteries— a great power in Bhutan as in all Mongolian States—to Pu-na-ka, one of the chief places in western Bhutan. I arranged for an increase of the yearly subsidy by half a lakh of rupees (£3,333). No smaller increase was possible, even had it been desirable, for Mr. White had already suggested an increase by this amount independently of any treaty, and his suggestion appeared to have come to the notice of the Bhutanese authorities.

When things were ready I went into Bhutan, accompanied by Captain Kennedy, the Medical Officer at Gyantse. Four days' travelling over rough tracks brought us to the inhabited zone with its lesser rainfall and open valleys.

The next stage was at Pu-na-gu, an ideal site for a hill-station, had it been in British territory. Grassy hill-sides free from undergrowth and from leeches, those pests of the

Crossing Lo-me Pass in the mist

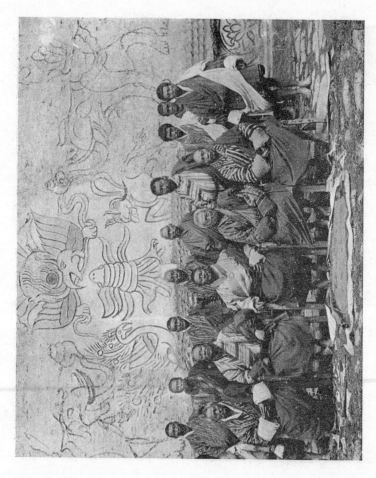

Maharaja of Bhutan and Council in 1906

eastern Himalaya, are watered by streams meandering down the easy slopes, which are interspersed with woods of oak, birch, and pine. In the Ta-ka Valley we noticed some huge honeycombs hanging from a cliff. The Bhutanese secure such combs, letting themselves down the precipices by means of ropes.

A day or two later, I learnt that five Chinese spies were ahead of us. I therefore decided, in spite of illness, to push on by double stages, and in three days arrived within six miles of Pu-na-ka. The etiquette of the Tibetan countries prescribes that your last march should be a short one, and that you should arrive in the forenoon. So we came to Pu-na-ka on the following morning, conducted by the Maharaja's escort and band, and met His Highness and the Council at the entrance to the camp which they had prepared for us. After our arrival I held the necessary interviews. I found the Council Members reluctant at first to place the external relations of Bhutan under the British Government, but I was able to gain their consent. The guarantee of non-interference in their internal administration helped me considerably in the negotiations. Most of the night was spent in making four copies of the treaty in English and Bhutanese, two for Bhutan and two for ourselves.

On the following day, the 8th January 1910, the four copies of the treaty were signed and sealed.[1] The Bhutanese seals included those of the Maharaja, each member of the Council, and the ecclesiastical Representative, and, at the head of all, the seal of the Dharma Raja, the Incarnation of Buddha, who presides over Bhutan as the Dalai Lama does over Tibet ; but with this difference, that the former is confined nowadays to spiritual functions, though his seal is necessary for governmental actions of prime importance. Thus, with the consent of all and with the blessing of its all-powerful priesthood, Bhutan was joined to the British Empire. When the treaty was completed, the Maharaja announced publicly that they were entirely satisfied with its terms.

[1] For a copy of this treaty see Appendix XI.

It was a pleasure to receive the congratulations of the Viceroy and the approval of the Home Government on the success of this affair. But the success was mainly due to three men. Firstly, to Mr. Paul, who laid the foundation of British friendship with Bhutan, and began the conversion of an aloof, hostile people to a condition of tolerance, though not of active friendship. Secondly, to Mr. White, who with greater opportunities had continued his good work, and had been present at the installation of the Tong-sa Penlop as the Ruler of Bhutan. Last, but not least, I was indebted to Kazi U-gyen, who was now to receive the title of Raja. His wise counsel did much for British interests and for those of his own people. He had the insight to see where these interests coincided. When he died a few years later, the Bhutanese Government lost a Minister of unusual merit, I, a faithful friend.

Captain Kennedy and I stayed several weeks in Bhutan, where I was able to cement friendship with the Maharaja and with the lesser Chiefs. His Highness is not only a very able Ruler, but is also universally respected both by his subjects and by his foreign friends. Though he has only twice in his life quitted his hermit land, he has all the broad-minded tolerance of one who has lived a cosmopolitan life. His perfect courtesy and quiet sense of humour are the common heritage of the Tibetan nobility. I shall always feel it an honour that he included me among his three chief friends. On my departure he presented me with one of the five gold medals which had been struck to commemorate his accession to the throne of Bhutan.

His relations with the Tibetan Government were amicable, but not closely cordial. Mr. White had crossed a corner of Tibet, south of Gyantse, to visit eastern Bhutan, three or four years earlier. The Tibetan Government remonstrated with Bhutan for allowing an Englishman to come to their country through Tibetan territory. The Maharaja replied somewhat as follows : ' Living as I do in the wilds of Bhutan, I am but a simpleton and have no doubt committed a serious mistake. But, as the Tibetan Government had

Druk-gye Dzong, 'The fort of Victorious Bhutan' near the Tibetan frontier

Band of the Pa-ro Penlop

permitted several hundred British soldiers, as well as some thousands of Indian soldiers under British officers, to come to Lhasa, the heart of Tibet, I thought that there could be no harm in a solitary Englishman travelling through an out-of-the-way corner of your country.'

' To that letter,' said His Highness with a twinkle in his eye, ' I received no reply.'

I became good friends also with the Pa-ro Penlop, who six years before had attempted to prevent my passage through western Bhutan. Personal intercourse removes many misunderstandings.

At the close of the following year the Maharaja attended the Delhi Durbar and paid his homage to the King.

The advantages of these treaty provisions with Bhutan are briefly as follow :

(a) Bhutan lies for two hundred and fifty miles along the borders of Bengal and Assam. Its mountains abut on one of the richest tracts in India, occupied by British and Indian tea gardens and by prosperous villages. The new treaty protects these from Chinese intervention.

(b) In both Bhutan and Sikkim the Nepalese population is increasing rapidly. The treaty helps us to keep a control over these.

(c) Bhutan is a very fertile country, and is capable of supporting one and a half million persons by agriculture. It could without difficulty have fed Chinese garrisons on the rice and other food which form their staple diet. There are at present neither British nor Indian troops near this frontier on our side. But if modern drilled Chinese troops were posted in Bhutan, tea gardens and villages over our border country would be hardly tenable, except by posting troops on our side of the frontier in one of the most unhealthy tracts in India.

(d) The treaty can be used effectually to prevent Chinese colonization in Bhutan. China had already, in 1909, made strenuous efforts to populate the inhospitable tracts round Batang in eastern Tibet with Chinese colonists. She was looking towards south-eastern Tibet, which is not far from

Bhutan, with the same object in view. Bhutan is an ideal climate for Chinese from southern and central China. Owing to the decrease of its population from monasticism, disease, and war, three-fourths of its land is uncultivated, and would quickly respond to the touch of the Chinese agriculturist.

(e) The treaty was gained without fighting, and gained therefore with goodwill on both sides, and without any of the bitterness which a military campaign must necessarily leave behind it.

That Chinese designs on Bhutan were real, admitted of no doubt. Mr. Chang, resorting to a recognized Chinese symbolism, had urged the blending of the five colours, i. e. China, Tibet, Nepal, Sikkim and Bhutan, and had likened Nepal, Bhutan, and Sikkim to the molar teeth lying side by side in a man's mouth. Such were the views of one who, after promoting a strongly forward policy as High Commissioner for Tibet, became the member of the Chinese Foreign Office in charge of Tibetan affairs.

When the Amban at Lhasa claimed Chinese sovereignty over Bhutan and ordered his Popön to establish the claim, he could hope for success, for Bhutan is of the same race and religion as Tibet, venerates the Tibetan hierarchy, and exchanges gifts with the Tibetan authorities. During my stay in Bhutan the Maharaja was arranging to burn lamps in the great Temple at Lhasa, as prayers for the soul of his brother-in-law. Race and religion are the strongest of ties, especially in the East.

Had China obtained control, she would not have forgotten her expressed desire to make Bhutan ' the gate on the south, which prevents entry '. Friendly relations between British and Bhutanese would have been barred and trade restricted. Now that we have the treaty, we may expect in time a large increase in the trade between India and Bhutan.

It is well that we have this treaty ; good for us and good for Bhutan, whose economic interests, as time goes on, will be seen to lie more and more closely in the direction of India.

An Abor house, a type common among the savage tribes of the NE. frontier (p. 107)

A Mishmi chief in
bear-skin hat

A Mishmi youth. A not
uncommon type

XIII

SECURING THE NORTH-EAST FRONTIER

THE treaty with Bhutan secured our needs over this portion of the frontier. But it had always seemed to me that this was not enough. East of Bhutan, between south-eastern Tibet on one side and Assam and Burma on the other, are a number of savage tribes, among whom the Abors and the Mishmis are the most prominent. Their territories are from seventy to a hundred miles in depth. Tibetans know them as lopas (savages), and divide them into Kha Lo, i. e. ' the savages at the entrance,' and Ting Lo, i. e. ' the savages at the bottom.' The former, who live on the borders of the Tibetan provinces of Kong-po and Po, trade in Tibet. The latter, living on the confines of India, hold no intercourse with their northern neighbour, but visit the Indian plains, where they sell rubber and buy salt.

Chinese soldiers were pushing into Tibet from western China under the leadership of Chao Erh Feng. Chinese officials had followed in their wake and were administering, or attempting to administer, large areas in eastern Tibet. The south-eastern portion of the country, being the lowest in elevation and therefore the most fertile, was bound to appeal to them as suitable for those Chinese colonies, which were being attempted even in the colder regions round Ba-tang. The Dalai Lama had long been absent from his country ; the Tibetan Government was disorganized ; there was no effective opposition.

I feared Chinese intervention and influence—and eventually a measure of control—in these tribal territories. They cover seven hundred miles of the Indian frontier, a hundred miles farther than from London to the Orkney Islands. The Indian Government had constituted me their adviser on Tibetan affairs. It seemed to me therefore that, although these tribal areas lay outside my own charge—Tibet, Bhutan, and Sikkim—I ought to point out the danger. Accordingly in July 1909, I suggested to the Indian Foreign Office that it should be ascertained how far the country of these tribes was cultivable, how far their hills and valleys could be depended on as a barrier for the plains of India, and whether any of the tribes had in any way recognized the suzerainty of Tibet or China. My recommendations were not accepted at the time, but my fears of Chinese intervention were confirmed in the following year, and I returned to the charge again and again. I communicated information, which I received—far away in Darjeeling—of the advance of Chinese troops into the territory of the Hkamti tribe on the north-eastern corner of India. Two months later a Chinese force arrived at Ri-ma in Tibet near the Mishmi border, and ordered a neighbouring Mishmi chief to cut a track from Tibet to India.

The Indian Government were at length aroused. In August 1910 one of the leading authorities in the Indian Government urged the importance of gathering information about the tribal territories and of losing no further time in doing so. At the same time I felt it necessary to advocate that the political officer or officers, to be appointed for dealing with these tribes, should be removed from all subordination to our local district officers, who have neither the time nor the knowledge for dealing with such matters, and should be placed directly under the Indian Foreign Office, or at any rate directly under the Assam Government. The latter suggestion was in due course adopted.

The exploration of this large area, some forty to fifty thousand square miles in extent, was carried out with thoroughness, and the tribes were brought under a loose but efficient control. Great credit was due to the officers and men who carried out the work of pacification in these border lands, where hostile tribesmen, trackless forests, and fever-laden swamps constituted a difficulty of no small magnitude.

This part also of the border was thus secured. The northern and eastern frontiers of India are now fenced off with a difficult mountain barrier, from Kashmir in the north-west to Burma in the south-east, a distance of over two thousand miles—five times the distance from London to Edinburgh.

XIV

THE DALAI LAMA'S FLIGHT TO INDIA

On my return from Bhutan—a country which has hitherto escaped the blessings of post and telegraph offices—in February 1910, I received the news of the Dalai Lama's flight to India.

On his way through the Chumbi Valley he left with Mr. Macdonald, our Agent there, a letter to the following effect :

' The Chinese have been greatly oppressing the Tibetan people at Lhasa. Mounted infantry arrived there. They fired on the inhabitants, killing and wounding them. I was obliged, together with my six Ministers, to make good my escape. My intention now is to go to India for the purpose of consulting the British Government. Since my departure from Lhasa I have been greatly harassed on the road by Chinese troops.' A force of two hundred Chinese Mongol infantry were behind me at Chak-sam,[1] and I left a party of my soldiers to hold them back. A small fight took place there, in the course of which two Tibetans and seventy Chinese were killed. I have left the Regent and Acting Ministers at Lhasa, but I and the Ministers who accompany me have brought our seals with us. I have been receiving every courtesy from the British Government, for which I am grateful. I now look to you for protection, and I trust that the relations between the British Government and Tibet will be that of a father to his children. Wishing to be guided by you, I hope to give full information on my arrival in India.' [2]

Five years of altered conditions in Tibet had evolved a great change. The Dalai Lama and his Ministers now turned to those, towards whom until recent years they had been invariably hostile. The position was unprecedented ; a few years earlier it would have been impossible. We had to consider how we should treat him and his Ministers, the heads of the country with which we had lately been at war.

---

[1] At the crossing of the Tsang-po, forty miles from Lhasa.
[2] Tibet Blue Book 1910, No. 311.

I was summoned to Calcutta to confer with the Government
on these matters. Lord Morley's instructions to the Indian
Government were to adopt a strictly non-committal attitude
on all points at issue between China and Tibet. But it
seemed important to utilize this opportunity of strengthening
our friendship with Tibet, by according good treatment to
the sacred personality of the Dalai Lama. The Indian
Foreign Office appreciated the position and allowed me
to place at His Holiness's disposal a house with retired
grounds on the outskirts of Darjeeling, and to give him
periodical presents of food and other things in accordance
with Tibetan custom. The total cost during the two years
or so that the Lama remained was, I think, less than five
thousand pounds, an insignificant amount, when compared
with the lasting good name that we gained. For His Holiness
not only occupies a commanding position throughout Tibet,
but wields also a very strong influence in Mongolia, and is revered by many throughout China and Japan, and even in
parts of Siberia and European Russia. Every year, for many
years, the Indian Government paid the Rulers of Afghanistan
twenty times this amount or more, but can hardly be said to
have gained their friendship, and frequently failed even to
keep the peace.

While he was in Mongolia and China, after the Younghusband Expedition, the Chinese Government met the entire
cost of food, residence, interpreters and other servants for
himself and his entourage, the entire cost also of his journeys
from place to place, no small item when several hundred
animals are requisitioned daily. Custom demanded it. The
cost to the Chinese Government must have been many
times greater than the cost to us, for their large expenditure
continued for over four years, while our small gifts lasted
for only two and a quarter.

We posted a small police guard over him and his Ministers,
for the latter persistently maintained that the Chinese had
offered a thousand rupees to anybody who would assassinate
them. They also feared injury to the Lama, the man who
of all others stood between the Chinese and the realization

of their ambitions in Tibet.   The fact that we afforded the
supreme Incarnation of Buddha a refuge from his foes and
showed him hospitality is even now perhaps the chief reason
why the British name stands high in Tibet.

I went to Darjeeling before the Dalai Lama arrived there,
and had my first interview with him immediately upon his
arrival.   After the usual complimentary exchanges, he dismissed all his attendants and we sat together alone.   He
then declared that the Chinese Emperor had promised him in
Peking that there would be no curtailment of his former
power and position as Dalai Lama, and that no harm would
be done to the Tibetan people.   These promises had been
broken, and later on China would menace India also.   At
subsequent interviews with him and his Ministers they
denied that Tibet was under Chinese suzerainty.   They
admitted that China had helped Tibet with troops in the
past ; so had Mongolia.   They admitted that China had
Ambans at Lhasa and that these helped, especially in the
management of foreign affairs.   They admitted that China
gave presents to the large monasteries.   But they denied
that these things put them under China.   ' The relations
between the two ', they used to say, ' are those between a
layman and his priest.   The priest receives help from the
layman but does not become his subordinate.   The Chinese
Government cannot produce any document to show that
Tibet has ever agreed to be under China.'   They repudiated
also the Convention of 1906, concluded at Peking, for they
had not signed it, nor had they even been consulted about it.
They asserted that China would not rest contented with her
control over Tibet, but would try also to get hold of Nepal,
Bhutan, and Sikkim.   This was regarded by many at the
time as fanciful, but events were soon to show that the
Dalai Lama's prediction was right.

On a chilly morning in early March, when the British
residents at Darjeeling were going about wrapped in winter
clothing, I conveyed the invitation from Lord Minto, the
Viceroy, for a visit to Calcutta.   His Holiness accepted
the invitation with pleasure.   He inquired whether His

Excellency spoke Tibetan and whether Calcutta was much
hotter than Darjeeling.   During his interview with Lord
Minto, Mr. Jelf, the Under Secretary of the Foreign Office,
showed the Ministers some of the sights of Calcutta.   He at
first proposed a visit to the Zoological Gardens, but this had
to be postponed for a day or two.   ' It would not be fitting ',
they said, ' that we should see all the strange animals before
His Holiness sees them.'

After the Dalai Lama's flight, on the 25th February 1910,
the Chinese Government again issued a proclamation
deposing him, as they had done during the British military
expedition of 1904.   To the British Government they
intimated that this step did not affect the Anglo-Chinese
Convention of 1906.   But the Tibetans paid no more heed
to this second deposition than they had paid to the first.
The Government of China also informed the British Minister
that they had no intention of altering the administration
of Tibet, still less of converting it into a province of China,
which, as they were careful to point out, would be a contravention of treaties.   Both promises were soon to be broken.
As a commencement the Chinese Amban at Lhasa took all
power into his hands, reducing the Tibetan Ministers to the
position of puppets.   It was not difficult for him to do so, as
China had now over three thousand soldiers in Lhasa and
central Tibet, while the Tibetans had neither troops nor
arms worth the name.

The Chinese having broken their pledges,[1] the Indian
Government then proposed that we should ask them for
definite assurances that the Chinese garrison in Tibet would
be limited to a number adequate for the maintenance of
internal order ; that a real Tibetan Government would be
maintained, and that our right of dealing direct with the
Tibetans would not be interfered with.   But Lord Morley
was still for retreating.   Recognizing perhaps that China
would not keep her promise to maintain the Tibetan administration, he stipulated only that British treaty rights

---

[1] A fuller account of the treaties and promises broken at this stage
will be found in the Tibet Blue Book of 1910, No. 336.

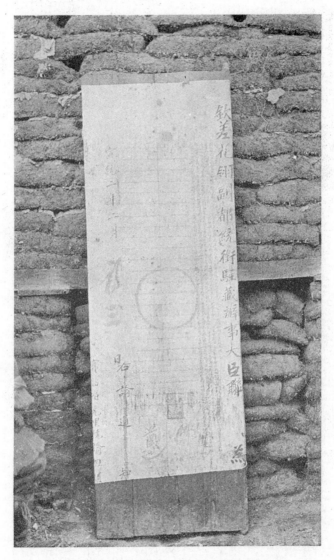

Chinese notice at Phari deposing Dalai Lama

should be observed, that the Chinese should co-operate with British local officials in a friendly manner, and not station troops on the Indian frontier.[1] Pious hopes these, but not destined to be fulfilled, for the British Government had tied its own hands by the treaties of 1906, 1907, and 1908, and had deprived itself of the means of enforcing its rights in Tibet and of making Tibet a bulwark for the Indian frontier. As regards Nepal, Bhutan, and Sikkim, China was to be told that we would protect the integrity and rights of these. Lord Morley's advice was acted on by the London Foreign Office.[2]

We were in effect driven out of Tibet and had to fall back on our barrier of Himalayan States. Our treaty with Bhutan was only just in time. Without it we should have had no right to include Bhutan in the barrier, and should have been in a dangerously exposed position.

In May 1910 I was instructed to inform the Dalai Lama that the British Government would not intervene between China and Tibet, and that they could recognize only the *de facto* Government,[3] i. e. that set up by China in Tibet in place of the Tibetan Government. The *status quo* and the promises of China went by the board. The Tibetans were abandoned to Chinese aggression, an aggression for which the British Military Expedition to Lhasa and subsequent retreat were primarily responsible.

When I delivered the message to the Dalai Lama, he was so surprised and distressed that for a minute or two he lost the power of speech. He could not, or would not, realize the extent to which we were tied and the attitude of the Home Government.

Finding the British Government so complaisant, China now threw out feelers as to whether it would induce the Dalai to go via Calcutta to Peking. It would have suited the Chinese book to keep him as a State prisoner, and, if harsher measures were necessary, it would have been easy to adopt them. But to such a betrayal our Government declined to agree, and the idea was accordingly abandoned. Had it been followed, there would have been an end of the Dalai Lama

---

[1] Idem, No. 345.   [2] Idem, No. 347.   [3] Idem, No. 354.

and an end of British influence in Tibet. There is a Tibetan prophecy, which says, ' The British are the road makers of Tibet ', meaning that the British will prepare Tibet for occupation by another Power. The Tibetans would then have felt that the prophecy had been fulfilled.

Feeling themselves secure in Tibet, the Chinese Government now turned their attention, as the Dalai Lama had from the first predicted, to Nepal and Bhutan. In June they claimed Nepal as a feudatory of China, and referred to the *sovereign* rights of China in Tibet, the *suzerainty* stage being now left behind. A subsequent Chinese Note claimed Bhutan also as a feudatory. During this year the Chinese Amban at Lhasa made several efforts to assert the Chinese claim over Bhutan. He demanded from the Bhutanese authorities explanations as to why they had allowed the Dalai Lama's servants to pass through their country. He issued a proclamation to them that Chinese rupees must be allowed to circulate in Bhutan.

But the Maharaja of Bhutan throughout abided loyally by the new treaty, and ignored the Chinese communications. We informed the Chinese that, as the external relations of Bhutan were controlled by the British Government, we, and not the Bhutanese, would always answer such communications. It is perhaps unnecessary to add that we did not promote the circulation of Chinese rupees, which would not only have shown Bhutan as subordinate to China, but would also have been irksome to the Bhutanese. Indian rupees are eagerly snapped up in Tibet, as they are required for trade in India. But Chinese rupees are not accepted by people in India and would be therefore but a trouble to the Bhutanese, whose trade is tending more and more in the direction of their great southern neighbour. The Maharaja subsequently promised that he would not receive any Chinese officials without first consulting the Indian Government, a valuable safeguard against Chinese intrigue.

The Dalai Lama and Tibetan Government appealed again to the British Government for assistance against Chinese aggression in Tibet. The refusal was repeated. The Lama read the letter, embodying the Government's instructions, three times, and could not speak for some time afterwards. The Ministers were surprised as well as distressed. The Prime Minister kept saying, ' Ha-le, Ha-le (Extraordinary ! Extraordinary !),' and added, ' we do not know where to go or where to remain ; we cannot show our faces after this.'

Shortly afterwards a Russian, Professor Stcherbatsky, visited the Dalai Lama with a letter from Dorjieff, written ten months earlier, asking His Holiness to permit the Professor to go to Lhasa, and to aid him in procuring copies of certain sacred books. As Professor Stcherbatsky did not speak Tibetan, I interpreted for him at the interview. The Lama returned a non-committal reply. At our next interview he said, ' Even had I been in Tibet, it would have been difficult to grant that request, for the Chinese would not have liked a European to come to Lhasa. But, as I have come to Darjeeling, the matter has been made easy for me.'

Towards the end of 1910, the Dalai wrote to our King for protection and also to the Tsar of Russia. The replies of both were necessarily non-committal, but the latter's reply was written in a more friendly vein than that which our Ministers deemed suitable for the King. This fact should be borne in mind by any who may be inclined to blame the Lama for communicating with Russia, whose power in the eyes of Tibet, even after the Russo-Japanese war, was limited only by the great distance intervening between the two countries.

The general policy of the British Government at this time was to abandon Tibet to China, but to attempt to keep the latter out of Nepal and Bhutan. Sikkim was safe for the present, as China had recognized its subordination to the British Government in the Convention of 1890. It is true that assurances had been taken from China that she would maintain her treaty obligations towards us in respect of Tibet. But it had already been made clear that no reliance could be placed on Chinese assurances. Information received from reliable sources, and in part admitted by the Chinese themselves, proved beyond question that they had taken much of the internal administration out of the hands of the Tibetan Government, though they had promised to leave it alone.

It was indeed not unnatural that the British Government should hesitate at that time to support Tibet, even to the extent of diplomatic representations on her behalf. From the events of the last hundred years or so she figured as a country at once hostile and weak. The earlier history of Tibet, which would have indicated the capabilities latent in her people, was unknown. But time was soon to show that the teachings of history could not be disregarded. It was to show that Tibet was not as weak as had been supposed, and that it was possible for India to maintain friendly relations with her northern neighbour to their mutual advantage.

Friendly relations with China are no doubt of high importance to the British Commonwealth. But the security of the Indian frontier is certainly no less important. And there is no reason why, if India maintains relations of neighbourly friendliness with Tibet, relations with China should thereby be imperilled.

It was during this period also that the Amban infringed the Trade Regulations of 1908 by forbidding the Tashi Lama and his officials to communicate with the British Trade Agent at Gyantse. The Chinese Government denied that this had been done, but we obtained a photograph of the prohibitory order, which rendered further denial useless.

In extenuation of Chinese action, one must remember their long and intimate connexion with Tibet, the measure of civilization which they had imparted to it, and the partial control which they had once exercised over it. Had they but exercised that control with understanding and sympathy, they would have had matters all their own way. But, as noted by Mr. Teichman of the British Consular Service in China in his illuminating review of recent Sino-Tibetan politics,[1] the Chinese are accustomed to treat the Tibetans as inferiors in a high-handed way, though the Tibetan officers are often superior in character and intelligence to their own.

[1] *Travels of a Consular Officer in Eastern Tibet*, by Eric Teichman.

Some years later, when I was in Lhasa, one of the Councillors (Shap-pe) left behind in Tibet by the fleeing Dalai Lama gave me an account of his dealings with the Chinese Amban. I will relate it here, for it is typical of Chinese administrative efforts and of Tibetan methods for nullifying these.

'Amban Len told me', said this Councillor, 'that I was a man of too low a family to be a Shap-pe and that he would employ me instead on making a cart road from Cham-do (the advance post of the Chinese troops in eastern Tibet) to Lhasa. I replied, "It is true, Great Amban, that my family is not among the high families of the land, but of road-making I know nothing." "You have got to do it," said Len, " and I will depute two Chinese officials to work with you."

'So I went to Cham-do, fearing I should be beheaded if I did not go. I worked till November, when I wrote to Len saying that the work could not be carried on during the winter. Len then recalled me, and, when I reached Lhasa, he sent for me.

'" I have four things against you," he said to me. "Firstly, you are not doing the road work well. Secondly, you have been receiving letters from the Dalai Lama ; you must show them to me. Thirdly, you told the Tibetans of those parts that the Tibetan Government is sick but not dead (meaning that, though weak at present, it would regain power later on). Fourthly, you have been recruiting Tibetan soldiers."

'" Your first charge ", I replied, " is quite true. Before you sent me I told you that I knew nothing about road-making. But I have received no letters from the Dalai Lama ; I did not tell the people that the Tibetan Government was sick but not dead ; and I have not been recruiting soldiers : it was quite difficult enough recruiting men under your orders to make a road without payment for their work ; it would have been beyond my power to recruit soldiers also. If you do not believe me, you can ask the Chinese officials that. you sent with me. I wish to know the name, Great Amban, of the man who has made these false charges against me."

'" Well, it was Chao Erh Feng " (who was in Cham-do at the time), said the Amban.'

' How did you manage with the two Chinese officials who accompanied you ? ' I inquired.

' They were great gamblers. They went into all the houses to gamble, did very little work and lost all their money. So I used to give them some of my money, and after that they could do nothing against me. When Len questioned them about me, they always spoke well of me.'

' How much of the road did you construct ? '

' As far as from here to Dre-pung (four miles) out of about six hundred, and that not fit for carts. Then we came to a river, which required a long bridge, and there we stuck. I had no wish to make a road which would bring Chinese soldiers, ammunition and other supplies to Lhasa.'

Next year Amban Len gave the Councillor permission to retire from Government service.

In December 1910 our Minister at Peking informed the Chinese Government that Nepal and Bhutan were both independent of China, and that, since the conclusion of the new treaty with Bhutan, the latter's external relations were under the British Government, which would not tolerate any attempt by China to exercise influence over either of these States.

A new extradition treaty, which the Indian Government concluded at this time with Bhutan, made it easier for the latter to recover escaped criminals. The former treaty, with its cumbrous and one-sided procedure, had made such recovery almost impossible.

The end of this year gave us another Secretary of State, though Lord Morley returned for six months during 1911. His term of five years at the India Office synchronized with the Peking Convention, the Anglo-Russian Agreement, and the Tibet Trade Regulations, each of which made it more difficult for us to show friendliness to our northern neighbour. Excellent as was Lord Morley's work in promoting the cause of Indian reforms, he appears to have lacked insight into the Tibetan question. To put one's blind eye to the telescope is a good thing occasionally, but it can easily be overdone.

It was, I think, during this period that Mr. (now Sir

Harcourt) Butler quitted the post of Foreign Secretary at Simla. The Indian Government owed much to this clear-sighted, imperturbable colleague, who worked at a time of exceptional difficulty, and did what little could be done to maintain British influence in Tibet and the border States.

During 1911 the Chinese further strengthened their hold on Tibet. They also attempted on two or three occasions to intervene in the affairs of Bhutan, but His Highness's common sense and loyalty to the new treaty were proof against their appeals.

Towards the close of this year the Maharajas of Bhutan and Sikkim attended the Coronation Durbar at Delhi. The former, though he had only once before been in British territory, was thoroughly at hóme. His first glimpse of the British troops showed him that they had a new rifle, some-what shorter than the old, and he wanted to know all about it, for the necessities of his position had made him quick to notice anything in the military line. Of all the events at Delhi, that which he appreciated the most highly was the military review in which fifty thousand troops were employed.

At the Maharaja's interview with the King I interpreted, for His Highness spoke only Tibetan, slightly tinged with the dialect of eastern Bhutan. His Majesty asked the Maharaja whether he often quitted his State. His Highness answered that only once before had he found it worth while to leave, and that was when His Majesty visited Calcutta as Prince of Wales.

The King next inquired how far His Highness had come to attend the Durbar.

' Owing to the excellent administration of the British Government,' came the reply, ' there is a railway up to the border of Bhutan, which brought me in two days to Delhi. I had also a journey of seventeen days in my own country.'

His Majesty directed me to express his appreciation of His Highness's loyalty in coming so far.

Bhutan's reply was instant. ' When coming to present myself before your Majesty, no distance seems far.'

It was during this year, 1911, that the revolution broke out in China, and this had a decisive influence on Tibetan politics. During November the Chinese garrisons mutinied. Some sold their arms to the Tibetans and departed to British territory ; others roamed at large over the country-side, looting and destroying. Fighting between the Chinese and Tibetans followed. The flame of revolt was fanned by the Dalai Lama's emissaries, and the Chinese troops were worn down by the superior numbers of the untrained yokels attacking them.

On the whole the Dalai Lama and the Tibetan Government understood the limitations imposed on them by residence in neutral territory. Occasionally, however, they made mistakes. One such occurred when an agitated telegraphist aroused the Deputy Commissioner of Darjeeling at midnight, showing him a telegram that had come from Tibet and the reply handed in on behalf of the Government of Tibet. The former was to the effect that a Chinese captain with two hundred soldiers had arrived at a certain Tibetan monastery ; what were they to do ?

The reply ran as follows :

' If they are stronger than you, send them on with soft words. If you are stronger than them, cut them off by the root.'

It is perhaps needless to add that the reply was not sent by the Indian Telegraph Department. It was of course a breach of neutrality, but the Tibetans were not well aware of the neutrality laws. No doubt this stoppage made them all the more anxious to own the telegraph line in their own country, so that, there at any rate, they might telegraph in what terms they pleased.

Party factions and internal jealousies hindered, as ever, the action of the Tibetan Government. The Tashi Lama's Government had secret relations with the Chinese, and offered no help to their Lhasan brothers, until compelled almost by force. The ten thousand monks in the Dre-pung Monastery, the largest in Tibet, sided with the Chinese, until some of their leading monks had been executed, and even then gave only a half-hearted support to the Head of the

Faith. For the largest college in this monastery is peopled
by monks from the borders of China, who are by no means
prepared to fight against the Power that overshadows their
homes. The Ten-gye-ling Monastery, whose head had been
imprisoned with such severity that he died, when the Dalai
came to power, and whose property had been attached,
fought openly for the Chinese.

However, in this turmoil of opposing races and factions,
the Dalai Lama's authority proved the strongest. The
Tibetan Ministers had frequently told me that the reason why
Chao Erh Feng found the subjugation of eastern Tibet so
easy was that the Dalai Lama had discouraged the Tibetans
from fighting. It does not accord with the Tibetan religion
that His Holiness should be associated with the idea of
fighting, and from the time that he ordered military opposition, the Dalai came in for a large measure of adverse criti-
cism. But when he gave these orders, the Chinese troops
began to lose their hold. Large numbers of them were
captured and deported to Sikkim. Encouraged by Mr.
Macdonald, my assistant in Tibet, who, throughout this
difficult and dangerous period, rendered admirable service,
their Tibetan foes treated them with great humanity, providing ample food for all, and ponies for the old and weakly
to ride. I persuaded the Sikkim authorities to prevent these
men from staying in Sikkim, for I could not but realize that
they would prove a focus of intrigue and danger on the
frontier. The Bengal Government allowed a number to
remain in Kalimpong, but later on found them troublesome
and shipped them back to China.

By June 1912 the Chinese were without power in central
Tibet. The Dalai Lama and his entourage accordingly
returned from their two years' exile, and settled for some
time at Sam-ding, on the shore of the ' Lake of the Upper
Pastures ' (Yam-drok-Tso). On his way through Yatung, he
told Mr. Macdonald that he would endeavour to settle with
the Chinese at Lhasa, but that, if he failed, he would ask that
I might be sent there to mediate. In a parting message he
was informed that it was the desire of our Government to see

the internal autonomy of Tibet under Chinese suzerainty, but without Chinese interference, so long as cordial relations were preserved between India and Tibet and treaty obligations were duly performed—a considerable advance on the attitude taken two years earlier, when the leading idea was to refuse him all political encouragement. The power latent in the Tibetan people was beginning to be recognized.

A few months after His Holiness's return to Tibet, the Chinese troops in Lhasa surrendered. They were deported by the Tibetans across the Indian frontier, receiving, as usual, kindly treatment on the way. The Ten-gye-ling Monastery was subdued, its monks expelled, and its large landed estates confiscated by the Tibetan Government. For many generations one of the leading monasteries in Tibet, sharing with six others the prized privilege of supplying a Regent during the minorities of Dalai Lamas, now its place knows it no more.

In eastern Tibet the Chinese were able to maintain most of their ground. The contest continued there, off and on, with varying fortune.

Chinese soldiers leaving Gyantse on deportation to India

Tibetan women threw dust after them and clapped their hands, a Tibetan mode of expelling devils

XV

THE PRESENT DALAI LAMA

AT this point I propose to touch a little more intimately on the appearance, daily life, and character of the mysterious divinity who rules this wonderful land of Tibet.

As the Vice-regent of Buddha on Earth, His Holiness the Dalai Lama occupies a position unique among the religions of mankind. Behind the massive walls of the Potala palace at Lhasa or within the enclosed gardens of his country-seat at Nor-pu Ling-ka in the environs of the capital, the 'Inmost Protector' is aloof from the crowds that come but to adore him and receive his blessing. And when they do come, they must bow down and remain with faces towards the ground, for it is not permitted to look on the countenance of the God-king.

But few Europeans have seen a Dalai Lama; fewer still have conversed with one. It was to me, therefore, a great privilege that I had the good fortune of being with the present Dalai in India for over two years, from 1910 to 1912, during which time I had numerous interviews with him. At these interviews he used to dismiss all his people, including even the indispensable Court Physician,[1] from the room. Thus, sitting together, our conversation was free and unrestrained, and wandered over many subjects, political, religious, and other. In these conversations with the Dalai Lama I found him singularly frank. Many were the opportunities for judging him, but I seldom found anything of importance which he did not tell me spontaneously. As time went on, political exigencies kept us somewhat more apart, but his personal friendliness did not diminish one whit on that account. He is undoubtedly a man of strong character, and, though some may account him headstrong, a clear and consistent line of policy runs through all his actions. Our mutual relations, in spite of the rebuffs

[1] *La-me Kempo* in Tibetan.

which he received from our Government, were close and cordial, so much so that, when he left for Tibet in June 1912, I felt that there were few Orientals whom I knew so well as the Vice-regent of Buddha.

Eight years later, when I visited Lhasa and stayed there for a year, I came to know His Holiness even more intimately. He chose a house for me near his own country palace, in which he almost invariably resided.

The name of the present Dalai Lama is Nga-wang Lop-sang Tup-den Gyatso. He was born in 1876 of humble parentage, at the village of Per-chö-de in the province of Tak-po, about 100 miles south-east of Lhasa. He is the thirteenth in the succession, and has held the reins of government since 1893.

His has been a chequered career. The first to hold the power for nearly a hundred years, things have not been easy for him. The attempt of the Regent, or his subordinates, to kill him by witchcraft must have weighed heavily on his young mind, for, whether the Regent was himself implicated or not, there is no doubt, from what the Dalai Lama told me, that he believed him to be so. The methods of killing by witchcraft are various. The name of the victim may be written inside a boot, suitable incantations uttered and the boot thrown into the water. Another way is to put the name into an animal's horn with certain drugs. Incantations are then performed by one of the Black Hat [1] Lamas, for this is the branch of the priesthood that deals in the Black Art. The person so attacked sickens and dies. Of these Ngak-pa priests it is said that if they do well in this life, they attain a higher Paradise, but, if evilly, a lower Hell than other mortals. Theirs is a risky profession.

But to return to the Dalai Lama. From time to time the Court Physician gives him a pill which, in the language of my informant, ' renews his vitality and makes his body shine '. It is possible that when the Regent or the Amban wished to poison the young Dalai Lama, they bribed the Court Physician to give him a poisoned pill.

---

[1] *Ngak-pa* in Tibetan.

The heavy punishment which fell on the Regent and on the revered Ten-gye-ling monastery, of which he was the head, occasioned bitter feeling among the adherents of this institution, which has not yet died down. Among other attacks the monastery lent the weight of its religious influence to a rumour, that there would be only thirteen Dalai Lamas. This was tantamount to asserting that the present incumbent, who is the thirteenth, could not reincarnate, as he was himself no true incarnation. The pronouncement did not mislead the better informed Tibetans, who are acquainted with the old and well-authenticated prophecy that there will be seventeen Dalai Lamas, but it was hoped to work harm among the ignorant crowds.

When the Grand Lama went to China after his flight from the Younghusband Expedition, he was received with great ceremony. For instance, on his arrival at Singanfu, the Governor of the province, accompanied by his officials, went outside the city walls to receive him. He was accompanied by fifty Tibetan horsemen, some of whom carried flags, while others carried guns or rifles. A string of five hundred camels and four hundred followers accompanied him. But whereas the fifth Dalai Lama on his visit to Peking had treated the then Emperor of China as one independent sovereign treats another, the present Dalai was made to feel his subordination. Yet even in their hour of defeat and impotence, Tibetan patience had its limits. Their refusal to acknowledge the dismissal of their Divinity by the head of the Chinese nation has already been noticed. The Chinese claim to have dismissed the sixth Dalai—who drank wine, consorted with women, composed popular songs, and generally conducted himself in an unorthodox manner—was strenuously denied. The Tibetans point out that the reincarnation of the sixth occurred in the usual way a few years after his death. When the sixth Dalai Lama passed away, the Chinese, indeed, endeavoured to introduce a nominee of their own, but the Tibetans consistently rejected him, and, as history shows, were able to establish him whom their religious guides identified as the true successor.

Modern Tibet, as has been mentioned above,[1] rejects the Chinese suzerainty and claims the status of an independent nation.

The present Dalai Lama has a somewhat dark complexion, which is pitted, but not very deeply, with the marks of small-pox. His form and features reflect his humble parentage, but he moves and speaks with the natural dignity that is inherent in his race and is still further emphasized by the high position to which he has been called. As is natural in one who has perforce to mix much in worldly affairs, his face has not acquired the quiet expression of saintliness that distinguishes his brother Prelate at Tashi-lhünpo. His moustache, high eyebrows, and keen, watchful eyes accentuate the impression of worldly cares, so that one who knew him but slightly would be apt to underrate his spirituality. In actual fact he is in some ways more strict in his devotions than even the Tashi Lama. The quick deprecatory smile that lights up his features when he speaks, and his courtesy, which never failed, even when receiving unwelcome letters from our Government, could not but impress those who conversed with him.

His ears are large but well set, his nose small and slightly aquiline, his hands neat and small. His eyes are a dark shade of brown, and prominent. During my stay in Lhasa they were very watery ; this condition is considered as one of the signs of Buddhahood. He is about five feet six inches in height, and thus somewhat below the Tibetan average. He seems even less when he walks, for he moves with the stoop of one who has spent nine or ten hours, almost every day of his life, seated cross-legged on cushions, meditating, reading, blessing, eating, but always seated. His outer robe for daily use is of thick yellow or red silk, after the Mongolian pattern, with an under-garment of thin yellow or white silk, and felt Mongolian boots reaching below the knee.

He stands the heat well, for, as he told me, his birth-place in Tak-po has an exceptionally warm climate. When several of his Ministers and entourage were suffering from dysentery

[1] Page 111

during May and June 1912 at Kalimpong—a station in the eastern Himalaya only 4,000 feet above sea-level—His Holiness maintained good health throughout. He has had in fact a robust constitution, which for many years withstood the effects of his early upbringing and later troubles and hardships, but is now, I fear, sorely tried by his constant anxieties and endless work. His Holiness has undertaken a gigantic task, by assuming detailed control of the secular administration in addition to his spiritual overlordship.

His flight to Mongolia after the British Expedition of 1904 did no doubt accustom him to journeys on horseback, but in his everyday life, residing as he does in or near Lhasa, he can take but little exercise. It was therefore no mean feat for him to ride in nine days from Lhasa to Sikkim, a distance of 270 miles, with three high passes to cross. This too in the latter half of winter, when the icy wind that sweeps the Tibetan table-land is at its fiercest, and strikes you full in the face as you come towards Sikkim. But both Chinese and Tibetans can often show unsuspected powers of endurance. The record from Gyantse to Yatung, a distance of 130 miles across the cold and windy Tang Pass, a land of gales, blizzards, and avalanches, was held by a young British officer. He covered it in three days. But the Chinese Agent at Gyantse, a man of sedentary habits and no longer young, having occasion to visit Yatung, travelled there in forty-eight hours, and did not seem to think that he had done anything out of the common. It is only fair to add that an Englishman and an Indian have since covered the distance in twenty-seven hours.

His Holiness lives at his country seat of Nor-pu Ling-ka (' The Jewel Park ') in the outskirts of Lhasa, with occasional visits to the Potala, when special ceremonies require this. At Nor-pu Ling-ka he takes exercise in the grounds, which are large, and in the Potala, on the roof. He has to stay in the Potala and in the Lhasa Temple [1] for three or four weeks during the ' Great Prayer ' Festival [2] at the New Year, and here to his regret he is unable to get any exercise at all.

---

[1] *Tsuk-la-kang* in Tibetan.   [2] *Mön-lam Chem-po* in Tibetan.

He does not like going out into the streets of Lhasa, as his presence draws the crowds. In Darjeeling he used to take regular exercise, and might sometimes be met on the paths in Birch Hill forest, accompanied by a single servant ; and along the secluded river bank outside Lhasa I have met him walking with but one attendant, who followed a few paces behind. To the Europeans and Indians in Darjeeling he was almost unknown, and any that met him were unlikely to recognize him. His Holiness has always disliked ceremony, whether in Lhasa or elsewhere. When in Darjeeling, he gave orders to the servants of the officials with him not to run away and hide themselves—as had been the custom hitherto—when he appeared, but simply to make way for him. The old custom, as he said, gave unnecessary trouble to the servants, and made him reluctant to appear.

Another reason which keeps the Dalai Lama out of the Potala and Lhasa is to be found in the dust and smells that permeate the city and almost always make him ill when he has to stay there. His Holiness is not slow to recognize the advantages of cleanliness. The palace and grounds at Nor-pu Ling-ka are clean and free of the polluted dust that whirls through the streets and lanes of Lhasa. His water supply is drawn from special springs at the foot of the ' Iron Hill ',[1] the only good water in Lhasa. These springs are walled in for his use : his own mules bring the water in vessels covered with white cotton cloth. When I came to Lhasa, he was careful to choose for me a house which was indeed cold, but had the supreme merit of cleanliness. And he allowed me the free use of his water supply.

He is fond of horses, dogs, and animals generally, but especially of birds. And flowers are an abiding joy to him, as I could not but realize when he showed me round the Forbidden Enclosure in Nor-pu Ling-ka. The grounds of this enclosure, surrounded by a high wall within which not even the highest in the land may enter, contain a small lake and masses of flowers tended with loving care. Here too is a large Bengal tiger in a somewhat fragile cage, who seems

---

[1] *Chak-po-ri* in Tibetan.

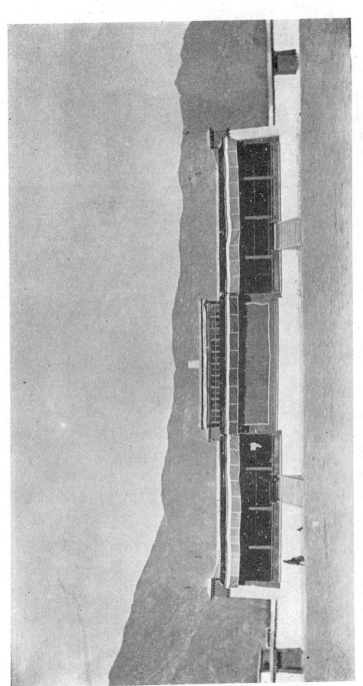

The Dalai Lama's private apartments in the Jewel Park

to quiet down when the Dalai Lama speaks to him. Interspersed throughout the grounds are Tibetan mastiffs, straining at their chains, magnificent specimens of the breed.

After we came to know each other, I found the Dalai Lama frank and open not only in his conversation but in his dealings generally. In both Darjeeling and Lhasa he put me in touch with political under-currents which I could hardly have discovered otherwise, though the information that he gave me was not to his advantage. In Darjeeling, no doubt, he was dependent on the protection of the British Government, and frankness was the wisest course. But, considering his antecedents and those of his Government, this man, who six years previously was unable to receive a letter from the Viceroy of India, might have been pardoned for keeping some things back. From fear of being taken to task for saying what they ought not to say, Tibetan officials used to be very guarded in their conversation on matters of government and politics, though I found them far more open as we became better acquainted. The Ministers, being under the Dalai Lama only, were less guarded, and, as time went on, most of them became entirely frank. But the Dalai himself, not being under supervision, was frank and open from a very early stage of our intercourse. Like most Tibetans, he is impulsive, cheerful, and gifted with a keen sense of humour. His eyes twinkled as he described to me the stratagems by which he evaded the pursuit of the Chinese soldiery. Many Englishmen criticized his flight to India as the cowardly act of a ruler who left his subjects to their fate. But this was not the Tibetan view. In their eyes he represents at once the Essence of Buddha on earth and the Tibetan National Party, which would have Tibet for the Tibetans and is against Chinese domination. Had he, the only one in Tibet who could withstand this domination, been captured, Tibet would have lain powerless in the grip of China. So he fled, and Tibet holds that he was right in doing so.

Both he and his Ministers were quick to show their feelings. When, more than once, I had to inform them that the

British Government refused to help them in their difficulties with China, their depression was extreme. The smiling faces were steeped in gloom. For a time they would not even drink tea, the national beverage, which is ordinarily consumed at least twenty times a day. But their innate courtesy never wavered.

The Dalai Lama is a shrewd judge of character, quick in understanding, and, unlike his compatriots, is not afraid of forming decisions. 'The Chinese way', he once informed me, ' is to say or do something mild at first, then to wait a bit, and, if it passes without objection, to say or do something stronger. If this is objected to, they reply that what they said or did has been misinterpreted and really meant nothing.' This view was certainly a true picture of Chinese policy in Tibet. If anything untoward happened, the Chinese officials in their loyalty would take the blame on themselves—if it could not be passed on to a brother officer —but never blamed their Emperor or their President. In discounting the judgments of the Lama and other Tibetans on Chinese motives, due allowance must be made for the sufferings which China has inflicted on Tibet during recent years.

The Lama makes it his duty to learn the news of Europe and America as well as of China and Japan. I gave him maps of the different continents with the place-names written in Tibetan. On pointing out Sicily he at once referred to the earthquake at Messina. Extracts from the English papers in India are sometimes translated for him. The Tibetan Trade Agents at Gyantse and Yatung and the high officers in Lhasa supply him and his Government with such news as they can glean from traders returning from India. From Mongolia Dorjieff sends information. So do the agents of the Dalai's bank in Mongolia, who still continue to send him instalments of the gold and silver coins—often in the shape of a small horse-hoof—offered to him when in Mongolia fourteen years ago, and deposited in this bank. His Holiness was under no illusion as to the power of Germany, and he had considerable knowledge concerning the resources of the leading nations of Europe and America, and of Japan. By necessity and inclination he is a student of world politics.

Of India he and his Ministers knew but little. After a considerable residence in Darjeeling, which, though not the country of the Bengalis, is included for administrative purposes in the province of Bengal, he and his Court Physician asked me where Bengal and Magadha [1] were. 'We read these names', they added, 'in our books, but we do not know where the countries are.' British methods in India were indeed observed and compared with Chinese methods in China and Tibet, but the chief interest centred on the places of pilgrimage where Buddha had lived and taught and died.

In spite of his pressing secular duties, His Holiness is very strict in his religious observances. When travelling in trains, he would not stop his religious meditations for taking the appointed meals. In the room below his at ' Hillside ', Darjeeling, the low tones of His Holiness's voice would continually be heard calling down blessings on suffering humanity, and not on humanity only, but on birds and beasts and the whole animate creation. Sunrise found him at his good work ; six hours every day he passed in study, meditation, and blessing. When in Tibet, he frequently goes into religious retirement for several months at a time, transacting only urgent business during these periods.

One day I discussed the doctrine of the Incarnation of Buddha with the Dalai Lama and the Court Physician, a high and able priest who afterwards became the Lord Chamberlain,[2] the head of all the ecclesiastical officials in Tibet. They told me that there were three main Incarnations of Gotama Buddha, namely, those of his Body,[3] Speech,[4] and Mind [5] respectively. The Dalai Lama is the Incarnation of the Body, Jam-pe-yang of the Speech, and Cha-na Dor-je of the Mind. The Jam-pe-yang Incarnation

---

[1] A Hindu kingdom in the time of Buddha situated in what is now Bihar.
[2] *Chi-kyap Kem-po* in Tibetan.
[3] *Ku* in Tibetan.
[4] *Sung* in Tibetan.
[5] *Tuk* in Tibetan.

is supposed to be found in the Chinese Emperors. ' But we doubt', said the Dalai Lama, 'whether the Chinese Emperors nowadays are Incarnations, as they do not appear to be truly religious.' The Cha-na Dor-je Incarnation is usually held to be in the Tashi Lama, though the Dalai Lama was not prepared to admit this, for there is an abiding friction between Lhasa and Tashi-lhünpo, and each is inclined to depreciate the other.

'Cha-na Dor-je's spirit', so the Dalai Lama's version runs, ' is in Chang Sham-ba-la—(a mythical country to the north of Kashmir)—but it will not reincarnate for another three hundred years, when Chang Sham-ba-la will become a powerful kingdom. At present it is inhabited by cannibals, among whom Cha-na Dor-je, as their king, is introducing religion and laws. But outside people cannot find either Cha-na Dor-je or Chang Sham-ba-la.' An old Tibetan prophecy says that a Mahomedan ruler will overrun the world, but three hundred years hence the ruler of Chang Sham-ba-la will emerge, defeat him, and restore Buddhism.

Though devout in the observance and zealous in the protection of Tibetan Buddhism, the Dalai Lama was not anxious to extend it to other countries. He put forward the somewhat curious idea that this would tend to weaken the religion in Tibet itself, with the result that food and other necessaries would become scarce, while disease and other evils would afflict the people. It is, as it were, a cloud which, increasing in size, becomes thin and breaks in the centre. This view is the Dalai Lama's own ; it is not shared universally by the Tibetan priesthood.

Devoted to his own religion, he liked to find other people earnest in theirs. One of his many criticisms of his Chinese enemies was directed against what he termed their materialism, their absence of religion. When I heard that he had described me to an acquaintance as a religious man, I knew that my influence with him would be no less on that account.

It may be of interest to note how the Dalai Lama spends an ordinary day at the Nor-pu Ling-ka Palace, on the outskirts of Lhasa.

THE JEWEL PARK. Lake in the inner enclosure. On the right the pavilion in which the Dalai Lama often sits and works. On the left the Serpent Temple

THE PAVILION BY THE LAKE   The Dalai Lama's verandah—sitting-room.   In it are valuable presents from Emperors of China.   The Lama sits on the rug by the low table on which is the jade teacup

Rising somewhat before six o'clock, he washes, dresses, and has one or two cups of tea. He then opens the day with prayer and praise. The Buddhas of past ages are invoked. Libations are poured and sacrificial offerings are made to spirits. He reads the Buddhist Scriptures and other devotional works, and invokes blessings on all human beings and the whole animal world. The morning devotions last ordinarily for about two hours.

He may then come out into the grounds for a few minutes, playing with his dogs. Breakfast follows. This may consist of rice with melted butter poured over it, curds, vegetables, and perhaps meat.

Shortly after breakfast he attends to private and semi-private concerns. A new piece of furniture is needed at Nor-pu Ling-ka, a religious emblem in the Potala needs alteration, and so on.

And now for official business. He peruses dispatches from his Ministers, and, by the quickness of his decisions, earns the reputation of promptitude which is gratefully recognized by his subjects. Throughout the day, and especially at this time, letters are brought from all parts of Tibet by the relatives of those who have died recently, making offerings to His Holiness and beseeching his prayers for the soul of the deceased. The Dalai will then leave whatever work he is engaged on, whether Government business or the morning or midday services. After he has said the necessary prayers, a statement to that effect is recorded on the letter, the seal of ' The All Knowing Presence ' is affixed, and the letter returned to the messenger. Such communications are frequent and take up much of the day.

From midday, for an hour or so, His Holiness will some-times hold a religious service with other priests who sit in a row below his throne. Prayers are read aloud by these, the Dalai replying at intervals, ' Let it be obtained.[1] Let it be performed ',[2] and so on.

Lunch follows. He is very partial to the pastry-puffs

---

[1] *Top-par gyur-chi* in Tibetan.   [2] *Drup-par gyur-chi* in Tibetan.

known as *momo*. His *momo* contain vegetables, cheese, raisins, and possibly meat. Tea and barley bread are also taken.

Work then occupies the Dalai again till about four o'clock. A good deal of the work during daytime is done on the outskirts of Nor-pu Ling-ka, in his pleasure house and grounds known as ' Clear Eye Park '. In this house he has a room fitted up in English style ; and during my year in Lhasa a house entirely on English lines was erected for His Holiness's use. Here the tedium of the daily task is occasionally relieved by watching the traffic pass along the road or through the neighbouring fields, a pursuit in which his field-glasses and telescopes are called into play. The God-king is intensely human. While loyally observing the restrictions which hedge in his divinity, for he recognizes their necessity, he still feels deeply the isolation to which his sanctity condemns him.

At about four o'clock he returns to Nor-p u L ing-ka takes a walk. His dinner at five to six o'clock may perhaps consist of macaroni, soup, bread, and fried vegetables. It should, however, be understood that these hours which I mention vary greatly, for, like most Orientals, Tibetans refuse to be tied to time. Discussing the time of a religious ceremony to be performed by the Dalai Lama, the latter's Secretary said to me, ' We Tibetans have no time. When the Dalai Lama has finished the preceding ceremony, he will take up this one ; it may be nine o'clock, or ten, or eleven.'

After dinner a brief talk with some members of the household staff. Some of the dogs or other household pets, but especially the dogs, are brought in, and a pleasant half-hour is passed.

The Lama's private evening prayer and meditation follow, lasting till about eight o'clock. He shuts his door, and quiet is observed throughout the building till he opens it again.

And from eight or nine till midnight, or even later, he deals with the most important problems that face him, for none are allowed to interrupt him at this time. He has three office rooms : one for dealing with religious matters, one for questions of the secular administration, and the third for his own private business. His two favourite attendants sit outside the door, but neither they nor others may enter, unless His Holiness rings his bell.

It should be noted that, in common with other well-to-do Tibetans, the Dalai Lama drinks tea every half-hour or oftener throughout his long day.

As mentioned above, the Lama's usual hour for rising is about six a.m. But he will sometimes rise as early as three ; as, for instance, if he has great arrears of work to meet, is starting on a journey, or has to attend a religious ceremony. And if the date be one of unusual importance in the Buddhist calendar, he may sit in meditation almost through the night. The late Lord Chamberlain confided to me that, having to be ready at all times for His Holiness's call, he seldom got more than four hours' sleep.

Some idea of the fullness of the Dalai Lama's day may be gathered from a description, though by no means exhaustive, of the work which he performs in addition to four or five hours spent in devotional exercises.

He deals with all the more important matters of both the religious and the secular administration. For instance, the chief questions affecting Government Revenue and Government Expenditure ; ecclesiastical matters from monasteries and temples, priests and oracles, throughout the country, whether under Tibetan or Chinese administration ; these all come before him for final decision. In criminal cases, the Prime Minister, a layman, has full control. His Holiness does not touch these ; the work is held to be unfitting for one of his spotless sanctity. But the important civil cases are submitted for his orders.

Is there a boundary dispute between the estates of two landed proprietors ? His Holiness must decide it. Or, may be, an Incarnate Lama dies leaving property worth four hundred *do-tse*. A *do-tse* equals four and a half to five and a half pounds sterling according to the varying rate of exchange. Another Lama takes away some of the property. The Dalai

Lama may order restitution, fix the amount to be spent on religious ceremonies for the soul of the deceased, possibly two hundred *do-tse*, and resume the balance of the property for Government purposes. The property left by the deceased Lama may be in money, clothes, barley flour, butter, firewood, and heaps of dried cattle dung. The last-named is of value in a cold country where firewood is scarce.

Or take the case of an inquiry into a riot. A Tibetan friend explains the matter thus. ' The Council proposes the name of a lay official and the Ecclesiastical Court [1] proposes the name of an ecclesiastical official. These two, on being approved by the Dalai Lama, inquire and report to the Council, who report through the Prime Minister to the Dalai Lama, recommending different alternative orders. The Dalai puts his red mark on the order which he finds most suitable. As for the two investigators, they *must* agree in their report ; the one with stronger will-power gets his way.'

It may be added that there are a hundred and seventy-five lay, and an equal number of ecclesiastical officials, in the regular employ of the Tibetan Government.

Any petitioner, high or low, by writing the Dalai Lama's name on his petition, can ensure that it will go to His Holiness for final decision, whether the matter at stake be large or small. Neither the Prime Minister nor the Council can stop it. But if the petition be found to be on a matter not considered worthy of the Dalai Lama's attention, the suppliant will be punished for his presumption. So this privilege is but seldom abused.

The higher appointments, not only in Government service, but those also of Abbots and other heads of religious institutions throughout Tibet, are made by His Holiness. When discussing the improved control which he exercises over the truculent monasteries round Lhasa, each with their thousands of monks, the Dalai Lama attributed this chiefly to the care with which he had selected their Abbots. Drepung has four Abbots, Sera has three. When-

---

[1] *Yik-tsang* in Tibetan.

ever I met any one of these men, I could not but be struck by his intelligence and commanding personality.

For the choice of Ministers or other high officials, the Council, through the Prime Minister, sends up two or three names, or more if the Dalai wishes it. The Lama makes his mark against the name he chooses : or, if he is so minded, returns the list for a further selection. He does not rest content until he obtains the man of his choice.

In addition to his religious devotions and his general control of the ecclesiastical and secular administration, the Dalai Lama has many other duties. Each of the monks in Drepung, Sera, and Ganden, and in some other monasteries, must be blessed every year. The day on which the ten thousand of Drepung receive each their separate blessing involves no little manual labour. Every novice also, whether peer's son or peasant's son, when he passes his examination for the priesthood, is entitled to the Dalai's blessing ; so too is every traveller starting on a far journey. And when the Dalai Lama himself travels, the whole country-side flocks to him for the same purpose. Every man and woman feels that such an opportunity is not to be missed. Each is blessed separately.

Numerous and lengthy too are the religious ceremonies over which His Holiness must preside. Again, it is for him to decide, especially in cases of dispute, as to which young boy is the true re-embodiment of Buddha, and of these there are many hundreds.

And yet, in spite of his manifold preoccupations, matters of apparently trivial import are often referred to him. A young Tibetan official was being sent to England for a further course of training in electricity, and the Tibetan Government asked the Indian Government to arrange his steamer passage. I asked the Prime Minister whether this was to be first class or second. The latter replied that he could not settle that point, which consequently was referred to the Dalai Lama for decision.

In addition to this heavy work, the Dalai Lama reads a great deal. He has a deep knowledge of the Lamaistic religion and philosophy, and is well acquainted with the events in Tibet, Mongolia, and surrounding countries. And, for a Tibetan, he has a good knowledge of the world at large.

It is perhaps permissible to add a few remarks—I will curtail them as far as possible—on the manner in which the Dalai Lama usually blesses those who come before him. He sits, cross-legged, in the position of a Buddha, on his throne on a daïs. If the reception is public, the throne is a high one ; if private, it is lower. In a public reception the suppliant removes his hat, goes forward with lowered head, hands the scarf of white Chinese silk to the attendant, bows his head, touching the ground, at least three times, then takes another step or two forward with the head still lowered, and receives his blessing.

When a high official calls privately on the Dalai Lama, he bows his head, lays his scarf on the table before His Holiness, and takes his blessing. Business can then be begun.

To bless those of the highest positions, the Lama places both his hands on their heads. Among this number are the Prime Minister, the Members of the Supreme Council, the Lord Chamberlain, the Chief Secretary,[1] the Kungs and the Incarnations of the highest order, known as Hutuktus, of whom there are only a very few.

With one hand placed on their heads, the Dalai Lama blesses all monks, even the youngest and lowest, and all ecclesiastical and civil officials.

For the rest he touches them only with a tassel which he holds in his hand. In this third class are included all laymen, except those—somewhat less than two hundred in number—already mentioned, and all women but one. This lady is Dor-je Pa-mo, ' The Thunderbolt Sow ' of Sam-ding, for she has the power of transforming herself into a sow. She, the only female Incarnation in Tibet, receives the one-handed blessing. Even the Prime Minister's wife and the wives of Kungs receive the tassel.

The Dalai Lama will not, as a rule, visit private houses, but monasteries and other religious buildings only. When

---

[1] *Dro-nyer Chem-po* in Tibetan.

Crowds awaiting the Dalai Lama's blessing

The Dalai Lama's palanquin

in the Chumbi Valley, however, he did visit the house of
the richest man in the valley, a resident of Che-ma. Here
he held a half-hour's service for the benefit of the household.
As an offering, a bag containing three thousand rupees (two
hundred pounds sterling) was laid before him.

' The Precious Protector's power is very great nowadays,'
remarked a Tibetan nobleman to me at Lhasa.

' Do Tibetans like to have it so ? ' I asked.

' All like his having supreme power,' my friend answered.
' For it is thus in accordance with the Tibetan saying :

> " The Ruler in this life ;
> The Uplifter in the hereafter."

The Inmost Protector is the one who can help us after death ;
it is best that he should rule us in this life also. We have
thus only one Authority to consider : this simplifies life's
problems.

' The Precious Protector knew how to assert himself even
against the Chinese Amban. For instance, a year or two
before the British Military Expedition to Lhasa, the Amban
appointed Ram-ba to be a member of the Council. The
Presence called up Ram-ba and said to him, " The Chinese
have appointed you as a Councillor, but you are not one of
my Councillors." On hearing this, the Council reported to
the Amban that Ram-ba had died. The Amban reported
similarly to the Chinese Emperor, though he (the Amban)
and everybody else knew perfectly well that Ram-ba was
alive. Meanwhile Ram-ba retired to his estate four or five
days' journey from Lhasa and remained there a year or so.
In due course the Precious Protector appointed another
Councillor.

' At that time, on account of the many false reports which
the Amban sent to him, the Chinese Emperor was known
to the people of Lhasa as " The Bag of Lies ".'

During his exile in India the Dalai Lama was criticized
by many Tibetans for taking part in secular matters. Among
these were the two late Rulers of Sikkim, Maharaja Tho-thup
Nam-gyal and Maharaja Sid-keong Nam-gyal, themselves
of Tibetan race, who maintained that he should have

abstained from politics and confined himself to religious duties, appointing a Regent to carry on the administration. ' His treatment of the Ten-gye-ling Regent, which resulted in the latter's death', said Maharaja Sid-keong, ' is considered by many Tibetans to be the cause of Tibet's present troubles. The Regent of Ten-gye-ling was a man highly respected. But Tibetans will of course express such sentiments only to true friends.' These views I too found to be widely held. And this was not only on account of the great respect in which the Regent of Ten-gye-ling was held and the widespread, though not universal, belief that he personally was innocent of the charge of witchcraft, but also on account of the deep-seated aversion among the Buddhists of Tibet to their spiritual Head being soiled by worldly affairs. This feeling lies deep down in the Buddhist and Hindu religions. It is still adhered to in Nepal and Bhutan, where the Heads of the States confine themselves to their ecclesiastical work, and do not intervene in mundane affairs : it used to be followed in many Indian States, and for long centuries it was followed in Japan.

It was clearly necessary for Tibet to fight the Chinese troops, if she wished, as she did wish, to free herself of Chinese domination. But by many it was taken amiss that the orders for fighting should have emanated from His Holiness. ' To take a share in destroying life ', said Maharaja Sid-keong, himself an Incarnation of Buddha, ' is a sin for a Buddhist, a great sin for a lama, and a terribly great sin for the highest of all the lamas.' It will easily be understood that these views, widely held as they were, added greatly to the Dalai Lama's difficulties. But his decision never wavered. He was and is determined to free Tibet as far as possible from Chinese rule. The majority of the Tibetan race are with him in this, and see in him the leader of the National Party and the only means of attaining their goal.

Soon after the Lama assumed power, he reduced largely the amount of bribes hitherto taken by the officials, and especially those taken by the Amban, by curtailing the latter's power as the sole donor of offices and decorations.

He reduced also the oppression of the common people of which many priests had formerly been guilty. One instance of this may be given. The fifth Dalai Lama, who was the first to rule as a king and is the most highly revered of the whole line, introduced the present system of administration, and, among other innovations, transferred the civil and criminal jurisdiction of Lhasa city to two monk-judges,[1] during the ' Great Prayer ' Festival each year. This festival takes place during February and March, immediately after the Tibetan New Year, and continues for twenty-one days. During this period the lay judiciary and the lay police lose their power ; the monk-judges with their henchmen hold control throughout the city. In former days they were not scrupulous as to how they exercised the control, provided that their coffers were filled. Many abuses resulted, heavy fines were imposed on trifling pretexts, and people used to flee from Lhasa to avoid the exactions. The young Dalai Lama sent for the two monk-judges.

' By whose authority do you exercise this power ? ' he asked.

' By the authority of the Great Fifth Dalai Lama,' they replied.

' And who is the Great Fifth Dalai Lama ? ' queried the Pontiff.

Though taken aback for the moment, the She-ngo did not fail to answer, ' Without doubt Your Holiness is he.'

' What I have given I can take away,' came the quiet reply, ' and I will assuredly do so unless you cease from your exactions.'

Since that interview the worst abuses have ceased, and the good people of Lhasa are grateful to the Head of the Faith for his intervention.

The leading priests and officials feared, and many of them disliked, the Lama during the early years of his reign, but were careful to conceal their feelings from the people. For the people not only revered him but were grateful for his strong administration.

---

[1] *She-ngo* in Tibetan.

The officials of Tashi-lhünpo, from the Tashi Lama downwards, are often opposed to the Dalai, for Tashi-lhünpo, at any rate during recent years, has from time to time endeavoured to gain complete independence of Lhasa. It would have welcomed the suzerainty of either China or Britain, if it were thereby assured of entire freedom in its internal affairs. But such a policy, even though Britain were the suzerain, would be disastrous to Tibet and harmful also to British interests.

The tendency towards the rule of abbots and barons remains strong in Tibet, which is still in the feudal age. This spirit of feudalism promotes the desire of cleavage in the Tibetan territories. A race of nomads does not readily come under the discipline of a distant government. It prefers not to look beyond its tribal chief. Still the movement on the whole is towards greater centralization, and the Dalai Lama's national policy has strengthened this tendency. His Holiness and the Tibetan Government accepted my constant advice to send administrators of better quality to their outlying territories, especially those of eastern Tibet, where China pushes in. And the result has been that the sturdy tribesmen of eastern Tibet, who formerly were wont to welcome the Chinese magistrate, as less oppressive than the Tibetan administrator, now call for the rule of their own compatriots. In this way eastern Tibetans add their wide territories to the rule of Lhasa and work for a large, united Tibet. Such a Tibet should be strong enough to gain freedom for itself, and strong enough to prove an invaluable buffer to our Indian Empire.

Suppliants sometimes evade the rule by which parties are not allowed to approach the Lama direct. They stand on the ground outside his windows and so gain his attention, or they push forward when His Holiness emerges in the streets. The suppliant may indeed be beaten for his interference, but cares little if he can gain justice.

The Dalai informed me that he had not allowed any capital sentence to be inflicted since he assumed power. This no doubt is so, but the punishment for deliberate murder is usually so severe that the convict can hardly survive for long. Visiting a prison one day in the village below the Potala, we heard groans proceeding from a room, dark and airless. In this room a murderer was confined ; he had been there day and night for three years. After leaving, I asked a Tibetan friend whether punishment of this kind did not kill a man.

'Yes, it often does.'

'Does it not make him mad ? '

'No, why should it ? ' was the reply. And indeed it is true that in matters of this kind Tibetans have nerves of iron.

Though his power is nominally unlimited, the ' Precious Sovereign ' finds it best to consult public opinion as far as possible. I asked him once whether he usually decided in favour of the large National Assembly or of the select Council of Ministers when the two disagreed. ' It is usually good ', he replied, ' to make the larger number contented.'

After the Dalai Lama returned to Tibet in 1912, orders were sent to each district in the two central provinces to send four representatives to give their opinion both on matters of external policy and on any features of the internal administration that seemed to them in need of reform. They were expressly forbidden to say, ' I am a man of no position and do not understand these things '.

Among the questions then discussed were :

(1) With what Foreign Power or Powers should Tibet make friends ?

(2) Whether to increase the size of the army ; and, if so, how to obtain the revenue to pay for this.

(3) What reforms, if any, should be introduced into the administration of justice ?

To the first question the usual replies were,

(a) ' Make friends with Britain ; she is the nearest to Lhasa.'

(b) ' Make friends with any one Power and then stick to her. Do not change from one to another.'

(c) ' Make friends with China ; she is strong and populous. Unless you can insure some other strong Power helping Tibet, China will take revenge on us later on.'

As regards the raising of revenue, the replies came :

(a) ' Make the landed estates of the aristocracy pay rent and give cash salaries to those who serve the Government, instead of paying them, as at present, mostly by their rent-free grants of land.'

(b) ' Make the monastic estates pay rent and give the monasteries subsidies in cash.' But others objected that the three great monasteries (Sera, Drepung, and Ganden) would never obey an order of that kind.

(c) ' Increase the size of the army. Pay the soldiers in cash and give land to their parents. Increase the amounts lent to the traders from the Government treasuries, and thus increase the revenue.'

The preoccupation of the campaign in eastern Tibet prevented much action being taken on the suggestions of the people. But the army has been increased, as has the amount lent to the traders. And to some extent the soldiers are now paid in cash.

The representatives were mostly managers of landed estates, large or small, government or private. They stated their opinions more readily than might have been expected, for it was the first time in the history of Tibet that such a gathering had taken place.

In difficult matters of foreign policy, however, especially where China was concerned, the Dalai Lama preferred to rely on the advice of his Ministers or on his own initiative. For the National Assembly took too long a time over its deliberations. And by writing conciliatory letters, the Chinese gained over a good many of its members to their side.

The Dalai Lama's family consisted of five brothers and one sister. His eldest brother was made a Kung in accordance with precedent ; a younger brother became the major-domo of his household.[1] The brothers of a Dalai Lama are

[1] *Sim-pön Chem-po* in Tibetan.

The Dalai Lama on his throne in the Jewel Park

not allowed to hold Government posts during his lifetime, for the family would thereby get too much power into their hands. There is, however, no doubt that his position as Sim-pön Chem-po gave this brother of the Lama great influence in government affairs.

Before leaving Kalimpong for Tibet, in June 1912, the Dalai Lama told me that he had come to know me well, and so wished to write to me from time to time, and hoped that I would write to him in return. A change indeed from the time when His Holiness would not exchange letters even with a Viceroy of India. We wrote frequently to each other from that time onwards, though the correspondence was somewhat restricted by the necessity on my side of adhering to the policy of semi-aloofness, still prescribed by our Government for the treatment of Tibetan affairs.

In accordance with the usual practice, the hour for departure was fixed by astrology and divination. So, at half-past four on a dark morning in the rainy season, I found myself at the large house belonging to the Bhutan Government and placed by them at the Lama's disposal. Here I bade His Holiness a very regretful farewell. After his return to Tibet the Dalai wrote to the Viceroy an appreciative letter regarding what he was pleased to term my ' vast knowledge of Tibetan affairs '; and continued : ' Unfailing in his duties to his own Government, he has been highly useful to me also, and has rendered me great assistance in the administration of Tibet.'

I continued to receive from His Holiness and from his Ministers frequent invitations to visit Lhasa. But the Indian Government were unable to permit me to accept any of these invitations or any of those from the Tashi Lama, who used to press me to visit him again at Tashi-lhünpo. It was not till I had retired from Government service and had been recalled that I was sent to Lhasa.

In a letter, written eight months after his return to Tibet, the Lama referred to a rumour that I was going to England on leave, and urged me not to go. He wrote that he had desired to ask me to go to England with the four Tibetan boys, then being sent there for their education, and the boys' guardians had also asked for this. But he added, ' As however peace has not yet been made between the Chinese and Tibetans, we refrained from making this request, for we know that you are the only man who is so well acquainted with Tibetan affairs as to be able to help us in all matters of importance. We now hear that you are soon leaving for England, which, if true, will kill Tibet, as a man who is strangled.'

I received many letters of this kind from His Holiness, as well as from the Ministers and others in the Government of Tibet. They show how easy it is nowadays for British and Tibetans to get on well together.

Although the British Government refused at the time to aid the Dalai Lama in his political designs, still the news of the kindly treatment which we gave him spread throughout Tibet, Mongolia, China, and Japan. The forbearance of the British Government in the hour of victory—when the British and Indian troops had captured Lhasa—made the first breach in the hostility of the Tibetans. But the protection and hospitality which we accorded to the Vice-regent of Buddha in his hour of need proved the real turning-point of our relations with Tibet. ' The whole of Tibet ', said a leading Tibetan to me, ' reverences the Dalai Lama beyond all earthly kings, for he is a Divinity walking on the earth. All, therefore, were grateful beyond measure, when the British Government afforded protection and hospitality to His Holiness and to our Ministers, although we had fought with you in Tibet.'

Sullen hostility was changed into cordial friendship. In 1904 Tibet fought the Younghusband Expedition. Ten years later, on the outbreak of the Great War, far from rejoicing in the difficulties of her erstwhile opponent, Tibet offered a contingent of troops to fight on the side of Britain. Seldom has a change in national feeling been so rapid and so complete. And if matters are managed on our side with sympathy and foresight, the present happy state of affairs should long continue.

I cannot conclude this chapter without expressing my high appreciation of this outstanding personality, His Holiness the Dalai Lama of Tibet, gained during a long and intimate connexion with him. Of his courtesy and consideration I need say no more. From the vanity and bombast which has infected many rulers, Oriental and other, he is entirely free. Finally, I cannot fail to recognize his strength of character, as well as the courage and efficiency with which he combats the difficulties that attach to his unique position.

XVI

THE SIMLA CONFERENCE

THE ball of Tibetan politics was again on the rebound. Tibet had shown that she had no wish to receive the Chinese and was in a position to make her wish respected. The British Government could not but recognize the changed position that was due to the outbreak of the Chinese revolution. And China herself gave ample provocation. A series of aggressions on Tibetan nationality culminated in Yuan Shih Kai's Presidential Order that Tibet was to be ' regarded as on an equal footing with the provinces of China proper '. The last remnant of Tibetan autonomy was to be swept away. Yet only two years earlier the Chinese Government had given the assurance that they had no intention of altering the administration of Tibet, still less of converting it into a province of China, which would be, as they themselves admitted, a contravention of treaties. It is not often that treaties are so frankly and fully broken.

The events of the last two years had shown clearly that we should not recognize any right on the part of China to control Tibet's internal administration. It was accordingly decided that we should, if necessary, apply pressure in this direction by refusing passage through Sikkim to Chinese officials going to Tibet. It was not difficult to justify this line by the occurrences of the preceding twenty years. Moreover it was a reasonable precaution, for the Tibetan Government was not willing to admit them to Tibetan territory. And to have permitted these officials to establish themselves in India or the border States near the Tibetan frontier would have been a source of embarrassment to both India and Tibet. The refusal of passage proved a weapon of considerable force, as the Tibetans consistently prevented the entry of Chinese through their eastern borders.

There was at this time a danger that Tibet might be driven to seek assistance from Mongolia, and through Mongolia from

Camels, a present to the Dalai Lama from spiritual subjects in Mongolia

Russia, which was at that time negotiating a Convention which placed that large country under Russian control. Mongolia and Tibet are closely related to each other in race and in general ideas. Each acknowledges the spiritual supremacy of the Dalai Lama, and they stand together in other ways as well. Should Mongolia go over to Russia, the latter would rule a large proportion of the Dalai Lama's spiritual subjects, for she had established herself also in northern Manchuria.

Manchuria is still somewhat akin to Tibet in religion. Not only in Manchuria and Mongolia, but in Tibet also, the tendency was to break away from China. This was a natural tendency, for it was largely based on religious grounds in countries where religion was all-important, and it had been intensified by recent Chinese aggressions. The Tibetan Government might well wish to follow the Mongolian lead, and would certainly prefer the suzerainty of Russia to the domination of China. This was what we had to fear, if we stood aloof. But if we helped Tibet now, she would prefer to deal with us, for we were near, and Russia far away.

The internal affairs of China having by this time settled down to some extent, the Government of the Szechuan province dispatched a force to Tibet to restore the Chinese position there. This was during the summer of 1912. Great Britain thereupon addressed a memorandum to China, to the effect that she would not recognize the right of China to intervene actively in the internal administration of Tibet, that she demurred to Yuan Shih Kai's Presidential Order, that she did not dispute the right of China to station a Representative at Lhasa, but that she would not agree to the stationing of an unlimited number of troops in Tibet. A written Agreement on the foregoing lines was asked for. China at first refused. Later on, however, recognizing the strength of the Tibetan position, she faced the facts and agreed to a Conference.

China agreed also to the transfer of the negotiations from Peking to India, and to the presence of a Tibetan Plenipotentiary on an equal footing with the Plenipotentiaries of

China and Britain. It was clear that, unless a Tibetan Representative attended, Tibet, as in the past, would refuse to recognize any resulting Agreement, and that, if the negotiations were conducted in Peking, the Tibetan Representative would be overawed.

At the end of 1912 Russia concluded her Agreement with Mongolia. In this Convention, concluded at Urga, she agreed to assist the latter to preserve her autonomy, and in return obtained privileges which gave her a strong grip, economical and political, over the country. Russian subjects were to be allowed to live and trade in Mongolia free of trade duties of all kinds, to open banks, to buy or lease lands for trade and cultivation, and to obtain concessions for mines, timber, &c. The Russian Government were empowered to appoint Consuls wherever they wished, to control the lands of Russian subjects independently of the Mongolian Government, to start their own postal service, and even to build bridges and levy tolls on them ; [1] the beginnings, in fact, of a complete control over Mongolia.

Towards the end of 1913 Russia and China concluded an Agreement [2] embodying the principles involved in the Urga Convention, and securing to Russia the privileges set forth in the Protocol accompanying the Convention. Chinese suzerainty over Mongolia was acknowledged by Russia, while China agreed to recognize the autonomy of Mongolia, and to refrain from colonization or military occupation.

It may be hoped, in the interests both of Tibet and ourselves, that we shall not endeavour to follow any such policy in Tibet. We should but increase our responsibilities very greatly without an adequate return : the Himalaya and Tibet would no longer form our northern barrier. But it showed clearly once again how necessary and urgent it was in our own interests to have an autonomous Tibet as strong as possible, a barrier against outside influences.

The Russo-Mongolian Agreement at Urga, the Mongolian capital, was followed, in January 1913, by what purported to

[1] For the full terms of this Agreement, and the Protocol which accompanied it, see Appendix XII.   [2] See Appendix XIV.

be a treaty between Mongolia and Tibet.[1] By Article 4 of
this treaty, Mongolia and Tibet agreed to ' afford each other
aid against dangers from without and from within.' The
Mongol Government was then under Russian control, its
army was being trained by Russian officers. Buriat monks,
Mongolian by race and living in Russian territory, had commenced the training of Tibetan troops at Lhasa. By Articles
5 and 6, Mongols were allowed to travel and trade freely in
Tibet and to open industrial establishments there. By
Article 2 of the Urga Convention and its Protocol, Russia
received a dominant position in Mongolia. Russian rifles
had already been sent to Lhasa by the well-established
Urga-Lhasa trade route. The boundary between Mongolia
and Tibet is doubtful. It was clear therefore that, if it acted
on the treaty, Russia could find indirect means of avoiding
the restrictions imposed on Russia and Britain by Articles
III and IV of the Tibet portion of the Anglo-Russian Agreement.

This ' treaty ' was concluded on behalf of Tibet by the
Russian Buriat, Dorjieff, tireless as ever in the work of drawing Russia and Tibet together. His authority was based on
a letter given him by the Dalai Lama, when the latter was
fleeing from the British Expedition to Lhasa. But the
Dalai Lama denied that his letter—which enjoined Dorjieff
to work for the Buddhist religion, a not uncommon request
—justified anything in the nature of a treaty. Nor does it
appear that the Lama or his Government ever ratified the
document. Still, there is a danger in such documents, for
arguments can be twisted in various ways, and if Russia had
insisted on regarding the treaty as genuine, as indeed she was
inclined to do, great trouble would have resulted.

As regards Tibet, whatever may have been the position in
the past, there was no doubt that she was inclining more and
more to deal with us, for we were the nearest Power able to
help her against China. If we failed her, she would turn to
Russia. If Russia too failed, she would join with Mongolia
against the common foe. For, as the Prime Minister

[1] See Appendix XIII.

informed me, whether Tibet and Mongolia were bound by a treaty or not, the two countries were united as closely by race, religion, and common ideas as it was possible for two countries to be.

While the Chinese Plenipotentiary was lingering in China, I met Lön-chen [1] Shatra in Gyantse. He was on his way from Lhasa to attend the Conference as Plenipotentiary for Tibet. He showed me some letters from the Chinese officials in eastern Tibet. These pressed the Dalai Lama and the Tibetan officials to negotiate with the Chinese officials at Cham-do, though they must have known that their Government had already accepted the invitation to the Conference in India. At the same time we received news of a Chinese attack on a Tibetan outpost in the Mang-kam province of eastern Tibet. The Tibetan soldiers were unprepared for attack. They assumed, not unnaturally, that hostilities would be suspended during the Conference.

Shatra also told me the terms which the Dalai Lama wanted in the Agreement. These were :

1. Tibet to manage her own internal affairs.

2. To manage her own external affairs, consulting on important matters with the British.

3. To have no Chinese Amban, no other Chinese officials, and no Chinese soldiers in Tibet, but Chinese traders only.

4. Tibet to include Nya-rong, Der-ge, Ba-tang, Li-tang, and the country as far as Tachienlu. It should be stated that all these districts form part of Tibet, but some of them had been brought more or less under Chinese control during the last two hundred years.

The National Assembly desired a British Representative at Lhasa. The Dalai Lama did not press for this at first, but did so later on, when he found that our proposals included the re-establishment of a Chinese Amban at Lhasa. At this time the Dalai Lama was consulting only the Ministers, for the National Assembly took too long a time over its deliberations, and the Lama recognized the necessity for prompt

---

[1] The title ' Lön-chen ' means ' Chief Minister '

A part of a Tibetan Library. The white silk labels give the titles of the books

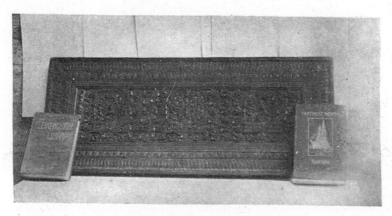

A Tibetan book-cover in richly carved wood

decisions. The Chinese, moreover, by writing conciliatory letters had gained several of the members of the Assembly over to their side.

When I met Lön-chen Shatra in Gyantse, I advised him to bring down all the documents which he could collect bearing on the Tibetan relationship to China in the past, and on the former's claims to the various provinces and districts which had from time to time been occupied by China. The prolongation of his stay in Tibet, while the Chinese Plenipotentiary hung back in his own country, gave time to amass a large collection of books and registers from the archives of the Government at Lhasa. The long, narrow sheets, strapped together between their wooden blocks and bound round with the many-coloured silks of China, were picturesque both in their trappings and in their title-pages. The *Feast of Pleasure for the Perfected Youths* gave an account, written in the time of the fifth Dalai Lama, of the early boundaries between China and Tibet. *The Golden Tree, the World's Sole Ornament* gave further information about the old boundaries. Registers of houses, monasteries, tenants, landlords, taxes, incomes ; registers of door-steps and fire-places, each door-step and fire-place connoting a family ; bonds of allegiance ; militia lists, and agreements showing the quotas of troops to be supplied by different districts ; laws, regulations, legal judgments and executive orders ; these and other proofs of actual administrative possession were brought down to support the claim of the Lhasa Government to rule their own countrymen in the various districts which had fallen, both in earlier and in later days, under the dominion of China. The bar on Chinese entering Tibet was useful in preventing them from influencing the Tibetan Plenipotentiary's assistants during this inchoate stage of the proceedings. When the Conference assembled and these matters came forward, it at once became evident that the Chinese Plenipotentiary had but little to oppose to the mass of evidence produced by his better-prepared colleague.

The Conference was finally summoned to meet at Simla. Sir Henry McMahon, the Secretary in the Indian Foreign

Department, was the British Plenipotentiary. Mr. Archibald Rose, of the Chinese Consular Service, was appointed to assist him on the Chinese side of the case; I was appointed similarly for the Tibetan side.

A characteristic hitch now occurred. The Chinese Representative still delayed in China. As it was, to say the least, doubtful whether he had any intention of coming to India, a limit of six weeks was fixed, and the Chinese Government were notified that, if he failed to arrive within that period, we should negotiate direct with Tibet. This brought the Representative of China at once. In October 1913 the Conference assembled at Simla. Lön-chen Shatra, the Tibetan Plenipotentiary, who had stayed on in Tibet, awaiting Mr. Chen's start from China, arrived a few days before the latter.

The discussions extended over six months, and dealt very fully with the whole Tibetan question. On the 27th April 1914 a Convention was initialled by the three Plenipotentiaries.

The chief provisions of this Convention were as follows :

1. Tibet was divided into two zones, ' Outer Tibet ' and ' Inner Tibet '. The former is the part nearer India, including Lhasa, Shigatse and Chamdo ; the latter the part nearer China, including Ba-tang, Li-tang, Tachienlu, and a large portion of eastern Tibet.

2. Chinese suzerainty over the whole of Tibet was recognized, but China engaged not to convert Tibet into a Chinese province.

3. Great Britain engaged not to annex any portion of Tibet.

4. The autonomy of Outer Tibet was recognized. China agreed to abstain from interference in its administration, which was to rest with the Tibetans themselves. She agreed also to abstain from sending troops, stationing civil or military officers (except as in (6) below) or establishing Chinese colonies there. Britain to abstain from all these things throughout the whole of Tibet, but to retain her Trade Agents and their escorts.

5. In Inner Tibet the central Tibetan Government at Lhasa were to retain their existing rights, which included among other things the control of most of the monasteries and the appointment of local chiefs. But China was not forbidden to send troops or officials or to plant colonies there. ' In Inner Tibet,' as the Tibetan Prime Minister remarked to me, ' the best man will win. Our Government should send honest officials there, tax the people lightly and keep up their warlike spirit.'

6. A Chinese Amban was to be re-established at Lhasa with a military escort, limited to three hundred men.

7. The escorts of the British Trade Agencies in Tibet were not to exceed three-fourths of the Chinese escort at Lhasa.

8. The British Agent at Gyantse was authorized to visit Lhasa, in order to settle matters which could not be settled at Gyantse.

The Convention also abolished the Trade Regulations of 1893 and those of 1908. In their place a fresh Trade Treaty was arranged, to govern the commercial relations between India and Outer Tibet. These new Trade Regulations are believed to be simple and practical. They should facilitate legitimate intercourse between India and the territories of the Dalai Lama.

The opportunity was also taken to negotiate the frontier to be established between Tibet and north-eastern India. From the east of Bhutan, along the northern and eastern border of Assam, round to the meeting-place of China, Tibet, and the Burmese hinterland, this frontier had never been defined. As narrated above in Chapter XIII, there was great danger of Chinese penetration here, and our reconnaissance parties during the last few years had been doing excellent work in exploring the territories and in bringing the tribes under a measure of control. It proved fortunately possible to establish the frontier between India and Tibet over eight hundred and fifty miles of difficult and dangerous country. We have thus gained a frontier standing back everywhere about a hundred miles from the plains of India.

The intervening country consists of difficult hills and valleys, and so constitutes an excellent barrier.

The treaty of 1910 with Bhutan safeguarded the two hundred and fifty miles along the Indo-Bhutan frontier. The reconnaissances in the tribal territories, followed by this agreement, safeguarded the remainder of the danger zone. The northern and north-eastern frontiers of India are now reasonably safe from foreign interference.

Two days after the initialling of the Convention, the Chinese Government disavowed the action of its Representative, and refused to permit him to proceed to full signature. On the 6th June the British Minister at Peking informed the Chinese Government that Great Britain and Tibet regarded the Convention as concluded by the act of initialling, and that in default of China's adherence they would sign it independently. In July the Chinese and Tibetan Plenipotentiaries quitted Simla. Two or three weeks later, the Great War broke out and threw Tibetan affairs into the background.

The negotiations with China broke down on one point only ; namely, the frontier to be established between China and Tibet.

The Tibetan Government claimed all territory in which the population was almost entirely Tibetan. This involved an eastern boundary passing through Tachienlu and a north-eastern boundary passing close to Si-ning in the Kansu province of China. Tibet in fact claimed the restoration of those Tibetan districts which China had annexed from time to time.

Far from agreeing to this, the Chinese Government claimed the above districts, and in addition all Tibetan territory which Chao Erh Feng had succeeded in occupying when his power was at its height. They accordingly pressed for a boundary through Gyam-da, only a few days march east of Lhasa.

On the British side a compromise was proposed, dividing the country into Outer and Inner Tibet, as already recorded. The boundary between these two was to follow in the main the frontier between China and Tibet established in 1727.

Nya-rong, however, was to be transferred from Tibetan to Chinese rule. It had stood by itself, an *enclave* administered by Tibet though on the Chinese side of this frontier, which passed west of Ba-tang, and thence north and north-west.

Tibet in particular objected to the loss of the rich territories of Der-ge and Nya-rong from her autonomous area. China especially objected to the inclusion in Inner Tibet of Ba-tang, Li-tang, and other Tibetan districts, which she had annexed nearly two hundred years before and regarded as part of the Szechuan province of China.

In the end, Tibet proved willing to accept the British award, in order to arrive at a settlement. China remained obdurate, but notified Britain [1] that, except as regards the boundary, she was willing to accept the Convention in all respects.

The terms of the Convention were advantageous to the three countries concerned. They would have ensured to Tibet a reasonable measure of that freedom for which she had so long striven. They would have given a chance of peace to the sorely-harassed districts of eastern Tibet, and enabled the Tibetan Government to consolidate its authority in central Tibet, where the Drepung Monastery with its strong Chinese influence, the Tashi-lhünpo administration with its yearning after independence, and the Ten-gye-ling Monastery with its legacy of hatred were serious sources of weakness. Drepung has over ten thousand monks, and holds landed property of enormous area. To China the Convention would have given a reasonable satisfaction, in spite of recent happenings, of her claims in Tibet. She would indeed have gained a more favourable boundary than she could reasonably claim at the present time. As for India, she would have gained what she most desired, peace and security on her long northern frontier.

Both Mr. Ivan Chen and Lön-chen Shatra were men of charming personality. The former had passed many years of his life in European chancelleries. Courteous and honourable,

---

[1] *Travels in Eastern Tibet*, by Eric Teichman (Cambridge University Press), p. 46.

he did what he could to maintain the attitude of his Government, but remained on terms of personal friendship with us all.

Lŏn-chen Shatra had but seldom left his native land. Yet he showed a knowledge of men and a grasp of political affairs that came as a surprise to many at the Conference. His simple dignity and his charm of manner endeared him to all who met him in Simla or Delhi.

The Tibetan Government was then aiming at a regular army of ten thousand men, both for defence against external aggression and for the maintenance of internal order. The intention was that this army should be divided into battalions of five hundred each. Each battalion was to be officered by one de-pŏn (colonel), four ru-pŏns (captains), ten gya-pŏns, (sergeants), and fifty chu-pŏns (corporals). A small force indeed for a country with an area of five hundred thousand square miles. Nepal, with a larger population than autonomous Tibet, but an area only one-tenth as large, has an army of thirty-five thousand men. But it is difficult to raise money to meet the expenses of regular troops, for large sums are spent on religious institutions ; and large estates which might otherwise be yielding revenue are vested in the monasteries as well as in the nobility. And if it is hard to find the money, it is still harder to find the officers. The traditions of the last few hundred years are all against military service, a result due to Buddhism and the influence of China.

The de-pŏns were to receive as yearly pay the equivalent of two thousand rupees, ru-pŏns seven hundred, gya-pŏns three hundred, and chu-pŏns one hundred. The private soldier was to be paid sixty rupees yearly, in addition to one thick and one thin uniform. De-pŏns, ru-pŏns, and gya-pŏns hold also landed estates from the Government, in return for which they are expected to render service. These estates must therefore be reckoned towards their salaries.

The Prime Minister told me that his Government were desirous of developing the mines in Tibet, employing British or Indian engineers for this purpose. They were very anxious to raise a revenue to pay for an army, and hoped to get a good deal from the mines. This is a matter in which the Indian Government can render substantial assistance, to the mutual advantage of India and Tibet. But care should be taken to keep the mines under Tibetan ownership. If Indians or British own mines in Tibet, we shall extend our responsibilities into the heart of this difficult country, whose proper function, at present at any rate, is to act as a protection to India, a second rampart behind the Himalaya. And with any kind of foreign ownership friction is bound to ensue.

Western education was another development on which their eyes were fixed. An English school in Lhasa or Gyantse was hoped for, as well as the dispatch of a few boys to England, a matter which will be mentioned in the next chapter.

The Tibetans, when in India, liked greatly to visit industrial establishments, and factories large and small, especially such as could help them to start or improve their factories in Tibet. An arsenal and a mint were of unfailing interest to them, but little places, where silk and cotton goods or gold and silver ornaments were turned out, were also eagerly examined. On the other hand they cared but little for old buildings, relics, and antiquities generally, other than religious. When the Prime Minister with his son and his chief assistant, now a Grand Councillor, visited the Fort at Delhi with me, they were solidly bored. A good Zoo always pleased them.

They kept good health on the whole, and preferred Simla to Darjeeling, because, being drier, they suffered less from rheumatism there. Delhi after the middle of February they considered unpleasantly hot, but they were able to keep well by abstaining from sweet foods. They found that they maintained their health best by keeping to their own barley-flour and other Tibetan food.

XVII

THE PERIOD OF THE WORLD WAR

AFTER the Tibet Conference the armed truce between China and Tibet continued, the troops on both sides holding their positions in eastern Tibet. The Tibetans, being inferior in arms and training, had to maintain the larger number. The burden of maintaining these lay heavy on the country, for the crops had been poor during the last few years. The Government revenue, such as it was, contemplated no provision for the support of a standing army; it had long been devoted in the main to the upkeep of religious institutions. But the Chinese in eastern Tibet and Szechuan now renewed their endeavours to negotiate direct with the Tibetan Government, and by threats and promises to open the way to Lhasa. Unless they cast off the alien British, and came to terms with their Chinese cousins, the troops of the latter would advance and devastate the land. ' I will not leave even a dog or a chicken alive in the country ', wrote the Chinese General to his opponents across the Salween. It was as necessary as ever for the Tibetan Government to maintain their troops at full strength.

When, however, the Great War broke out, the Dalai Lama, in spite of his own needs, immediately offered a thousand Tibetan soldiers to fight on the British side. He further ordered that special services for the success of the British arms should be offered in the main monasteries throughout Tibet. A verbal message which I received during 1916 from the Dalai Lama and Tibetan Ministers ran as follows: ' Tibet, being a nation of priests, has not been able to do much for the British Government during this war in the way of military assistance. But we have held religious services for the British from time to time in the leading monasteries. And we have transferred privately to the credit of the British Government a number of the services held for the

Priests attending service in the Temple at Lhasa

Tibetan Government. Had we held them all for the British, our people would have suffered needless alarm.'

These services were continued throughout the war and involved a considerable expenditure out of the scanty government revenue. In appraising the value of the Tibetan contribution we must remember both that it cost them sums of money which they could ill afford, and that, believing intensely, as they do, in the efficacy of prayer, it was to them a real and substantial contribution. To the people of our race the transfer of religious services to our credit and advantage by a mere stroke of the pen may no doubt seem absurd or even sacrilegious. But it is along defined lines of this kind —somewhat mechanical though it may appear to us—that the Tibetan religion proceeds.

The feelings of the Dalai Lama and the Tibetan Government were indeed changed from the time, only ten years before, when they had refused to have any dealings with the British, and His Holiness had fled from Lhasa on the approach of a British military expedition. The offer of troops could not be accepted, but it was eloquent of the change in the Tibetan situation.

The extent of this change was well expressed by Mr. (now Sir John) Shuckburgh, Political Secretary at the India Office, when speaking a few years later at a lecture given by Mr. Coales, of the British Consular Service in China, on his travels in eastern Tibet. In the course of his remarks Sir John Shuckburgh said :

' It seems to me that perhaps the most remarkable thing about Mr. Coales's most remarkable journey, and it does not perhaps strike one at once, is the fact that it ever took place. When we consider what the Tibetan attitude was, even within a few years ago, towards travellers of any kind, it seems strange that Mr. Coales is able to march, apparently without any difficulty, through the country occupied by these people, and be, apparently, entertained everywhere with a complete courtesy and good feeling. It is only a very few years ago that the relations of the Government of India with Tibet were so strained that it was found necessary to send up an expedition, under Sir Francis Younghusband, to the heart of Tibet to occupy the Tibetan capital. That was in 1904. The fact that relations are so much better now between the Tibetans and ourselves is, I think, due to two things. First of all to the generous use which the British Government and the Government of India made of their military victory ; and, secondly, to the admirable pioneer work which has been · done since then by officials of the Indian Political Department and by officers of the Chinese Consular Service, such as our lecturer this evening. I should like to quote one instance of how well that work has been done. When the great European War · broke out in August 1914, it was just ten years after the time that Sir Francis Younghusband and the British Expedition had occupied Lhasa, the capital of Tibet. One might perhaps have thought that the Dalai Lama, the ruler of Tibet, and the Tibetan Government, would have been pleased to see their old opponents in such difficulties. That was not the case. So far from being pleased and from sympathizing with our enemies, the Dalai Lama telegraphed to His Majesty the King offering to furnish a contingent of Tibetan troops and telling His Majesty that the abbots and lamas throughout Tibet were praying for the success of the British arms. And only a few weeks ago another telegram was received congratulating His Majesty on the glorious results of the Great War. I think that a very striking instance of the way in which British foreign policy in these out-of-the-way countries is carried on ; and I feel confident that we may look forward in future to excellent relations with the Tibetan nation.'

The Tibetan Government had at this time to maintain some ten thousand men to guard the roads through eastern Tibet. These were mostly untrained militia armed with any guns that might be obtainable ; but they were stiffened with a small nucleus who had received such training as Lhasa could supply and were armed with the new rifles. During the Younghusband Expedition, according to common report, the few soldiers who received modern rifles had been warned that they would be fined five hundred rupees if they lost them ; and many in consequence preferred to leave their rifles behind in safety before they went into action. But there was no reason for such tactics at this later stage.

During his stay in Darjeeling I had advised the Dalai Lama to send some Tibetan boys to England for education, for it seemed to me that not only would they be useful to Tibet on their return, but also they would in various ways, provided they were treated well in England, help to draw closer the bonds between the two countries. Four lads of the upper middle class had been sent ; Rugby and other places had helped to give them such education as their few years' stay in England allowed. One was set to learn about mining ; another, whose school report certified him as fonder of a town-and-gown row than of his books, did nevertheless manage to acquire some knowledge of survey and map-making ; the youngest, a bright, clever boy, took up electrical engineering, after his school course was completed. The eldest, Gong-kar, was given a military career, serving ten months with the 10th Yorkshires and nine months with the artillery at Woolwich. During these periods he came to realize how stiff military training can be in war-time.

The Indian Government contributed towards the cost of the scheme, for the Tibetan Government was poor, and various signs indicated that both Russia and Japan would be willing to pay the entire cost of such education. Unfortunately the lads were sent back to Tibet before their training was completed. Thus the experiment has not hitherto gained such success as greater care might have ensured to it. Still the lads have done some good work, and the youngest has recently returned to England to make good the deficiencies in his earlier education.

Gong-kar was the first to return to Tibet. He rendered useful service in helping to train the raw Tibetan soldiery at Lhasa in up-to-date methods. Both he and two young officers, who had received a measure of training at Gyantse, drilled the Tibetan troops as far as their experience permitted. As each year passed, the Tibetans became stronger for the defence of their country. Gong-kar's death a few years later was no small loss to Tibet.

A Russian Buriat and a Japanese had for some time been training Tibetan detachments according to their own methods. The Tibetan Government had engaged these at the time when the attitude of the British Government was doubtful, if not unfriendly. Now that friendliness had been restored, they stopped the Russian and the Japanese drill and adopted British methods throughout their army. The three systems were subjected to a formal inspection, at which it was decided that the British system was the best. A month before it happened I had heard of the proposed inspection and of the decision that would be taken thereat.

To meet their new military charges, the Tibetan Government had, in 1914, imposed two taxes. The first was on the salt which is produced in large quantities in the Chang Tang ; the second on hides. These being insufficient, they proposed to levy a tax on wool, which is one of the chief products of their country and their chief export to India. For fear of possible objection, under Article IV of the Lhasa Convention, they asked the permission of the Indian Government to levy this, at the rate of approximately one rupee per maund—equalling thirty-six shillings per ton, i. e. about five per centum *ad valorem*. The Indian Government gave their consent. This new tax helped materially to ease Tibet's financial difficulties.

The uniforms of the soldiers were made in Lhasa, the woollen cloth coming mostly from the Tsang province and from the districts south of Lhasa. The food was supplied from the Government granaries, which are found throughout Tibet, for a large portion of the Government revenue is paid in grain, meat, butter, tea, &c.

The stationing of an officer in our Chinese Consular Service at Tachienlu helped greatly to keep us informed of developments in eastern Tibet. Tachienlu, on the border between eastern Tibet and China and on the main route between the two countries, is the head-quarters of the Chinese administration which deals with Tibet. These Consular officers have occasionally made journeys in the disputed regions and added very materially to our knowledge of them.

During my visit to Tibet this year (1915) I met a consignment of baths and buckets on its way to Lhasa. Since the visit of the Dalai Lama to Darjeeling, many Tibetan gentle-

'Four lads of the upper middle class had been sent' (p. 163)

A Tibetan hermit

Nuns travelling

men take hot water baths once a week and find that they keep better health by doing so. In various ways the standard of cleanliness at Lhasa has risen.

A less pleasant importation was a swarm of locusts which passed up the Chumbi Valley this summer, borne along on the south wind which blows throughout the summer and part of the winter. They travelled daily farther and farther north until they died on the cold uplands and passes of the interior. At Gyantse I saw only one, which fluttered feebly into the court-yard of the Government rest-house, to die a few minutes later.

In the interior of Tibet locusts are rare, though once, thirty or forty years ago, they came as far as Lhasa. In Nepal, Sikkim, and Bhutan they are more common and do much more damage than in Tibet, where the small oases of cultivation are scattered among vast tracts of grass and shale. The Tibetans and Lepchas believe them to be re-incarnations of persons whose funeral ceremonies have not been properly performed.

During the preceding two or three years the crops had been poor. People in want of food had become desperate, and robberies were rife. Hermitages and nunneries, being defenceless, suffered severely. ' The robbers ', I was told, ' do not scruple to attack even saintly lamas, if alone ; they have no religion, but seek their own well-being only. They will however seldom rob anybody, even a woman, belonging to a family that exercises power, such as that of an official or large landlord, for fear of being caught later on and punished.'

This year (1915), however, the thefts and robberies decreased, for the crops were unusually good. There was abundant rain, the yearly fall at Gyantse being twelve inches as against an average of seven or eight. The extra supply of water was not in itself a very great matter, for the Tibetan communities maintain efficient systems of irrigation, and water for this is always procurable from the mountain streams. But the frequent rain brought cloudy nights which kept off frost, the chief enemy of the Tibetan cultivator.

If cloudy nights, and consequent absence of frost, can be obtained on the plains and valleys round Gyantse to the end of August, the crops are fairly safe. Hailstorms, though furious indeed in this cold land, ravage the crops only here and there. They are not feared so much as frost, which in a few cloudless nights will blight the crops over hundreds and hundreds of miles. Round Gyantse we find barley, mustard, peas, and a little wheat ; and these are reaped during September.

While I was in the Chumbi Valley, a messenger from Lhasa arrived with a letter and presents from the Dalai Lama. From now onwards this became the rule whenever I visited Tibet.

Shortly after my arrival at Gyantse I received invitations from the Dalai and Tashi Lamas to visit them at their respective capitals. At Lhasa the Tsa-rong Shap-pe offered me his new house, which had been built in European style ; at Shigatse a palace recently completed was placed at my disposal. Henceforward I always received such invitations from Lhasa and Shigatse when I came to Tibet, but political exigencies prevented our Government from allowing me to accept them. In 1916 the Dalai Lama's invitation was twice repeated.

During these years the Government of Tibet was confronted by a double anxiety. They had to guard against an advance by the Chinese troops in eastern Tibet, and they had to wait for the outcome of the World War. They hoped that if the latter were favourable to the Entente Powers, the British Government would be able again to attend to Tibetan affairs, complete the Simla Convention, and bring about Tibetan autonomy.

As the training of their troops improved, the Tibetan Government felt less fear of the Chinese. The latter, it is true, had a few machine guns and mountain guns, while the Tibetans had none of these. But in other respects the Tibetan equipment was not inferior, and their training was sufficient to be of some use. Moreover, they were naturally hardy, and were learning how to make use of the difficulties of their own country. The intense anxieties of 1915 yielded by the spring of 1916 to a fair measure of self-confidence.

But the anxiety as to the result of the Great War continued. Reports that Germany was winning were general in Lhasa and elsewhere during 1915 and 1916. There were, so the Tsarong Shap-pe informed me, about five hundred Chinese at Lhasa in poor circumstances, and many of them circulated false rumours. A number of these were accordingly put across the border into Sikkim, and I passed them across to British territory.

An instance of the ubiquity of German intrigue came to my notice at this time. I was informed by an exceptionally good authority that when the Dalai Lama was in Peking, after his flight from the British Expedition of 1904, the German Minister told some officials on the staff of His Holiness that Britain had oppressed Tibet shamefully and that the German Government was willing to send arms to Tibet through Russia and Mongolia. This offer, however, was not accepted.

In 1917 the Chinese General in command in eastern Tibet, finding that neither his promises nor his threats induced the Tibetan Government to forsake the British connexion and deal with him direct, decided to attack. The Tibetans were unprepared, for they relied on the Chinese observing the truce, as they had observed it. The attack was made when the Tibetans were celebrating one of their religious festivals, and the latter were driven without difficulty out of one or two advanced posts. They then rallied, recaptured the posts which had been lost, pursued their advantage and gradually drove the Chinese out of Mang-kam, Tra-ya, and Cham-do and recaptured most of the territory which had been seized by Chao Erh Feng several years before. Later on, a truce was made, the Tibetans retaining the lands which they had reconquered but advancing no farther. They thus regained the greater part of eastern Tibet.

Mr. Teichman, of the British Consular Service in China, who was in Tachienlu at the time and took the leading share in concluding the truce, has recorded the events of this period in detail.[1] He writes that, if the fighting had continued, ' another month or two would possibly have seen several thousand more Chinese prisoners in Tibetan hands, and the Lhasa forces in possession of all the country up to Tachienlu.'

In this event the Tibetans would have reconquered the whole of south-eastern Tibet, including Nyarong, Ba-tang, Li-tang, and the other districts which had been annexed to the Chinese province of Szechuan two hundred years ago and held by them ever since. But the Chinese would not have recognized any settlement that took from them areas which they regarded as part of China proper, and the Tibetans were not strong enough to hold their outposts so close to Chinese armies and the centres of Chinese population. It may be hoped that in due course China will recognize the justice of permitting the annexed and controlled districts of eastern Tibet to rejoin their own administration, where they wish to do so. There can be no final peace in Tibet till this is done.

At any rate this campaign has shown that the Tibetans are willing to make sacrifices in order to recover their territory from Chinese rule. It has also shown that the Tibetans are at last learning again how to fight. In time, with arms, equipment, and training, they may be able to defend their own country tolerably well.

Public anxiety in Tibet as to the World War was relieved by the assurances of the Dalai Lama that Britain would be victorious in the end. A prophecy in 1915 by the lamas under the headship of the Lord Chamberlain, himself a lama, was to the effect that Germany was an elephant, which is pulled down eventually, though it takes a long time to do so.

When the war ended in the defeat of the Central Powers, justifying the prophecies of the Dalai and other lamas of Tibet, His Holiness telegraphed his congratulations to His Majesty the King. Thus did this hermit nation in the heart of Asia feel her fortunes linked closely with those of the island far away to the west of Europe. The enemies of yesterday had become the friends of to-day. The sullen aloofness of

[1] *Travels of a Consular Officer in Eastern Tibet*, by Eric Teichman (Cambridge University Press).

Altar in a Tibetan chapel

By colour photography

former times had passed away, never, let us hope, to return, for an autonomous Tibet looks forward to close co-operation with Britain.

Wars may rage and their country suffer from invasion, but the spiritual side of life is never far from the heart of this people. For some time past the Tashi Lama had been fashioning an enormous image of the coming Buddha, the ' King of Love ',[1] at Tashi-lhünpo, and was building a temple of great height to house it. Report stated that His Holiness had himself carried the first stones for the building, and so fired the enthusiasm of all. A Tibetan friend of mine explained the object of the new work as follows :

' It is a request to the King of Love to come quickly. The age of Gotama Buddha has seen its best days. The dark days alone remain, days in which the span of human life will gradually shorten to ten years, and the stature of human beings to a cubit. It is a life, in which one is born to-day, and to-morrow one is old enough to ask for fire to cook his food. Two thousand five hundred years of the age of Gotama still remain, but the Tashi Lama hopes thus to shorten them. A work of merit, like this of the Tashi Lama, brings prosperity in countless other ways also. The good crops of this year (1915), the best for the last ten or twelve years, are attributed by many to the building of this image and of the temple in which it is enshrined.'

[1] *Gye-wa Cham-pa* in Tibetan ; *Maitreya* in Hindi.

XVIII

AUTONOMOUS TIBET

THINGS were now easier in Tibet. The Tibetans were in a fairly strong position, and peace between Tibet and China was assured for the present.

In Sikkim too, a State of Tibetan origin and originally part of Tibet, we had completed another stage of political development. The treaty of 1890 between Great Britain and China declared a British Protectorate over Sikkim. A British Political Officer was appointed to take a leading part in the administration of the State, which was supervised by the Bengal Government. Tu-top Nam-gyal, the Ruler—to whom the Indian Government has always given the Indian title of Maharaja though the Chiefs of Sikkim are of Tibetan, not Indian, origin—being thus deprived of his former power, held sullenly aloof. Later on, he attempted to flee through Nepal to Tibet, but was arrested by the Nepalese and made over to the British. He was then kept as a State prisoner near Kurseong. There can be but little doubt that our relations with Sikkim were mismanaged at this time ; too little tact and sympathy, too much of the hobnailed boot. Sikkim no doubt was small and powerless, but the news spread through Tibet and Bhutan, where people said, ' Sikkim has been turned into mud ', and feared closer contact with a Power which might inflict similar treatment on themselves.

On the other hand it must be entered to the credit of the British authorities of this period that the resources of the country were increased, greater freedom given to the tenantry, and various changes introduced, many of which at any rate were recognized as improvements by the succeeding generation of Sikkimese. Mr. Claude White, the Political Officer, did much excellent work in a difficult position, and during his long incumbency developed the resources of Sikkim out of all recognition.

When I joined my post in 1908, I was able to increase

to some extent the powers of Tu-top Nam-gyal and of the leading men in the State. During my two years of land settlement work in Kalimpong, where the races are the same as in Sikkim, I had gained experience of the administration from the village life upwards, for the great advantage of settlement work is that it brings one into close contact with the everyday life of the people. I was thus able to promote in some degree the development of the country, and at the same time, seeing where the shoe pinched, to ease life for the peasants, who form over nine-tenths of the inhabitants of Sikkim.

Among other measures the Council agreed to a few changes in the rent laws, in the debt laws, and in the general administration of justice. We conserved large areas of forests, which were being rapidly felled, and introduced rules for their management ; a necessary provision and less unpopular than most of its kind, because we left the profits to some extent in the hands of the landlords. I classified the rice lands and assessed the rents of each. To afford shade on the hot mountain sides I arranged for certain kinds of trees to be planted along all the roads. The heir to the Sikkim throne took over this work, by which some seventy thousand trees in all were planted and preserved. Through the same agency I reserved lands for the needs of villagers in respect of free grazing and fuel, as I had done in Kalimpong.

Speaking to me in 1912, this young Prince of Sikkim, who was in many respects an outspoken critic of British and European methods, expressed appreciation of the altered conditions in his country. He said, ' The leading men in Sikkim are pleased by the changes effected by British rule ; e. g. the improved administration of justice, the increased trade resulting in an increase of wealth, the larger bazaars, the knowledge of the outside world, and the conveniences of Western civilization. They say that formerly they used to live like animals, and they hope that they may live to see another generation in Sikkim, in order to witness yet another stage in their country's prosperity.'

Some months before the outbreak of the world war the

Maharaja of Sikkim died, and was succeeded by his son, this Prince, who also died after a short reign. The youngest son, Prince Ta-shi Nam-gyal, was called from an English school to succeed the latter. During the last three years his English Assistant, under my superintendence, had been teaching him how to rule the new Sikkim, increased fivefold in population and tenfold in material resources since the British took over the country thirty years before. Though there was opposition in some quarters, the Indian Foreign Department entirely supported my proposals for giving the Ruler full ruling powers, so that for the first time since Sikkim joined the British Commonwealth, its king might rule in fact as well as in name. It was left to the priesthood of Sikkim to choose the auspicious date for the Installation. Their choice fell on a date early in April 1918.

Tibet was now at rest for the time being, and in a position to consolidate her recent gains. In Sikkim our initial work had attained fruition ; the country, with largely increased resources, was restored to its Ruler. Bhutan, a State of Tibetan origin and still inhabited mainly by people of Tibetan stock, was more than contented with its position since our treaty of 1910 : we had given it security against external foes, and had fulfilled our promise to abstain from all irritating interference in the internal affairs of the State.

I decided accordingly to take leave, of which I had only had three short spells during the last ten years. It had been necessary to be continually on the alert as to events and political tendencies, throughout the wide areas of Tibet, and in Bhutan. The responsibility was considerable, and was not lessened by the difficulty of pressing necessary measures on the Indian Government, which, war or no war, was pre-occupied with Afghanistan, Persia, and the other countries to the north-west of India.

The Maharaja of Sikkim asked me to postpone my leave, that I might be present, as the Indian Government's representative, at his Installation in April 1918, for, as I had done my best to guide him so far, we both felt it to be suitable that I should see him into his new environment. I was able at this Installation to express my appreciation of the cordial friendship accorded to me by His Highness, and by his Highness's father and brother.

In March 1919 I retired from Government service. Shortly afterwards the Chinese Government proposed to our Minister in Peking, that the negotiations broken off at the Simla Conference should be resumed. They pressed that the Ba-tang, Li-tang, and Tachienlu districts of eastern Tibet, which had long been controlled, and in large measure administered, by the Chinese authorities, should be annexed to the Szechuan province of China. They were willing to agree that Gya-de, Cham-do, Mang-kam, and Tra-ya should be incorporated in autonomous Tibet. They claimed also to have Chinese Commissioners at the Trade Marts in Outer Tibet, viz. Gyantse, Yatung, and Gar-tok. Such were the main modifications which they proposed.

The British Government, while not binding itself to accept the Chinese terms, expressed itself as willing to regard them as a basis for negotiation. The Tibetan Government was however not consulted until August, when they rejected all the Chinese modifications. At the same time came the news that the Chinese had themselves backed out of their own proposals.

The provinces of Szechuan and Yunnan have long had chauvinistic ideas as regards Tibet, which they—especially Szechuan—regard as their own particular appanage. There arose the usual rumour that British troops were entering Tibet. That it was entirely baseless mattered not at all. Meetings of protest, attended by students and others, were held in various places. The Chinese Government found the opposition too strong and withdrew, temporarily as they said, from the negotiations, which they themselves had initiated. There were indeed good grounds for believing that the opposition was fomented by Japanese advisers, whom of late years Japan has pressed on the Chinese Government. The powerful military party in that Government was largely under Japanese influence. For Japan had taken advantage of the world war to fasten her grip on China, and did not hesitate to use her newly gained advantages to the detriment of her ally, Britain. She too may have felt that the British Government had not accorded her all the privileges that should rightly belong to such an alliance.

After the breakdown of these negotiations the prohibition against Tibet importing munitions from or through India was continued. Their scanty store of reliable ammunition being by now almost exhausted, the Tibetan Government found it impossible to continue the long, unequal contest with China ; and, feeling that our Government was not helping them as had been promised, consented at last to receive a Chinese Mission in Lhasa. This was the first time such a Mission had been admitted since the break between the two countries, and it showed that—from necessity, not from choice—Tibet was turning from Britain to China. Hitherto the Tibetans had refused to meet a Chinese Representative, unless a British Representative also was present to see fair play and to join in any Agreement that resulted.

And in truth Tibet can hardly be blamed for the course that she followed. For, from 1913 onwards, we had encouraged the Tibetans to trust in us. At the signing of the Convention of 1914 they were promised the diplomatic assistance of the British Government. They were promised also that they would receive help to a reasonable extent in obtaining munitions. In pursuance of that promise we had from time to time permitted them to purchase ammunition in India. But for the last two years our Government had barred them absolutely from obtaining ammunition or other military supplies.

A large measure of foreign assistance had been supplied to China in the equipment of arsenals. By denying facilities to Tibet, we were placing that country at the mercy of the Chinese. Thus, Tibet, whose friendship we had at last gained, would fall back into an attitude of hostility, feeling that the British Government had broken their pledge and betrayed her. Chinese pressure, backed possibly by Japanese influence, would steadily grow into a real menace along the north-eastern frontier of India. In our own interest we need a Tibet that is contented and as strong as may be.

It might indeed be argued that the Entente Powers had agreed that they would not supply arms to China till her Government was more settled and order re-established. But Tibet was in effect—and had been for several years—independent of China. As from the Nepal Government, so from the Government of Tibet, no Mission had been sent to Peking for the last nine years. Tibet too was settled and orderly. A reasonable import of arms and ammunition would not cause disorder, but would on the contrary further promote the stability of the country. There was no chance of such munitions finding their way to China, for the Tibetan Government could be trusted in their own interests to see to that.

By barring Tibet from buying munitions in India, the British Government were breaking their definite pledges, were undermining Tibet's hard-won freedom, and were jeopardizing the security of the northern frontier of India.

Tibet in effect was war-weary. For several years she had had to maintain an army in her eastern territory, and the strain on her slender resources was severe. The people everywhere recalled the prophecy made some thirty years before to the effect, ' The British are the road-makers of Tibet.' Our people would come and work in their country for a while, and then depart, leaving the fruits of their toil to others. Throughout Tibet great importance is attached to prophecies, proverbs, and the sayings of old times, for it is held that these were divinely inspired.

After my retirement I had remained in Darjeeling for various Tibetan studies. Having completed these, I was leaving for England. But shortly before my departure the Indian Government asked me to return to work. After some hesitation—for I had been long absent from my native land—I agreed to return for a year, and arrived at Gangtok, my headquarters in Sikkim, in mid-January 1920.

At the same time the Chinese Mission, after a long journey through eastern Tibet, arrived in Lhasa. In due course they proposed new, and ostensibly favourable, terms of settlement to the Tibetan Government, requesting the latter to depute their Representatives to China to negotiate a final Agreement. They did not, however, succeed in effecting anything definite. After a stay of four or five months, in April 1920 they quitted the Tibetan capital and returned to China. But Chinese influence in Lhasa was considerably augmented.

The general position appeared to me tangled and unpromising. I therefore urged that I should be permitted to accept the Dalai Lama's oft-repeated invitation to visit him and the Tibetan Government in Lhasa. I had been many times so invited, but our own Government had hitherto not seen their way to permit me to accept. The Tibetans were almost in despair at our turning the cold shoulder to them. The Chinese Mission had done what it could to poison the minds of the Tibetan Government and people against us. If I went to Lhasa, I could explain the position in personal conversation with the Dalai Lama and the members of his Government, and do my best to restore confidence and friendliness.

At the end of September, when the time for my departure for England was drawing nearer, I received a letter from the Dalai Lama, who had evidently heard of my impending departure. In this letter he urged me to stay on until the dispute between China and Tibet was settled. His Holiness wrote also to Kusho Palhese—an unusual step—instructing him to press me with all the emphasis at his command to remain at work. From the Tibetan Council too I received a letter to the same effect.

It was about this time that the Indian Government acceded to a request made by the Government of Tibet during the world war and now repeated. This was for the construction of a telegraph line to Lhasa. It was surveyed during the autumn and, after a suitable design had been arranged and a system agreed upon, it was erected a year or two later. Thus Lhasa was enabled to communicate with Simla and to receive a reply on the same day, whereas, formerly, this took seven days, for the telegraph line ended at Gyantse, three days by post from Lhasa.

Tibetan postal service.   Changing couriers on the Gyantse-Lhasa road

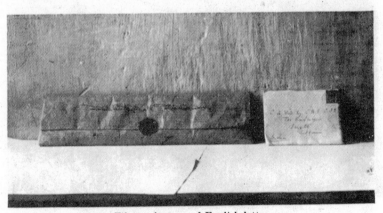

Tibetan letter and English letter

The Tibetans have had for several years a limited, but remarkably efficient, postal service of their own in central Tibet. This service they appreciate highly. Formerly they were put to the trouble, expense, and loss of time entailed by the necessity of finding a person to carry their letters for them.

In October of this year (1920) I concluded my usual summer visit to Yatung and Gyantse and was preparing to return to Sikkim, for winter sets in early at these high elevations. But the question of my visiting the Tibetan capital had meanwhile been decided, and accordingly I received a telegram from the Indian Government, asking me to conduct a Mission to Lhasa, in order to convey to His Holiness the Dalai Lama friendly greetings from the British Government and to explain the present political position.

We left Yatung, in the Chumbi Valley, for Lhasa on the 1st November 1920. The gales of the Tibetan winter were setting in, and an area where an infectious and highly fatal type of influenza was raging had to be crossed ; but the prospect of Lhasa was alluring to us all, on personal as well as on public grounds. My staff and private servants were nearly all Buddhists, few of whom had hitherto had the opportunity of visiting their Holy City. The only Englishman with me was Mr. Dyer, the Medical Officer of my Political Agency, who accompanied us temporarily. I had arranged that my old friend, Lt. Col. R. S. Kennedy, D.S.O., M.C., of the Indian Medical Service, should join us in Lhasa. Some years previously he had spent two or three years in Gyantse, and at the end of his time there, in 1910, had accompanied me on my Mission to Bhutan. He spoke Tibetan well and kept on good terms with the people. His medical skill was invaluable, not only to us of the Mission, but to the Tibetans of Lhasa and surrounding districts as well. To me his companionship was a pearl beyond price. For nearly a year we saw no other white man.

As my Personal Assistant I took Rai Bahadur A-chuk Tse-ring ; as my Attaché, Kusho Pa-lhe-se. To these two I looked as my chief confidants and advisers on the troubled sea of Tibetan politics.

XIX

MY MISSION TO LHASA

OUR journey to Lhasa and our return journey a year later were full of interest, and still more so was our long sojourn of eleven months in the centre of Tibetan Buddhism. For visiting Lhasa, as I did, on the repeated invitations of the Dalai Lama and his Government, I was welcomed everywhere and all facilities were accorded for my seeing the festivals and ceremonies, the manners and customs in palace and cottage ; in fine, all that goes to make up the life of this strange and interesting people. I had already of necessity acquired a good knowledge of the Tibetan language, and a considerable acquaintance with Tibetan life—as indeed who but the stupidest of mortals could fail to do after so many years of residence ?—and thus was able to understand and appreciate what I saw and heard. But to deal with these things in the present book would be to overweight it with matters which, however interesting in themselves, are foreign to its purport. I will therefore reserve them for a future volume, and in this one touch in the main only upon such events as bear directly upon the political life of the country.

On the 2nd November we covered a long stage of 37 miles from Gau-tsa to Tuna over the Tang La, avoiding as much as possible the intervening town of Phari, for it was the centre of the influenza epidemic. We could not, however, avoid changing our transport animals there ; and, whether from this or other cause, the infection caught us and took its toll of our party. For in high altitudes, with the consequent difficulty of breathing, the pneumonia that supervenes on an attack is more than ever deadly.

The cold was intense ; there was ice everywhere, but no snow, for the air was too dry. The winds were strong, but less severe than usual at this season of the year. I went via Gyantse and Nan-kar-tse, crossing the Ka-ro La and

Kam-pa La, the former somewhat over, the latter somewhat under 16,000 feet above sea-level. At Gyantse I was met by an emissary deputed by the Dalai Lama to conduct us to the capital. At Chu-shur, on the banks of the great river—which is marked on maps as the Tsanpo or Sanpo, but is known to Tibetans as the Tsang-chu—I was met by one of His Holiness's secretaries, sent to bring me the last forty miles of the journey, to welcome me to Lhasa, and to convey an invitation to lunch or dinner, whichever I might prefer, though, of course, His Holiness could not himself be present at this. This secretary, named Lo-trö, i. e. ' Wisdom ', was usually known as the Tsen-drön, i. e. the ' Secretary at the Peak ', the term ' Peak ' being commonly used for the Dalai Lama's palace of Potala, which is situated on a small hill. He was a man who in any country would be singled out as the fortunate possessor of exceptionally high intelligence. The Tsen-drön and Ne-tö Dzong-pön, the officer who conducted us from Gyantse, a priest and a layman, were attached to my Mission when I arrived in Lhasa.

I halted for a day at Chu-shur in order to arrive at Lhasa on the 17th, an auspicious date in the Tibetan calendar. I arranged to call on the Grand Lama on the 19th, this being another auspicious date, the 8th of the tenth Tibetan month. When dealing with Tibetans, one should be careful to utilize dates of good omen as far as possible, for it is a matter to which they attach great importance.

Here, at Chu-shur, a rumour reached us that there was a European in Lhasa, a man with grey eyes, who came on one occasion to change gold, mostly in the form of gold medals, with a trader in Lhasa. The report, however, proved to be without foundation, and was probably due to the presence of several Buriats in Lhasa. These people are Mongolians who live in that portion of northern Mongolia which has long been annexed by Russia to her Siberian territory. They trade a good deal in Russian merchandise, and many, living, as they do, in the latitude of southern England and in a Canadian climate, have grey eyes and fair complexions.

The representative of the Ladakhi community in Lhasa met me at Chu-shur with a scarf of welcome. These people from Ladakh [1] number several hundred souls, all Mahomedans, who have been settled in Lhasa for many decades and earn their livelihood by trade. It is believed that the settlement had its origin in the prisoners captured by the Tibetans from the Dogra Army, under Zorawar Singh, that attacked western Tibet unsuccessfully in 1841.

Eight miles out of Lhasa, the diplomatic Agent of Bhutan in Lhasa came to greet me, followed by the land agents of my old friends, the heads of the Pa-lha and Do-ring families. Our party growing thus larger and larger, we rode on till, two miles from our destination, we were welcomed by representatives of His Holiness the Dalai Lama, as well as by those of the Prime Minister and the Grand Council of Tibet. Here a tent had been erected, picturesque with its blue designs on the roof, after the manner of Tibetan tents, and we were regaled with rice, biscuits, and tea, all after the Tibetan style. In the tea butter, as well as soda, is boiled, so that a scum forms on the surface. This you blow aside before drinking; and each time that you drink, even though but a little, your cup is immediately refilled. You must drink once again after the first refilling, and then, if you like, you can stop. Europeans almost invariably dislike this tea, but it is well boiled and is not unwholesome. No Tibetan drinks less than fifteen or twenty cups a day, and some drink sixty or seventy.

Outside the tent we were met by the Captain in charge of the small Gurkha detachment which had been sent as a Guard of Honour by the Nepalese Agent in Lhasa. A second Guard of Honour was furnished by a hundred Tibetan infantry, drawn up by the wayside under their officers. Stalwart fellows they were, and, dressed in their modern khaki uniforms, adopted from India a few years ago, they appeared a workmanlike body. The crowd growing larger and larger, we were by now a veritable cavalcade and could sample to the full the restless unending dust of Tibet.

The Grand Council had proposed to accommodate us in

[1] See page 8.

The Prime Minister's daughter (right) with a friend

Lhasa city from the Potala

the house in which Sir Francis Younghusband and his Staff
were lodged in the Expedition of 1904, but the Dalai Lama
wished me to be nearer to him, and so we were given the
summer residence of a former Regent of Tibet.   It lay on the
bank of the river, about half a mile from the entrance to the
grounds of the Dalai Lama's country Palace, known as
' The Jewel Park ' (Nor-pu Ling-ka).   The Regent had never
lived in this house during the winter, and it was feared that
we might find it cold then ; but it was chosen because it
was clean.

On the next day the Ministers who constitute the Grand
Council made a joint call of ceremony upon me.   Among
them was my old friend the Commander-in-Chief, whom
I had first met in Darjeeling in 1910, when he was an
attendant in the private household of the Dalai Lama.   By
the favour of His Holiness on the one hand, and by his own
energy and devotion on the other, he had risen to his present
rank, and furnished an example of that rare phenomenon
among the laity of Tibet, a man of humble birth raised
to a high position.   I say ' laity ' advisedly, for in the
celibate ranks of the clergy, separated from their families
and having an independent status, such events are of
common occurrence.

My reception by the Dalai Lama, in the Jewel Park, was
of extreme friendliness.   He was not seated in formal fashion
on his throne, as is usual, but received me in his private
apartments, as he had done in the old days at Darjeeling,
when he came to us in trouble and we did our best to make
things easy for him.   His eyes lighting up with pleasure, he
rose from his European chair, and coming to meet me,
grasped both my hands in his, as he told me how glad he
was that I had come.   We sat together alone, as we always
had done, and I noticed, when I came out of the room, that
there was nobody even within earshot.   Thus we could talk
freely.   In all my subsequent visits similar privacy was
observed.   Business had to be held over for my second visit ;
it would have been contrary to etiquette to have discussed
it at this first one.

I then visited my old friend, Lön-chen Sho-kang, who, as the only survivor of the three Chief Ministers, may rightly be termed the Prime Minister. From him too I received an extremely cordial welcome. ' When I heard ', said he, ' that you had come as far as Gyantse and then returned to the Chumbi Valley, I was almost in despair of our ever meeting again. But I used to set your photograph before me and pray that somehow this might be brought about. And thus has my prayer been granted.'

An old man now, he spent some two hours daily in prayer, offering supplication for himself, his family, and his native land ; and not for these only, but for the whole human race ; nor stopping even there, but also for all ' mind-possessors ' (*sem-chen*), i. e. for birds, beasts, and fishes, the entire animal creation.

He gave me one good piece of advice. ' You will find it best ', he said, ' to conduct all your business direct with the Dalai Lama, and not with the Grand Council nor even with me. Otherwise, all kinds of people will come to know secrets which ought to be kept from them, and harm will result.'

He paid his return call on me in an hour's time. I had some difficulty in restraining him from paying it at once, but I insisted, for I felt sure that he needed a rest. The sooner a call is returned, the greater is the honour done to the caller.

Visits and entertainments, on the Tibetan side and on ours, now occupied us a good deal, especially for the first two or three months. For the Tibetans are a hospitable people, very fond of entertaining and of being entertained. Ceremonies and etiquette are to them of prime importance, a fact which anybody who has dealings with them does well to recognize.

At this time therefore we were often in the streets of Lhasa. The Tibetan gentry prefer to live in their town houses during the winter, rather than in their villas scattered over the neighbouring country-side, for the town is warmer than the country. Crowds gathered to stare at us for the

Shop in Lhasa with owner's daughter. Fruit, &c., for sale

Vegetable and meat shop, Lhasa

Corpse being carried away for the last rites. Ceremonial scarves are placed on the sack

The last scene

first week or two, as we rode past, for many of them had never seen a white man before. But we met with no rudeness. The Tibetan, from prince to peasant, unless greatly incensed, is essentially courteous and dignified.

An interesting personality in Lhasa at this time was the Governor of the Ili Province, in the north-western corner of Chinese Turkestan, on the Siberian border. There were good grounds for believing that this official—a Mongolian by race, and therefore akin to the Tibetans—had come to Lhasa to negotiate on behalf of China with the Tibetan Government, in order to bring Tibet back to the Chinese fold and to oust British influence from the country. The Tibetan Government were well aware of the risk of Chinese domination that was likely to result from negotiations unattended by a British Representative. But prevented, as they were, from importing ammunition from or through India, they were of necessity considering how to make the best possible terms with China. My arrival in Lhasa was opportune, in that it frustrated the further progress of this Mission.

Three or four months before I came to Lhasa, the Royal Geographical Society and the Alpine Club had requested our Government to ask the Government of Tibet for permission to ascend Mount Everest from Tibetan territory. Our ally, Nepal, had refused permission to attempt the ascent from the Nepalese side. I felt sure that, if I wrote, the Tibetan Government would grant the permission, for I do not think that the Dalai Lama has ever refused me anything that I asked for. But I felt bound to oppose the project of writing to the Tibetan Government for this permission ; for I knew that the scheme would raise suspicion in the mind of a people circumstanced as are those of Tibet. They would not understand the plea of geographical and scientific aims, and would suspect that some secret and possibly sinister object lay behind the proposal. They would also fear that, whatever our motives, the spirits of the place would be disturbed. The fact that the part of Tibet to be visited lay near the Nepal frontier would further increase their uneasiness, since Tibet and Nepal were not on the best of terms. Difficulties of this kind cannot be smoothed out in letters ; personal conversation is essential. The Indian Government and the Home Government agreed with my views.

When, however, I came to Lhasa, the Indian Government asked me to sound the Tibetan Government on the subject, provided that I saw no objection to doing so. The matter being thus left to my discretion, I did ask and obtain permission for the Everest Expedition. Personal conversation, direct between the parties, no interpreters being present, enables suspicions to be removed or minimized, when each side trusts the other. In this, as in all talks with the Dalai Lama, I found him full of tolerance. It was certainly a noteworthy fact that Tibet should grant to Britain, her former enemy, a privilege which Britain's own ally, Nepal, had consistently refused.

On the 11th December Rai Bahadur Achuk Tsering died of heart failure, brought on by a combined attack of influenza and gout. His death was a great shock to us all, and especially to me. We had worked together, almost continuously, for just twenty years, having been first associated in the census of the Kalimpong sub-division. He was a man of great acumen, whose opinion on questions of Tibetan, Bhutanese, or Sikkimese politics was invaluable. I applied immediately for an old friend, Sardar Bahadur Laden La, a Sikkimese in the Bengal Police, who had on my behalf looked after the Dalai Lama and his Ministers during their stay in India from 1910 to 1912. A considerable time, however, elapsed before he was deputed to my Mission, so that he did not join me until the 15th March.

My private conversations with the Dalai Lama, which were frequent, ranged over a wide variety of subjects. Sometimes the power of Tibet to defend itself came under discussion. During one of these conversations—which were entirely informal—being asked my opinion, I expressed my view that the Tibetan army was inadequate. It consisted only of some five thousand men. I thought that it should be increased gradually, as funds and equipment became available, till it reached about fifteen thousand. This seemed the lowest number that would offer a reasonable prospect of defence against foreign foes and internal disturbances; at the same time there was no hope of finding funds to pay for more.

When I found that the Dalai Lama and the Tibetan Government intended to adopt the opinion, which I had expressed, as a settled line of policy, I expressed it in more detail, suggesting that the increase should be gradual, that recruitment should be spread as evenly as possible over the whole country, that not many should be taken from the district round Lhasa, that in no circumstances should monks be recruited, and that neither the monasteries nor the landed estates should be subjected to direct taxation to meet this expenditure. Whenever mentioning this subject, I also made it clear that my views were entirely my own; that they did not emanate from, and were in no sense inspired by, my Government. The Tibetan Government framed their scheme substantially on the above lines, and commenced acting on it as circumstances permitted.

Many of the monks no doubt were opposed to any increase in the army. Some even urged that, since Tibet was useful to India as a barrier against outside foes, it should be protected by British and Indian troops. But this was not the view of the Tibetan Government, and not even of the responsible heads of the monasteries themselves. The latter control the Assembly, and the Assembly voted for the increase of the army.

The leaders were able to realize that Chinese domination in Tibet, though accompanied by subsidies to the monasteries, would in the end harm the religion and their own influence more than the domination of their own Government. They knew that with modern rifles they could keep out large bodies of Chinese troops. Those on the frontier knew it also. For, when volunteers were called for in eastern Tibet, the usual reply was, ' Lend me a good rifle and I will come '. They were well aware of the uselessness of men without training or equipment; they had not forgotten that a dozen or so of Chinese soldiers had kept the whole of Sera monastery at bay.

During January the Indian Government pressed me to come away from Lhasa, but I urged the necessity of remaining, on various grounds, and this view ultimately prevailed. The Tibetan Government were greatly relieved ; they were surprised and distressed at the idea of my leaving before our Government replied to a letter which they had written on my arrival in Lhasa. The Dalai Lama, the Prime Minister, and the Councillors all urged me to remain. The Prime Minister, who came twice to see me on the subject, said, ' I was ill for some months, but your coming here has made my illness better. We are old friends. When I looked at your photograph, I used to pray that you would come to Lhasa. The Dalai Lama prophesied that you would come here and settle the Tibetan question. When I heard you were coming, I felt that the prophecy would soon be fulfilled. If you leave now, with nothing accomplished, you will be rubbing my face in the dust.'

The leading priest official said to a friend of mine : ' We will first beg Minister Bell with folded hands to stay. If he does not agree to stay, we will throw our arms round his neck to keep him. If he still insists on going, we will hold on to him with our teeth, so that he will have to knock our teeth down our throats before he will be able to get away.'

February is the beginning of the Tibetan New Year. The festival known as ' The Great Prayer ', the chief festival of the whole year, takes place and lasts for three weeks. Lhasa as usual was crowded with monks. Owing to quarrels between the leaders of the monks and certain military officers, there was at this time a grave danger that the monks, of whom there were some forty thousand in the neighbourhood, might break out, loot and kill. The Dalai Lama was aware of the danger and did the most sensible thing by putting Lhasa out of bounds for the military. The good people of Lhasa were openly terrified, and many of them removed their belongings and hid them in villages far and near. Lhasa has an unenviable reputation for murderous

The Butter Festival, known as 'The Offerings of the Fifteenth'

The 'Offerings' (some 45 feet high) representing deities and sacred emblems are made of butter on a frame-work of wood and leather

outbreaks in which many people are killed and a great deal of property is destroyed. In the towns of Darjeeling and Kalimpong, on the Indian frontier, rumours were rife to the effect that we of the Mission had been assassinated.

The Tibetans everywhere attributed to me the increase in their army which was destined to curtail the influence of the powerful priesthood. And no doubt they had good reason for thinking so, for His Holiness had apparently taken the suggestion from me and was pushing the matter through with characteristic energy. When, therefore, I announced my desire to attend the Butter Festival, which takes place at night in the heart of Lhasa, those in authority were very nervous. There were a good many monks in Lhasa at the time, the streets were narrow and unlighted, and a stone could easily be dropped or a shot discharged from the darkness of a neighbouring house. The monks, as the Dalai Lama said, act without reflecting, and, being celibate, have neither family nor property to consider.

But I had been present at other ceremonies, and people would have drawn wrong conclusions if I had not been present at this also. As we left his house, the Commander-in-Chief offered Colonel Kennedy a revolver, which the latter fortunately refused. Twelve soldiers accompanied us and six monks armed with long staves. The atmosphere was indeed somewhat electric, but we were well treated everywhere. And indeed throughout this period of unrest, though we rode and walked unescorted day by day, neither I nor other members of my party received anything but courtesy and kindliness from the people.

Owing to the Dalai Lama's personality and skill, the trouble was eventually averted. Out of the four Councillors on the Grand Council, which constitutes, under the Dalai Lama and Prime Minister, the Government of Tibet, one was dismissed and two were fined. Three colonels were dismissed and two lesser military officers, including the Dalai Lama's nephew, were fined. The leading priests were summoned before His Holiness and warned to keep the monks under strict control. They were reminded that, if fighting broke out, their monasteries would be seriously damaged and they themselves heavily punished.

It was more than sixteen years since a Councillor had been dismissed from his post. He had to remove his official dress then and there at the meeting, in the presence of his fellow councillors, and to go home in ordinary garb.

Shortly afterwards His Holiness fell ill, and this caused renewed anxiety, for none can hold Tibet together as he can. Always a worker, he remained at his tasks when he was in no fit condition to do so. Thus, growing steadily worse and worse, he became dangerously ill. His physician, who had some years previously been promoted to the headship of the priest-officials, was seriously alarmed, and, after bowing his head to the ground as usual, addressed him as follows : ' Your Holiness, please instruct me what you intend to do. I asked you not to go to the Potala to conduct the ceremony, but you went there. I keep asking you to rest, but you continue working. Do you intend to change your body (i. e. give up this present life), or to remain with us ? '

The Dalai Lama laughed and replied : ' There is no harm done ; give me your medicine.' After that he was more careful. He was in fact too ill to work, however much he might wish to continue. The Court officials wisely kept their counsel regarding the gravity of the illness, for, had it been known, there might have resulted a panic in Lhasa and grave uneasiness throughout the whole of Tibet.

Another outbreak occurred five months later in the Dre-pung Monastery, but on a smaller scale, only five thousand monks being involved. It was not directly con-nected with the former outbreak, having originated in a question of internal discipline. The monks threatened to attack Lhasa. Affairs of this kind are apt to turn against the foreigner of alien religion who has penetrated into the land. The priestly classes, scenting in the foreign influence a menace to their religion and themselves, are especially inclined to be hostile. We had, however, by then been long enough in Lhasa to gain the good will of all classes. So far from our being an object of suspicion, some leading members of the Tibetan Government desired me to intervene with advice ; and the monks themselves went so far as to desire my arbitration in the entire dispute. This was undesirable, but I tendered advice on certain aspects of the case in the proper quarter ; and this was acted on.

The Tibetan Government summoned three thousand troops to Lhasa and besieged the monastery, which in due course submitted. The affair was settled with a wise admixture of force and leniency. As the Dalai Lama himself informed me during one of our conversations, ' I had to show myself the master. Otherwise, Sera, Ganden, and other large monasteries would be encouraged to break out when they wished to gain any end of their own.' But having shown his power, he used it with the utmost moderation. Even uprisings of this kind help to show how much more orderly is the administration of Tibet than that of China, a fact that is brought home to those Europeans in China who visit portions of Tibet under the Dalai Lama's rule.

XX

QUESTIONS OF POLICY

WHEN I had been three months in Lhasa, in close touch with the Tibetan Government and people, and had gained such an insight into Tibetan feeling as could be afforded only by a residence in the capital, I wrote to our Government, explaining once again my views on Tibet's position as regards international politics, and setting forth anew my suggestions as to the policy which, in my opinion, we ought to follow.

I pointed out that in 1904 British and Indian troops invaded Tibet, drove the Dalai Lama from his capital, and, in the fullness of their military strength, made a treaty with the Tibetan Government. Subsequent events were the direct outcome of this, and therefore the British Government was in some measure responsible for the present Tibetan problem.

It is unnecessary to recapitulate here the steps by which the Tibetan question had arrived at its present stage ; these have been set out, I hope, with sufficient clearness in the preceding pages. In short, China had oppressed and misgoverned Tibet ; and, when doing so, had endeavoured to gain power over the states and tribes of the Himalaya, which formed the inmost barrier along India's northern frontier. She refused to negotiate such a treaty as would meet Tibet's needs. And these needs coincided in the main with our own.

What did we need from Tibet ? Put briefly, our main requirement was that Tibet herself should be strong and free. With their scanty population and their dread of hot climates, the Tibetans could be no serious menace to India. On the other hand, they would furnish a northern frontier for India of unparalleled strength. No other land frontier in the world is so strong as the great Northern Plateau of Tibet to the north, buttressed by the Himalaya to the south.

And we wanted Tibet free also. For unless she is free, she cannot be really strong ; and what she wants most of all is to live her own life without interference from those around her.

In Tibet also we had an ideal barrier against Bolshevist influence, for the latter is abhorrent to the orderly Tibetan mind and to the religion which inspires it. Chinese soldiers, stationed in Mongolia, had been found to be infected with Bolshevism. If China re-occupied Tibet, their troops stationed in Lhasa, and even further south, might well form a focus of Bolshevist intrigue against India.

By maintaining close friendship with the Dalai Lama we gained also the goodwill of Mongolia and the Buriats, and thus secured the friendship of the nations from the Himalaya to the far-distant frontier of Siberia, and beyond.

But what was the present position ? We were continually protesting our friendship for Tibet, but we were not acting up to our protestations.

We had been able, by using every opportunity, to gain the goodwill of the Dalai Lama and of his leading Ministers. But His Holiness's life was necessarily uncertain and his health was not what it had been ten years before. Should he die, the Regent that succeeded him would of necessity have far less authority.

The National Assembly of Tibet is composed of representatives from the most powerful monasteries and of the officials, lay and cleric, high and low. It is a body, therefore, whose opinions carry great weight. The pro-Chinese element in this Assembly was steadily growing.

The most influential member in the Grand Council, who was also strongly anti-Chinese, was believed to have received promises of pardon and future favours, provided that he threw in his lot with China. A remark which another of the Councillors made to one of my friends was significant. He said, ' The British Government does not help us. It even prevents us from obtaining ammunition. It seems that we shall have to consider the situation.' Then, with a half-laugh, he added, ' You know what I mean.' In other words, the abandonment in despair of friendly relations with Britain and a submissive return to China, such as was bound to mean the loss of Tibetan freedom.

One indication of the impending change appeared in the coming to Lhasa of the Chinese Mission, which negotiated direct with the Tibetan Government, in the absence of any British representative. Another sign was to be found in the arrival at Lhasa of the Governor from Ili. And Dorjieff, who had caused the British Government so much trouble in the past, had an agent in Lhasa watching the situation.

Far and near in Tibet at this time one could notice a growing admiration for the other Island Empire, the Empire of Japan. It was felt that Japan had aided Mongolia against the Bolshevists, that she was a strong Power, and that she was steadily advancing nearer to Tibet. Mongolia was flooded with Japanese rifles, cheap and serviceable. If the British rifles were held back, let the Japanese be obtained.

What then would have been the outcome of continuing our policy of aloofness ? Tibet would be compelled to turn to China and Japan, and the north-eastern frontier of India would fall more and more under combined Chinese and Japanese influence. No longer would India have as its frontier the plateau of northern Tibet. Fifteen hundred miles from east to west, three to five hundred from north to south, never less than sixteen thousand feet above the sea, and almost uninhabited, this inhospitable tableland is the real barrier of India to the north. Instead of this barrier, India would have as her frontier a band of narrow Mongolian [1] States, greatly liable to fall under the influence of Japan and China, the two leading Mongolian nations. In the east too Burma, itself a Mongolian country, would be liable to fall under the same influence.

In these circumstances it may be understood that the policy—if such it can be called—of standing aloof might well bequeath to India a legacy of serious trouble. Hitherto

---

[1] The term is here used in its widest sense, as referring to the Mongolian family of nations.

MUNITIONS. Blacksmiths working in the Lhasa Arsenal

Soldiers of the new army on parade in Lhasa

we had been able to leave north-eastern India almost without troops, because our neighbour there had no desire to infringe the frontier by attack or intrigue ; and even had the desire been present, there was not, and could not be, sufficient strength to back it. But if these other influences pushed in, India would have to maintain considerable bodies of troops at great expense and in damp, unhealthy regions.

Another, and not unimportant, reason for permitting Tibet to import munitions was the preservation of internal order. Tibet on the whole governed herself well, far better than the China, that wished to govern her, was able to govern herself. But the chief obstacle to good government lay in the turbulence of the large monasteries, as I myself had seen in Lhasa. These could be controlled only by considerable bodies of troops, well trained and well equipped. The preservation of internal order in a country whose frontier marches with that of India and the Himalayan States for nearly two thousand miles, may fairly be termed an Indian interest.

China could not reasonably object to Tibet importing munitions through India, for Tibet had for several years at any rate been independent of the Chinese Government. Any objection on the part of China would be further discounted by the fact that Chinese officers and soldiers in Tibet and China had frequently and openly sold rifles and ammunition on a large scale to the Tibetans. One Chinese General alone had sold three hundred rifles. And for us to bar their passage from or through India was not the right treatment to show towards a friendly neighbour.

To meet the situation I proposed such measures as seemed necessary to enable Tibet to maintain freedom and good government ; in short, to live her own life. Put briefly, my proposals amounted to :

(a) Permission to import yearly from India a small and specified quantity of the different kinds of essential munitions.

(b) Assistance to a limited extent in training and equipping their troops.

(c) Assistance in engaging mining prospectors to discover mines ; if discovered, mining engineers to test them, and, if necessary, work them. There are numerous areas in Tibet where minerals have been found, but it was not yet known whether any of these could be worked at a profit. It was desirable that the Tibetan Government should retain the full ownership of the mines and that they should engage only trustworthy firms and agents to develop them.

(d) The establishment of an English school for the sons of leading Tibetans. To be opened at Gyantse ; and moved later on, if desirable, to Lhasa.

I pointed out that the above would cost us nothing, for Tibet would pay in full for all facilities accorded. Seeing Tibet thus developing and strengthening herself, China might come forward and complete the peace treaty. For she must realize that the longer she held back, the less likely would she be to gain any connexion with Tibetan affairs. Meanwhile, whenever any opportunity offered, we must press the Government of China to complete the treaty, for the Tibetan Government laid great stress on this ; and, in view of the past history of the negotiations, they had every right to expect it.

Such were the advantages to be derived by Tibet. As for India, her long north-eastern frontier would be secured. And, so long as she treated Tibet well, the latter might be willing to remain dependent on her for the above facilities, which she would chiefly use in keeping possible enemies from the Indian frontier. In fact, Tibet would promote Indian interests by promoting her own.

The question as to whether a diplomatic Representative of the British Government should be permanently stationed at Lhasa has long been a subject of discussion among those concerned in Tibetan affairs, and some were in favour of it. To me, however, it seemed that such advance was un-desirable, at any rate for the present. The extent to which we had, little by little, during the last fifteen years, gained Tibetan goodwill, had been in large measure due to our moderation. We had not gone forward in any matter, until responsible Tibetan opinion was strongly in favour of our doing so. We had in fact hung back too often, but at any rate the Tibetans had come to understand that we did not wish to interfere in their country. A good many of them were in favour of having a permanent British Representative at Lhasa, but now that the Chinese Representative had been expelled, the majority did not desire this. They thought, maybe, that to admit the British Agent would renew the demand for the admission of the Chinaman.

My residence in Lhasa had shown me that the thirty thousand monks who live in the vicinity of the capital would for some years to come be a potential danger, since, as was admitted on all hands, they act without thinking, and so are liable to sudden outbreaks. Our Representative there would be practically beyond the reach of military assistance. By putting him there we should materially increase our commitments.

If the Chinese Amban had perforce to be readmitted, it would probably be necessary to station a British Agent also in the Tibetan capital. But for the present it would suffice to send a British official temporarily to Lhasa, whenever both the British and Tibetan Governments should find this necessary.

It seemed to me, nevertheless, desirable that a gradual advance should be made in the direction of opening Tibet to foreign visitors, British and other. It is not possible in these days for any country, however large and however inaccessible, to remain closed against the pushful races of mankind. A political vacuum cannot be long sustained.

In these circumstances I suggested that Tibet be thrown open—but as far as Gyantse only—to both British and foreign visitors, except such as the Government of Tibet or that of India found good reason to exclude.

Thus the people of this hermit land would gradually accustom themselves to the ways of those living beyond their borders, so that a further advance in this direction could be made when the time was ready for it. Tibet had been so long out of the world, that to bring her too suddenly into contact with it would infallibly harm her. My long connexion with Bhutan and Sikkim had shown me clearly that it was best for these Mongolian countries to advance slowly. Let Tibet do the same.

This deliberate but sustained advance would be promoted by the establishment of an English school in Tibet. Tibetans of the upper classes were averse from sending their boys or girls to schools in India for education, and wished to see a school established in Gyantse or even in Lhasa itself.

The late Prime Minister, Lönchen Shatra, discussed the question with me in 1914. His views of the subjects that should be taught showed that even leading Tibetans are slow to realize the limitations of Western education and the long years that it requires. The school was to be for boys of twelve to twenty years of age, and the subjects to be taught were as follows :

(a) English.
(b) Engineering.
(c) Military training.
(d) Carpentry.

(e) Weaving.
(f) Working in leather.
(g) Working in iron.
(h) Utilization of horns and bones.

The suggested curriculum was at any rate useful as showing the subjects in which Tibetans desired fuller knowledge. Another influential Tibetan, speaking to me, a few years later, urged the claims of drawing and surveying.

He said, ' Drawing should be taught only to talented boys of the upper middle classes. These would then be able to draw portraits of deities for the chapels in monasteries and private houses, also portraits of the Dalai Lama, Tashi Lama, and other high Lamas, as well as portraits of the aristocracy.

' A knowledge of surveying would be useful to us in planning houses and roads and in measuring fields for revenue purposes.

' The boys should stay at this school between the ages of twelve and twenty, more or less.'

' What would they learn before they go to this school ? ' I inquired, ' and where would they learn ? '

The British Mission to Lhasa. Lt. Col.-Kennedy is on my right
(seated third from left)

The Tibetan Council, one priest (left) and three laymen, in the Council Chamber

' They would learn at home. They would be taught to read and write simple sentences in their own language. They would learn how to eat and drink properly, and how to behave themselves in the company of others. In fact, they would learn good manners and etiquette, the things that their parents should teach them.'

All with whom I discussed the matter insisted that the head master should be British.

Now that I was at Lhasa I was able to go into the question with the Tibetan Government, and to include among my proposals to my own Government one for the establishment of a school, which, it may be hoped, will promote Western education on reasonable lines.

It was a lasting satisfaction to me that, before I left Lhasa, in October 1921, every one of my proposals—even those in which I differed from other authorities—had been accepted by the British Government. On my departure I was therefore able to set before the Dalai Lama and the Tibetan Government the lines along which British policy towards Tibet would proceed.

It will perhaps not be considered out of place to record briefly a few of the incidents that occurred in connexion with our Mission to Lhasa.

Our good friends the Nepalese were uneasy at our presence in Lhasa. In times past they had been to a large extent the intermediary between Tibet and Britain. Anything in the nature of direct dealings between their two clients necessarily lessened their own importance. When one of our party was lunching with a Tibetan Minister, the two were amused at observing a Nepalese who was lying down, half screened from view, in the verandah of a neighbouring house, and was endeavouring to see what was happening. There were other incidents of a like nature, not very skilfully worked out, for the Gurkhas are of the solid stuff from which first-class soldiers are made, and are not deft at intrigue.

For various reasons the Tibetans and Nepalese were not on good terms. These will come under review in a later chapter. Here one item only need be set down, as affecting my Mission. Shooting and fishing, especially near the holy city of Lhasa, were forbidden, the prohibition resting on religious grounds, than which none could be stronger. The Nepalese, however, indulged in both shooting and fishing. They had for several decades enjoyed extra-territorial rights in Tibet. Their magistrates refused to convict Nepalese subjects who shot or fished, and this the Tibetans very naturally resented. In consequence of my request, made before we reached Lhasa, none of the members of my Mission did either. Our abstention in this respect was patently necessary, but it seemed to worry the Nepalese somewhat at first. Before we left, however, several of them acknowledged that this little piece of abstinence, apart from other considerations, had gained for us a large measure of goodwill among Tibetans of all classes.

From India also came a measure of opposition to my work in Lhasa. Some English and Indian newspapers asserted that I had gone to Lhasa to demand from the Tibetan Government the payment of money said to be due, as well as for loans said to have been contracted by the Dalai Lama during his residence in India. It had to be pointed out that there could be no collection of debt, for no money had been advanced.

Another Indian paper declaimed to its readers that I had gone to Lhasa to carry out sinister designs against the independence of the Tibetans and to bring them into a state of slavery. My object in going to Lhasa, as has been shown above, was the exact opposite of this. The fact that such reports are disseminated far and wide in the press in India shows the necessity for greater publicity in such foreign affairs as can without danger be discussed, when once definite action has been taken or a definite line of policy settled.

Although the Mission was working in the interests of India, for the security of the Indian frontier and in other ways, yet such examples as came to my notice seemed to show that Indian influence was exerted against us. In addition to the articles in the Indian press, personal influence was brought to bear in Lhasa itself.

The members of the Mahomedan community in Lhasa visit Calcutta frequently for trade purposes. On their return they brought to the Government and people reports to the effect that Germany was again fighting with Britain ; that Turkey was steadily growing in power and had driven out the French and recaptured large territories ; and that India had rebelled against the British and introduced her own currency notes. The first of these appeared to refer to our occupation of German territory, the second to the French retirement in Asia Minor, and the last to the notes, very much after the style of the Government's treasury notes, circulated at this time by the Khilafat Committee in India.

Two Indians, dressed as Sadhus, i. e. religious mendicants, came to Lhasa. One went on to the east ; the other remained at the capital, staying in the grounds of the Nepalese Agency. It was reported that he was speaking slightingly of the King-Emperor and pushing as far as he could an anti-British propaganda. Later on, he was joined by another Indian, who was said to have lived for many years in other parts of Tibet, to have taken a Tibetan name and to profess faith in Buddhism.

The anti-British feeling in India was very strong at this time, and it was natural that it should spread to Lhasa also, when my Mission went there. Indians are frequently credited by Tibetans with supernatural powers and, when this is so, gain the influence that fear bestows. On the matter being brought to the notice of the Nepalese Government, the stay of these gentlemen in the grounds of the Nepalese Agency came to an end. The Tibetan Government then took steps to have them both deported by Tibetan officials out of Tibet, across the Indian frontier.

Without wishing to touch unduly on the thorny question as to how far or how soon Home Rule is desirable in India, I may perhaps be permitted to record how conscious I was of a certain weakness in my own position. I was continually urging our Government to press on China the need for Home

Rule in Tibet, while I was aware that they could not point to Home Rule in India. The Chinese Government had not failed to make use of the discrepancy between the two positions. The cases indeed are not precisely parallel, for the Tibetans are more closely related to their neighbours the Chinese than are Indians to British. They stand more nearly in the relationship which Canadians, Australians, or South Africans stand towards ourselves.

But, whatever might be the requirements of India, my residence on the north-eastern frontier had impressed on me strongly the desirability of Home Rule in our States of Bhutan and Sikkim, as well as in Tibet itself. For, firstly, the people themselves preferred it. Secondly, our recognition of the autonomy of Bhutan in 1910 and our restoration of the autonomy of Sikkim in 1918 had done much for our good name, and thereby increased our influence on the long Tibetan frontier and far beyond. In Tibet and Sikkim alien Government had been the exception, not the rule ; Bhutan had always been self-governing.

It was indeed remarkable on the north-eastern frontier how the need produced the man. Tibet, Nepal, and Bhutan had long been accustomed to govern themselves. Outside Powers had on the whole left them alone. Their form of government was autocratic, tempered in the case of Tibet and Bhutan by many democratic traditions and tendencies among their peoples. In the result one found three rulers of outstanding ability, the Dalai Lama of Tibet, the Prime Minister of Nepal, and the Maharaja[1] of Bhutan. And the leaders of the people possessed an innate political consciousness. Isolated in their mountain homes, without roads or other modern means of communication, their knowledge of the world outside was necessarily small. But, as must be, outside events impinged upon them, and their political insight and balance enabled them to learn from these new experiences.

During the summer the Chinese charged the Tibetans with

[1] The title by which the Indian Government recognize His Highness. He and his people use the title *Gye-po*, *Desi*, &c., signifying the head of the civil, as contrasted with the ecclesiastical, power.

having sent troops across the provisional frontier arranged under Mr. Teichman's armistice. Inquiry proved that the charge was unfounded. What had happened was that some Tibetan troops had in their own territory pursued a large party of robbers who, after ravaging districts in Chinese Tibet, which the Chinese administration failed to protect, had turned their attention to a district under the Tibetan Government. A leading member in the Tibetan Government expressed the opinion that the Chinese allegation was due to fear. Their defeat by Tibetan troops a few years earlier had seriously impressed them. As a matter of fact, the Tibetan Government, far from planning an invasion, had actually reduced the number of their troops on the Sino-Tibetan frontier.

The monks of Chatreng, an unruly Tibetan monastery in Chinese Tibet, which by past uprisings had captured a number of Chinese rifles and ammunition, rose once again, captured towns and villages, and advanced on Tachienlu itself, the seat of the Chinese administration. A letter from the Dalai Lama reached them, telling them to go home again. And home they went accordingly.

The state of Chinese nerves and their capacity for making unfounded charges may be gauged by their complaint made at this time, and repeated, to the effect that the Indian Government was moving several thousand troops through Bhutan and Sikkim to overawe the Tibetans. There was of course not a grain of truth in this fantastic assertion.

But, though they proclaimed the need for maintaining peace in these border lands, and charged the Tibetans with breaking the peace, they themselves broke it by launching a large military expedition against the Golok territory in north-eastern Tibet. As this territory lay in that portion of Tibet which had been reserved for Chinese penetration, there was perhaps insufficient reason for diplomatic interference. But the action of China was unlikely to conduce to a permanent and satisfactory peace between that country and Tibet.

Our postal service with India—which was under the

Indian Government as far as Gyantse, and from Gyantse to Lhasa under Tibetan management—was remarkably efficient Letters and newspapers took eight to eleven days only from Calcutta to Lhasa.

From the newspapers we learned in due course that the Conference at Washington was to take place in November. Questions relating to the Pacific were to come under discussion, and of these, Chinese affairs would form an important part. There seemed to me a danger that the Chinese Representatives might bring up the Tibetan question, though no Tibetan Representative had been invited to attend and therefore Tibet's case could not be fully represented. On consulting the Tibetan Government, I found that they too were of the same opinion. They added,

(a) That, even if now invited, there would not be sufficient time to instruct and send a Representative, for the journey from Lhasa to Washington would take him some three months.

(b) References would have to be made from time to time, and America was much too far away for these. They desired negotiations either in Lhasa or India.

(c) They were unwilling to enter on negotiations, unless I were present at them.

I passed on these views to our Government as usual. As far as I am aware, Tibet did not figure among the Chinese questions discussed at this Conference.

Our postal service with India

Crossing the Jelep Pass

XXI

CONCLUSION OF MISSION

THE spring of 1921 was exceptionally dry. For eight months there was no rain and there were only two falls of snow, one in November, the other in March, and each so light as to have but little effect on the parched soil. The young crops were on the point of withering. As was to be expected, the blame fell on the foreigner. ' This is the result ', exclaimed an influential priest, more outspoken than his fellows, ' of miscellaneous kinds of people coming to Lhasa.'

Fortunately the monsoon, though it began late, was a full one. Its late ending kept off the frost, the chief enemy of Tibetan crops. Accordingly these were above the average. ' Had they been bad,' as a Tibetan friend remarked to me, ' everybody would have said, " The Sahibs have come to Tibet, and so the crops have failed." The crops being good, many pay no attention to the matter ; while those who do, say, " The Sahibs came to Lhasa, but no harm has resulted." This is how our people speak.'

The time for my departure was now drawing near. Although the Tibetans would have been willing for the Mission to remain another year, and many would have welcomed it, this would have been undesirable on various grounds, and was indeed unnecessary. For the British Government had accepted my recommendations as to our future policy, and the Tibetan question was therefore, as far as possible, settled. It was an especial pleasure to the Mission to receive the Viceroy's approbation, as well as that of the Secretary of State for India, before we left Lhasa.

Apart from this settlement, my Mission had been able to smooth away misunderstandings and to re-establish confidence between the British and Tibetan Governments. Of this increased confidence there were many signs, too numerous to mention. The case of a monk, convicted of counterfeiting the currency notes, newly introduced into the country, was sent to me for my decision as to the length of imprisonment to be imposed, and my opinion on the point was accepted without further question.

A few weeks before my departure the Dalai Lama, the Prime Minister, the Grand Council, and the National Assembly each wrote a letter to the Viceroy, asking that I might remain in Lhasa until they received a reply from the British Government to their representations; and that, when negotiations with China were resumed, I might be the British Representative. A deputation from the National Assembly called on me to urge the same requests. On this deputation were Representatives of the three principal monasteries, including the one which had recently been in rebellion.

At the great New Year Reception, held by the Dalai Lama on the second day of the first month of each year, the chief Reception of the year, we were given the place of honour. As far as I am aware, we were the first white men to attend this ceremony. At the State departure from this Reception, His Holiness the Dalai Lama twice stopped the procession by turning round and smiling at me, an event noticed and commented on by the whole gathering. On reaching his Palace, he sent me a letter of thanks for observing Tibetan customs both at the Reception and elsewhere.

I might indeed naturally suppose that when I visited a country where I was received with such friendliness, the least I could do was to observe carefully the etiquette and the courtesies to which my hosts attached importance. But the Tibetans felt that when the representative of a great Power observed these matters, the agents and subjects of smaller States would find it difficult to reject them. They hoped also that the precedent established would be followed by others who came afterwards.

During August the Dalai Lama gave his annual theatrical entertainment, lasting for five days. Here we were given the place of the Grand Lama of Sa-kya, who ranks higher than the Prime Minister, the Dalai and Tashi Lamas alone taking precedence of him. The performance was not allowed to

'A monk, convicted of counterfeiting the currency-notes' (p. 203)

A currency-note

Police Court below Potala.

The three magistrates, in red overcoats and yellow Tam O'Shanter caps,
with their clerks.   Court records fastened to walls and pillars

Court-room with prayer-wheel (right centre), chests, and records
fastened to the walls

commence until I arrived. To these performances the Chinese Amban receives no invitation.

At the invitation of the Tibetan Government we visited many places and attended many interesting ceremonies hitherto jealously guarded from European eyes. But it would be tedious and egotistical to multiply instances of the courtesies extended to us.

One result of the confidence which we had gained was that all classes told us freely their hopes and fears on political and other subjects. And in this the priests also, usually so suspicious of the foreigner with his alien religion, were not a whit behind their lay brethren.

Buddhists, like Hindus, believe in transmigration. Not once or twice, but frequently and from all classes, I heard that I was generally believed to have been in my last life on earth a Tibetan, a high lama who prayed on his death-bed that he might be reborn in a powerful country so as to be able to help Tibet. Thus they explained why I had been engaged for so long and so profitably on Tibetan affairs ; why, though of delicate constitution, I had been able to come to Lhasa in winter without injury to my health, and had stayed in Lhasa longer than any Englishman had done before. A former Ganden Ti Rim-po-che—the highest of those lamas who are not incarnations of Buddha— prayed a similar prayer on his death-bed a few years ago. As regards myself, I heard the idea even from the Nepalese.

My prayer having been granted, this, according to the Buddhist creed, became for me a destined work,[1] left over from my last life, and therefore bound to be carried through in this one.

The requests which the Tibetan Government had made to our own were indeed modest ; such as one friendly neighbour had every right to expect from another. Yet the granting of these requests gave great pleasure, for it removed an anxiety that had gnawed at Tibetan minds for many years. The Prime Minister, an old man, in his farewell call on me, showed the pleasure that he felt. ' Now ', said he, ' I can die happy ; it matters not whether I live or die. But if you had

[1] *Le* (ལས་) in Tibetan.

returned to India some months ago with Tibet in a dangerous and almost hopeless condition, I should have died in misery.'

My farewell visit to the Dalai Lama was a sad event for both of us. The last words that His Holiness addressed to me were, ' My great hope is that you will return to Lhasa as the British Representative, to complete the treaty between Britain, China, and Tibet. We have known each other for a long time, and I have complete confidence in you, for we two are men of like mind.[1] I pray continually that you may return to Lhasa.'

Having to choose the exact day of departure, I selected a Wednesday, for, out of the seven days in each week, Wednesday is the Dalai Lama's ' life-day '.[2] Each individual has a life-day, fixed according to the year in which he or she was born. For instance, all persons born during the ' Iron-Bird ' year have the same life-day. This and the ' soul-day '[3] are the two lucky days of the week for such persons. It is best to start on a journey or to commence any new enterprise on one or other of these. The life-day of the Dalai Lama is of universal application. Its selection caused pleasure and was expected to insure us against illness and accident.

The receptions, guards of honour, &c., on our departure, were similar to those on our arrival, with a few added compliments. But there was one addition, which was somewhat remarkable, in view of the seclusion which enfolds the sacred person of the Dalai Lama. As we passed down the public road, His Holiness came and stood on the roof of a house near by, in view of ourselves and of the people that thronged the wayside. And thus we each gave to the other our last farewell.

The labouring classes of Lhasa, men and women, are fond of composing topical songs about their own officials, high and low. These, which are usually of an uncomplimentary character, they sing in the streets in loud voices, especially when going to and returning from work. No check is put upon them ; it is one of the ways in which public opinion finds expression. Such a song was composed about me after I left Lhasa ; but, fortunately, I am able to record that it was couched in complimentary terms. It was somewhat on

---

[1] In Tibetan, ང་གཉིས་མི་སེམས་གཅིག་པ་རེད །

[2] In Tibetan, སྲོག་གཟའ་

[3] In Tibetan, བླ་གཟའ་

On the way home. Twelve miles from Lhasa

the lines of a nickname which the Tibetans had given me several months earlier.

Our return journey to India was not without interest, but there is nothing of political import to record. We stopped a night on the way with the elder brother of the Maharaja of Sikkim, who would now be the Ruler of that State but for a political disagreement some thirty years ago. He has adopted the peaceful life of a Tibetan squire and seems to bear no envy towards his younger brother immersed in the cares of government. As a painter and as a musician his skill is beyond the ordinary. To his neighbours he is known as Gyal-se Kusho, ' The King's son '.

We had thirty-four degrees of frost when crossing the Himalaya in November, and a fairly strong wind in our faces; but the taking of a few precautions insured our travelling in reasonable comfort.

Three or four weeks in Delhi enabled me, in consultation with the Indian Foreign Department, to work out the details of the new settlement with Tibet, and to apprise the Tibetan Government of these details. My Mission was now ended. As far as I am aware, I was the first white man to visit Lhasa by the invitation of the people themselves. And Colonel Kennedy and I had been in the Tibetan capital longer than any white man had been there for one hundred and seventy years.

Out of the Government's allotment for the Mission expenditure, apart from salaries and travelling allowances, I found it possible to return about 40 per cent. A good deal can be done in Tibet with a comparatively small expenditure ; for it is not money that Tibet looks for, but the opportunities to help herself.

I left for England in December, and arrived in London on New Year's Day 1922. Two months after my arrival, I received, through the courtesy of the Government, a copy of a letter from the Dalai Lama to the Viceroy. In it His Holiness emphasized the cordial relationship between Britain and Tibet and the strengthening of this by my recent visit to Lhasa. He concluded, ' Thus all the people of Tibet and myself have become of one mind, and the British and Tibetans have become one family.'

XXII

CHINA IN TIBET

THE Chinese connexion with Tibet goes back into the mists of antiquity. Both nations belong to the same main branch of the human race. The religious tie through Mongolia, and in a lesser degree through Manchuria, has long been a powerful one. Even in far-distant Peking we find Tibetan settlements and a Lamaïst temple. The two languages, different though they are, have certain principles in common. This connexion between Tibet and China, sometimes stronger, sometimes weaker, but appearing always in the history of past centuries, is based on contiguity and natural affinities, and is likely, in some measure at any rate, to remain.

In the old days Tibet and China waged war with each other on fairly equal terms. Once at least China seized the Tibetan capital ; once at least Tibet captured the capital of China. During the seventh and eighth centuries of the Christian era, neither China nor India escaped invasion by the Tibetans, though their lack of organization and culture, combined with their inability to live in hot climates, prevented the latter from holding their gains.

But, when the softening influence of Buddhism extended its hold over the country, the power of the Tibetans in war gradually declined. From Nepal, Kashmir, and India came priests preaching the new religion ; from China also priests and the main arts of civilization. Internal dissensions, always ready to break out in this country of loosely-knit tribes, were encouraged by the struggles of the new religion with the old, and left Tibet an easy prey to the incursions of their Mongolian cousins. Meanwhile, Chinese civilization and influence spread little by little. Silks and brocades, some articles of food, ornaments of porcelain, lacquer, and jade, and Chinese manners and customs were largely adopted in Tibet, especially by the aristocracy and other wealthy classes.

Thus it was that, in the eighteenth century, the early Manchu Emperors, then at the zenith of their military power, were able to establish for China a considerable measure of control over Tibet. The former's large population and resources, her defeat of the Gurkhas, albeit with the assistance of Tibetan troops, her superior civilization, more effective armaments, and astute diplomacy, contributed to this end. Chinese troops were posted at Lhasa, Shigatse and Cham-do, in eastern Tibet. Magistrates supported by military police were also stationed at these places and at Lha-ru-go in eastern Tibet, all under the superintendence of two Ambans, who resided at Lhasa. The influence exercised by the Government of China in Tibet was not, however, as complete as that which Chinese governmental regulations and Chinese writers claim. Of this there is abundant evidence.

The wish of China to control Tibet was mainly due to the desirability of gaining the influential aid of the Dalai Lama, the head of the Lamaïst Church, in promoting Chinese policy both in Tibet and throughout Mongolia and Manchuria. These latter dependencies, especially Mongolia, lived under the religious influence of the Dalai. And the possession of the kindred land of Tibet rounded off the Chinese dominions in a natural and homogeneous manner.

During a conversation in Lhasa with the Lord Chamberlain—the head of the ecclesiastical officials, who hold half of the Government posts throughout the country and exercise also the influence due to their priestly status—the relations between China and Tibet came under discussion. The Lord Chamberlain remarked, ' China wants to keep Tibet not only for the sake of retaining Tibetan territory, but also because the Chinese know that, if Tibet breaks away, Mongolia will follow, by reason of the religious connexion between the two countries.' And in Tibet, even more than in Mongolia, the Dalai Lama speaks with an inner authority which no Chinese potentate, however ample his resources, can hope to gain. In the heyday of Chinese power over Tibet, the monks of Cha-treng, for many decades under Chinese rule, seldom failed to seize any opportunity, however desperate, of rising against their masters. But, when these monks had defeated their old enemies and were marching victoriously against the chief town on the border, the residence of the Chinese High Commissioner for Tibetan affairs, at a word from the Dalai Lama they halted and returned to their homes.

When the military power of China waned under the feebler rule of the later Manchu Emperors, she had to rely more and more on diplomacy to maintain her position in Tibet. The Chinese have an exceptional aptitude for gauging the temper of those with whom they negotiate, and thus discovering how far they can bluff with safety. The Tibetans, especially in early times, were no match for them in this.

The Chinese civil and military officials helped to keep alive the prestige and influence of their country. The greater honesty of the Chinese magistracy contributed to this result. In 1905 Tibetans used to tell me that they preferred the Chinese to their own countrymen as magistrates, as they did not take bribes to the extent that the Tibetans did, when trying cases. They were indeed somewhat afraid to go to the Chinese, as these were frequently transferred, while the Tibetan officers, at any rate those of the lower grades, remained, and had thus the greater power which attaches to permanency. Still the Chinese magistrates enjoyed by comparison a high reputation.

Gradually, however, the power of China declined more and more. A favourite Chinese way of claiming authority over subordinates is by giving them seals of office, and this practice was followed by giving a new seal to each Dalai Lama. In the case of the last two, however, the Tibetan Government was strong enough to refuse this token of subordination. In the election of the present Dalai Lama some forty-five years ago, the Tibetan authorities definitely refused to place his name in the golden urn. And when he returned to Lhasa from Peking, it was the Tibetans who presented him with a golden seal. The last vestige of Chinese control over Tibet was at an end, and of political influence but little remained. After the Sikkim Expedition of 1888 China did indeed make her treaty with Great Britain, but could not enforce its observance by the State which she claimed as her vassal.

The war between China and Japan at the end of the nineteenth century showed Tibet her protecting Power in the inglorious rôle of the vanquished. The advance of the British Expedition to Lhasa in 1904 showed its impotence to protect Tibet against a foreign foe. And the Chinese advance to Lhasa between 1908 and 1910 showed China as an oppressor, and, worse still, as violating the holy religion. The gorgeous ceremonial and the high-handed methods of the Amban, which had served to impress the unsophisticated Tibetans of earlier times, now served not at all, except to arouse feelings of anger and ridicule.

I have quoted above [1] the Amban's appointment of Ramba as a Councillor and the manner in which the Dalai Lama rendered this appointment ineffective and even ridiculous. This example was typical of others.

Four miles beyond Nan-kar-tse, on the way to Lhasa, is a grove of willow trees, planted some seven years ago by the Dalai Lama's orders. It is carefully fenced and regularly watered. An earlier grove, planted by the order of one of the Ambans, had died because nobody would look after it.

The Chinese Mission was in Lhasa for four and a half months in 1920. During that period they were permitted only two interviews with the Dalai Lama ; and, before going into the presence of His Holiness, each member's person was unceremoniously searched to make sure that he was not secreting arms.

When I took my Mission to Lhasa in 1921, I frequently visited the Dalai Lama, who used to rise from his seat, grasp my hand cordially, and make me sit at the same table as himself. The contrast could not have been stronger.

That Chinese cast of mind, which the Tibetans stigmatized as lacking in religion, had always caused resentment in the Tibetan heart, and was further emphasized by recent events. The Dalai Lama informed a Sikkimese friend of mine that

[1] Page 139.

the British and Tibetans were both religious peoples, and could therefore live in amity together : the Chinese having no religion, the Tibetans could never be real friends with them.

Between 1906 and 1908, during the period of Chinese ascendancy in Tibet, the Amban tried to induce the Tibetan Government to dismiss the more ignorant monks and make soldiers of them. This Amban was more powerful and popular than most, for he endeavoured to strengthen Tibet against British aggression, which was at that time still feared by the Tibetans. He was, however, told that there would be unceasing opposition to this proposal from the monks themselves, for they had decided on a religious career in this religious country and would not abandon it easily. Moreover many of the monks, e. g. Mongolians and dwellers in the province of Gya-rong, were not subject to the Tibetan Government. This Amban further urged that some of the monastic revenues should be used for the upkeep of the army, arguing that the number of monks would be reduced by the conversion of monks into soldiers, and therefore the revenues of the monasteries could be appropriated by the Tibetan Government proportionately to that reduction. But the Government and people were scandalized at what appeared to them an irreligious innovation, and the project had to be abandoned.

This same Amban turned his attention to the prophet, or oracle, of the great monastery of Sam-ye, and expelled him on the charge of prophesying falsely. His action in the matter was resented, but, as China at this time was powerful in Tibet, his order was perforce obeyed. The oracle went to Bhutan, where the Maharaja of that country helped him, and was recalled to Tibet by the Dalai Lama, when the latter returned to his country from India in 1912.

There is an old Tibetan prophecy that the prosperity of China depends on the happiness of Tibet. Tibet is the ' root ' of China. If therefore Tibet is maltreated, China's prosperity will decrease. So the Tibetan Prime Minister and his colleagues informed me in June 1910, when the God-king of Tibet had been driven from his capital by the Chinese invasion. A year or so later the Revolution broke out in China, and the Emperor was in his turn removed, an occurrence which Tibet interpreted as the natural sequence of events.

The deposition of the Manchu Emperor still further weakened the tie between the two countries. For the Manchus are regarded in Tibet as followers of the Lamaïst religion and the Manchu Emperors as incarnations of the Buddha of Wisdom, while the Chinese are regarded as indifferent, if not actually hostile, to the religion of Tibet. The Tibetans maintain that their political connexion was with the Manchu Emperors. These having been removed, the political connexion was severed.

The increase of Tibetan power during recent years has been accompanied by a greater stability in the administration, while the Chinese level has been lowered. The result is that, as foreign travellers in eastern Tibet do not fail to note, the districts of Tibet ruled by the Dalai Lama's Government are not only governed better than those districts which are subject to the Chinese, but better also than the neighbouring districts in China itself. Brigandage is more effectively suppressed and the whole tenor of the administration is more orderly. In their officers too the Tibetans have now the advantage. As Mr. Teichman [1] has noticed,

' Tibetan officers from Lhasa and Shigatse, whom the Chinese profess to regard as savages, are nowadays more civilized and better acquainted with foreign things than their equals in rank among the Chinese military of western Szechuan. The reason for this state of affairs lies in the fact that it is much easier for the Tibetans of central Tibet to come and go between Lhasa and India than it is for a native of western Szechuan to visit Shanghai or Hankow.'

The Tibetan is the more virile of the two ; stronger physically and mentally, and endowed with greater force of character.

While the Tibetan officers have improved, the Chinese

[1] *Travels in Eastern Tibet*, p. 122.

have deteriorated. In eastern Tibet the Tibetan soldiers are imperfectly rationed on account of the great difficulties of transport. Inevitably therefore they loot the people to some extent. But even here the Tibetan peasantry prefer Tibetan to Chinese rule. The bias in favour of Chinese magistrates has disappeared. The common religion, the common race and language, and the memory of Chinese oppression have combined to ensure this result.

The Tibetans too are gradually coming to hear of the headway which Bolshevism has made in parts of China. To the people of Tibet, as to those of Mongolia, Bolshevism is abhorrent.

At the same time there is undoubtedly a pro-Chinese party in Tibet among the officials, the priests, and the people. This is due to the natural affinity and the long connexion between the two countries. The Chinese Government, in order to draw the powerful priesthood of Tibet to their side, gave subsidies to certain monasteries, and especially to ' The Three Seats', the collective title of Sera, Drepung, and Ganden near Lhasa, the most influential of all the monasteries in Tibet. These are naturally loth to lose their grants, and thus it happens that some of the priests, especially in Drepung, are still in favour of China. Again, the lamas and the monks cannot fail to realize that their former influence is being curtailed by the new army which the Dalai Lama and the Tibetan Government are fostering.

Among the peasantry too we hear from time to time of those who express a wish that the Chinese would return. A Tibetan friend of mine put the position as follows : ' The farmers in Tibet, when treated badly by their own magistrates, say that they do not like Tibetan officials and want the Chinese back. They usually talk in that way. But in their hearts they do not want the Chinese back, for they remember how they destroyed the country when they were here.'

The pro-Chinese element in Tibet should not be underestimated, but, if money can be found to pay for an increased army, the Dalai Lama and the Tibetan Government should be able to control the priests. And the gradual improvement in the Tibetan officers will probably remove the occasional discontent among the peasantry.

One of the Chinese Mission was reported to have urged the Tibetans to come to terms with China and to keep the British out. When the Tibetan Government refused negotiations, unless a British representative also were present at them, he was said to have argued that it was perhaps good to make friends with the British, if the Government of Tibet could be sure that the latter would stick to them ; but, if the British fell away, China would be certain to exact severe retribution from Tibet. The argument was used at a time when many Tibetans thought that the British had failed to act up to their previous undertakings. But the Tibetan Government, having at last made friends with us, preferred to trust us a little longer in spite of various disappointments and anxieties.

It may be argued that, whatever might be the opinion as to Chinese actions in Tibet, the country was undoubtedly under the suzerainty of China. But Asia does not think along European lines. The Tibetan Government maintain that the Dalai Lama is the spiritual guide and the Chinese Emperor his lay supporter. All who are well acquainted with the East know what this relationship involves. It is the duty of the layman to help his priest in all ways possible, but the priest does not on that account become the layman's servant. Whatever help China may have rendered to Tibet was rendered in that capacity and does not in any sense put Tibet under China. ' You will find no treaty ', they used to continue, ' by which Tibet recognizes that China is her overlord.'

When I pointed out to a representative Tibetan of the governing classes 'that the foreign relations of his country were for a long time conducted through the Amban, who had also exercised considerable power in the internal administration, he put the matter in this way : ' The Amban and his soldiers were first posted at Lhasa as a bodyguard to the Dalai Lama. The Chinese, being cleverer than us Tibetans, gave presents frequently to the Dalai Lama, to the leading monasteries, and to the most influential officials. The Amban gradually converted into a bodyguard for himself the soldiers who had been sent originally as a bodyguard for the Dalai Lama. In ways like these China gradually worked Tibet into a position resembling political subordination.'

In the Treaty of 1856 between Tibet and Nepal the Tibetan and Gurkha texts run side by side. Article II in the Tibetan text begins, ' Gurkha and Tibet have been regarding the Great Emperor with respect.' The corresponding Article in the Gurkha text states, ' Gurkha and Tibet have been regarding ——— with respect till the present time ; ' the words ' the Great Emperor ' being omitted.

If it should be argued—a doubtful point—that this constituted at the time a Tibetan admission of Chinese suzerainty, the reply of many Tibetans would be as follows :

' You Chinese at this time managed our foreign affairs under the former agreement, and thus were able to have this reference to China inserted in the treaty. Moreover Tibet owned all Sikkim down to Titaliya near Siliguri in India. You did not keep this territory for us against the British ; it would be of no use our telling the British now that this territory is under us. Again, you afforded us no help in the British military expedition of 1888, nor in their subsequent expedition against Lhasa in 1904. You have not kept your part of the bargain. We will not keep ours.'

For a long period it was the custom for both Tibet and Nepal to send periodical Missions, usually regarded as tribute Missions, to Peking. The Tibetan Mission was dispatched once in every three years, the Nepalese once in every five. But both have been discontinued during recent years. The Mission from Tibet was styled *Ten-che* in Tibetan, which means ' commodities ' in general and—according to the Tibetan authorities—' articles for presentation ' in particular. This Mission has not been sent for the last twelve or thirteen years. One of the Ambans who was in Lhasa when the Tibetan Mission was discontinued is said to have urged both the Tibetan Government and the Nepalese representatives in Lhasa to continue sending these Missions, but without success. It is clear that for the last twelve years at any rate the Dalai Lama's dominions have been *de facto* independent of China. Their independence was demonstrated in 1912, when the Tibetans fought and drove the Chinese troops from central Tibet, and again in 1918, when they ejected them from many of their eastern territories.

Such is the position of Tibet with regard to the Chinese claim to either sovereignty or suzerainty. There is no doubt that they desire to be free of Chinese control in their political affairs. They are a homogeneous people and, though they are akin to the Chinese, the relationship is no closer than that between Frenchmen and Italians.

China, however, will not willingly abandon her former position in Tibet. It remains therefore to consider how far the Tibetans have the power to support their claim to self-determination. In August 1913 the late Prime Minister gave me his opinion as follows : ' If we could raise the revenue necessary for equipping an army, obtain good rifles, and improve the facilities at Lhasa for the manufacture of cartridges, Tibet could keep 20,000 Chinese troops at bay. Tra-ya and Cham-do could each put 7,000 men into the field and Mang-kam 5,000, all good fighters. Der-ge could muster 10,000 to 15,000, but of somewhat inferior quality. Even if the Chinese retain Ba-tang, Li-tang, and adjoining districts under their rule, the people, being Tibetan in race, religion, and language, will always seize any opportunity for throwing off the yoke.' And it is a fact that these districts rose against their Chinese masters when the outbreak of the revolution threw the latter into confusion, and at other times also on the smallest of opportunities.

The campaigns of 1917 and 1918 showed that with modern rifles Tibetan troops were more than a match for troops from southern China. The northern Chinaman is no doubt physically finer and a better soldier than his compatriot from the south. But, with a further improvement in the equipment and training of the Tibetan army and some increase in size, it may well be that they will be able to resist invasion by

Chinese northern troops. Their mountains and valleys and their cold, desolate plains are an important item on the Tibetan side of the account. And as regards physical strength and hardihood, there are few, if any, finer races in the world than some of the tribes in eastern Tibet.

Though bent on freedom from Chinese control, the Tibetans do not, it would appear, desire a complete severance of their long-standing political connexion with China. When I was in Lhasa, the Tibetan Government sent to Peking three priest-officials,[1] all young men. The two senior ones were to teach the Tibetan language to Chinese schoolboys ; he of lowest rank was destined to act as an interpreter in Peking. These three replaced predecessors who had died within recent years. They were all of good birth and had been given the rank of priest-official to enable them to take up this work. Having received the Dalai Lama's blessing, they started on their long journey. They would remain many years, possibly their whole lives, in Peking. The Chinese Government pay salaries sufficient to support the officials themselves ; the Tibetan Government maintain their families. It is only a slight bond ; but no doubt there are others.

The name of the Chinese Emperor is still held in respect by some sections of the community, including the larger monasteries which were subsidized by the Government of China. Over the main entrances of many monasteries, as well as over some of those in the mansions of the nobility, are to be found name-tablets, the gift of some former Chinese Emperor. The name-tablet over the portal of the Kün-de-ling monastery, whose large grounds on the outskirts of Lhasa accommodated my Mission, contains the name of the monastery in large gold letters, in Chinese, Tibetan, and two other languages. The tablet is enclosed in a wooden frame beautifully carved. It is noteworthy that, in spite of the hostility entertained towards China in so many quarters, these name-tablets given by former Emperors of China are everywhere preserved and respected.

The walls of rooms in Tibetan houses, and especially those

[1] *Tse-trung* in Tibetan.

'Over the main entrances of many monasteries . . .
are to be found name-tablets, the gift of some
former Chinese Emperor'

in the country villas of the aristocracy, are often covered
with Chinese frescoes and other Chinese paintings. They are
not, as are those by Tibetan artists, of a religious nature.
Favourite subjects are animals and birds, gardens and
summer-houses, and especially old men and large trees with
perhaps rocks and streams as emblems of long life and dura-
bility. One Chinese painting of exceptional beauty is to be
found in the country villa of the Kung of Pün-kang, a few
miles from Lhasa, painted on the inside of the glass, over
wooden panels. But perhaps the most beautiful specimens
of all are to be found in the inner, and forbidden, grounds of
the Jewel Park.

Food, dress, utensils, and ornaments are all imported from
China in large quantities. In many of the great monastic
dances the actors wear robes of wonderful brocade, almost
beyond value. Different sets are used for different dances,
so that every monastery of any size has a large store of silk
dresses, all of which come from China. A considerable
portion of the wealth of Tibet is spent on dress.

But the chief import from China is tea, all of which, except
an insignificant fraction, comes from China, for Tibetans do
not like Indian tea.

The chief exports from Tibet to China are wool, hides,
musk, medicinal herbs, &c. The medicinal herbs of Tibet are
famous in China and India, as well as in other countries.

This trade connexion with China is the only strong connexion that Tibet as a whole desires. Both countries realize
its value. Many a time have Tibetans said to me, ' We want
no Chinese officials ; the only man we want from that side
is the Chinese trader.'

XXIII

JAPAN AND RUSSIA

THE war between Japan and China, and that between
Japan and Russia, kindled Tibetan interest in the growth of
the Island Power, whose relationship with themselves, both
in race and religion, afforded them natural gratification.

Before these victories, Japan was no more than a name
to the Tibetans. But during the last two decades some
half dozen Japanese have penetrated into the country and
resided at Lhasa. One of these, Mr. Ekai Kawaguchi, has
recorded a highly interesting account of his adventures—
for he travelled in secret and under a disguise—and his
impressions of Tibetan life.[1] Subsequent Japanese travellers
have lived openly in Lhasa ; one of them was employed by
the Tibetan Government in the training of troops. During
my year in Lhasa there was one Japanese in the Se-ra
Monastery. He was studying hard and was comparing the
Buddhist scriptures of Tibet with the Buddhist scriptures of
Japan. He had been there eight years. His eyesight had
suffered, probably from the prolonged study of the Tibetan
script in the darkened rooms of the monastery ; and in this
matter Colonel Kennedy was able to be of service to him.

It is not only from the few Japanese in their own country
that the Tibetans have learnt about Japan. When they
travel in China, they see how Japanese influence has grown
there steadily. In Mongolia the people of Tibet are still
more at home, and here they find Japanese power and
prestige strongly established. They find that power used
for an end which they regard as essentially right, the
endeavour to stem the Bolshevist irruptions from the north.

Tibetans have thus come to understand and admire the
power of Japan. Feeling that the latter is not on good terms
with China, they are all the more drawn towards her. When

[1] *Three Years in Tibet*, by Ekai Kawaguchi (Theosophical Society,
Adyar, Madras).

it seemed beyond their power to persuade the British Government to permit the import of arms through India, the
authorities at Lhasa turned their eyes to Mongolia, which
was flooded with Japanese arms and ammunition of a cheap
and serviceable kind.   A machine-gun, a few rifles, and some
bombs were imported across the plains of northern Tibet.
They arrived while I was in Lhasa and were found to be
satisfactory.   It was proposed then to import ten to fifteen
thousand such rifles, the idea being to economize in the cost
of carriage by bringing the barrels only and by making up the
stocks from walnut wood in Tibet.   It was reckoned that
each camel would carry from twenty to thirty barrels, and
that its hire would be from seventy to one hundred rupees.
If the import through India had continued to be barred, there
is no doubt that the Japanese munitions would have been
obtained.   And training by Japanese instructors might well
have followed.

A few Tibetans have visited Japan.   Prominent among
these are the Commander-in-Chief, whose energy and
capacity have brought him into conflict with powerful
interests, and an ecclesiastical official whose high intelligence
has gained for him a considerable measure of influence
among his countrymen.   The latter, while professing entire
loyalty to the Dalai Lama, deplored the rigid conservatism of
Tibet.   Pointing to Colonel Kennedy's dog, a Lhasa terrier,
he remarked, ' I too have a strap round my neck.'   Among
all who travel far afield the same result is to be noticed, and
is indeed inevitable.   It may be hoped, however, that such
changes as must come may develop gradually and on such
lines as to enable the Tibetan Government and people to
assimilate them and profit by them.   It is the duty of Tibet's
neighbours and of those who are in her confidence to help, as
far as may be, towards this end.

Articles on Tibet appear from time to time in the Japanese
newspapers.   One of these, written towards the end of our
stay in Lhasa, commented—regretfully, as it seemed—on
the increase of British prestige in Tibet.   And from various
other indications it is abundantly clear that the Japanese,

both officials and non-officials, take a great and increasing interest in Tibetan affairs.

Until the outbreak of the Great War Tibet looked on Russia as the strongest Power in the world. Her enormous Empire, concentrated in eastern Europe and Asia, and ever pressing forward like the rising tide of a mighty sea, as well as her large army, was bound to impress the Tibetans more forcibly than the more distant possessions and smaller armies of other Powers. Britain was regarded as second in strength, and, since India was nearest to Lhasa and Russia was still far away, as the Power most favourably situated for helping against China. But a watchful eye was kept on Russia. For it was felt that, if Russia occupied Mongolia, Tibet's natural ally, and came nearer to Tibet itself, while the British Government maintained its attitude of aloofness, it would then be well to seek Russian protection against the Chinese adversary. The Tibetan Government wished, and still wish, to keep out of the hands of China, if this is in any way possible. Dorjieff did much to foster the belief not only in Russia's strength but also in her wish to aid Tibet.

After the British Expedition of 1904 the Dalai Lama fled to Mongolia. Russian assistance was hoped for, but it was not forthcoming. This was the first set-back to Dorjieff's influence with the Dalai Lama and to the Tibetan belief in Russia's desire to help. Their belief in her power remained.

But the world war has modified this. They see Russia now divided against herself, and her great strength lessened. They doubt whether she will re-unite, at any rate for many years to come. As a protector for Tibet, she is therefore out of consideration. And these events have robbed Dorjieff also of his influence with the Dalai Lama and the Tibetan Government.

Russia's chief connexion with Tibet has been through her Buriat subjects. These are Mongolians whose territories have been annexed to the Trans-Baikal and Irkutsk Governments in Siberia.

Together with other Mongolians, many Buriats live in Lhasa for years together, studying in the large monasteries, for the Dalai Lama is their spiritual head, as he is of all Mongols. Others join the caravan from Mongolia which visits Lhasa twice yearly.

A Buriat priest came to Lhasa when I was there, from the vicinity of Chita, having been a year on the journey. Some information which he gave me is perhaps worth recording. He assured me that the Buriats, while the Tsar lived and ruled, valued their position in the Russian Empire : now the majority would prefer to be re-united to Mongolia with the Grand Lama of Urga, Je-tsün Tam-pa, as their Ruler. Many educated Buriats were looking admiringly towards Japan ; but the mass of the peasantry found the Japanese administration too strict for their taste.

My Buriat friend had come to Lhasa to repay money borrowed by his lama from monasteries at Lhasa. He wished to return via India, but not until the affairs of his native land were in a more settled condition.

Among some Tibetans, the Buriats have the reputation of being adept miners. If profitable mines should be discovered in Tibet, it is possible that they might find employment in them.

Another bond between Russia and Tibet is to be found in the trade. Silk from Russia is highly valued. It is seldom that any silk comes from Russia other than that of first-rate quality.

To Tibet at present Britain is the most powerful of all the nations. For many years America has been looked on as the wealthiest nation, but as one which takes great enjoyment in comfort and luxury, and is therefore less powerful for war. The strength of France and of Japan are also realized.

XXIV

MONGOLIA

To the east and south of Tibet certain countries and districts of the Tibetan race have fallen within the orbit of China and Britain respectively. Ladakh, Sikkim, and Bhutan are examples of these on the British side, while large areas in eastern Tibet have been annexed to the Chinese provinces of Kansu, Szechuan, and Yunnan.

To the north-east of Tibet lies Mongolia, a country of vast extent. Tibetans state that the two countries are coterminous, but the maps usually show them as divided by a strip of the Chinese province of Kansu. It is asserted that the people inhabiting this strip are mainly Tibetan or Mongol. But the Chinese treat it as part of Kansu, wishing perhaps to maintain direct access to the province of Chinese Turkestan.

In Mongolia, as in Tibet, disruptive influences have been at work. Her wide but sparsely inhabited plains have for long been subjected to encroachment from the over-flowing population of northern China, creeping in from the south. And on the further side Russia, advancing across the whole length of Asia, annexed a large portion of her northern territory, the lands of the Buriat tribe, which are now controlled by the Siberian governments of Irkutsk and Chita.

The encroachment on Mongolia by the Chinese peasantry was, and is, a continuous process. The advance of the Russians was, however, stayed until recently. In 1903 the Russian Foreign Minister had informed the British Government that Russia had no designs upon Tibet, but could not remain indifferent to any serious disturbance of the *status quo* in that country. The British military expedition to Lhasa, with the resulting treaty, was pushed through in 1904. Eight years later the Russian warning materialized in the Russo-Mongol Treaty of 1912, subsequently reinforced by a tripartite agreement between Russia, China, and Mongolia.

The effect of these negotiations was to put northern Mongolia into Russian hands.

But the world war has, temporarily at any rate, lessened the power of Russia in these parts ; while China seems to be endeavouring to break through this treaty, and to regain the hold which a divided Russia can hardly grasp. The Mongols are at one with the Tibetans, both in their dislike of Bolshevist ideas and in their distrust of the overlordship of China under present conditions. When in Lhasa, I was informed that the Mongols have a natural liking for the Manchus and might be willing to be under China if a Manchu Emperor were on the throne. I repeat the statement for what it may be worth. Speaking for Tibet, the Dalai Lama and his Ministers used often to tell me that a political connexion with China might have been possible with a Manchu Emperor on the throne. For it was felt that the Manchus are a Buddhist people, while the Chinese are not.

It was not until recent years that Japan began to exercise influence in Mongolia. The world war gave her the opportunity required. By the seven articles in the second group of her ' Twenty-One Demands ' she showed clearly her desire to gain control, political, military, and economic, over the south-eastern portion of that country. Through their opposition to the Bolshevist advance, the Japanese have earned the goodwill of the Mongol people. It may be doubted whether the latter as a whole desire any intimate political connexion with Japan. Yet this may become inevitable, if it be found that Japan, and Japan only, is able to protect them against the subversive doctrines of those who are ' without law and without custom '.

Political necessity may cause Mongolia to cling to this nation or to that, but her natural affinity is with Tibet. In race the two peoples are closely akin ; you can hardly tell one from the other until they speak. In religion they are one : both acknowledge the spiritual sovereignty of the Dalai Lama. The Grand Lama of Urga, the immediate Head of the Mongolian Church, has invariably been a Tibetan ; the present incumbent was born under the walls of the Potala.

The connexion between the two countries is maintained in various ways. One is by trade. The caravan from Mongolia assembles at Kün-bum, near the Koko Nor Lake. With it come men from Am-do and the Koko Nor, and even Buriats from distant Siberia. All march together, finding in their large number their protection against the brigands of the Go-lok country. At Nag-chu-ka, some ten days' march from Lhasa, the danger from robbers being now past, the large company breaks up ; and, the formal permission of the Dalai Lama having been obtained, proceeds in driblets to Lhasa. Twice yearly the caravan, merchants and pilgrims together, crosses the ' Northern Plains ' of Tibet, once in the floods of summer, and once when this desolate expanse, several hundreds of miles across, seventeen thousand feet above sea-level, and swept by hurricanes of wind, is in the grip of an Arctic winter. Camels, yaks, and ponies are used both for riding and for carrying loads.

During August 1921 Colonel Kennedy and I, making a journey from Lhasa to the north, met numerous parties of the summer caravan on their way to the Tibetan capital. Here a party of Mongols with ponies from Sining, in the Kansu province of China, for sale to those who are willing to pay the price for ponies of this superior quality. Here a Mongol greybeard come to revisit the Holy City once again before he dies. And a little farther on, a party of fifteen young peasants from Am-do, the home of Tsong-ka-pa, in north-eastern Tibet, seated in a circle on the bank of a stream to eat their frugal lunch. Barley meal, raw meat, and tea are all they need at this stage. They are on their way to join the great Sera monastery, where they hope to spend many years, benefiting both themselves and others by lives devoted to religion. Anon, a small child of six, strapped on a mule ; he has come a four months' journey in this way. But he is not the youngest member of the caravan. For at another stage I see two small specks of humanity, little more than babies, each strapped into its box of yak-hide. The yak to which these boxes are secured, one on each side, wanders here and there, grazing over the stony fields. Sunshine or

' And even Buriats (right) from distant Siberia '

storm, the little ones sit in their square cases, placid and happy, while the elders of the party prepare the evening meal. In this primitive manner they have come a four months' journey from their homes across the frozen wastes of the lofty Northern Plains. As they come and go across Tibet, the Mongols seem almost at home ; by no means strangers in a strange land.

Some of the parties were returning northwards by the summer caravan, after staying only one month in Lhasa. Others were to wait for the winter. But a good many intended to remain in Tibet till the summer of the following year. The summer caravan leaves Lhasa in September. The flood season is then over ; and the grazing on the Northern Plains is at its best.

The gifts which the Dalai Lama receives every year from his Mongol worshippers are both numerous and valuable. One such gift, a dozen fine Mongolian camels, used to graze up and down the river bank on the outskirts of our park in Lhasa.

During my first few months in Lhasa a Mongolian brigand, by systematically robbing merchants and pilgrims, had become a source of anxiety and loss to many. But it was found possible to influence him, for he too wished to come to Lhasa and to prostrate himself before the Head of the Faith.

It is not only through trade that Tibet and Mongolia know each other. Each caravan brings parties of Mongols, like that of the peasants from Am-do, thirsting to study in the great monasteries at and round Lhasa. Their willingness to come so far is a measure of their zeal for the religious life ; and, cut off as they are from family ties, they are able to follow it without distractions. Thus it comes that the Mongols share with the men from eastern and north-eastern Tibet the reputation of numbering among their ranks the keenest students and the most learned professors in Lhasa. At the Dalai Lama's New Year Reception, which I attended in February, two Doctors of Divinity held religious disputations between the various performances. Men of the highest powers are selected for these posts of honour ; it is significant that, in this case at any rate, both men were Mongolians.

The highest religious post in Tibet, outside the ranks of the great incarnate Bodhisatwas, such as the Dalai and Tashi Lamas, is the headship of the monastery of Gan-den, twenty-eight miles from Lhasa. The incumbent of this post holds office for seven years and is known as *Gan-den Ti-pa*, ' The Enthroned One of Gan-den ', and sometimes as *Gan-den Ti Rim-po-che*, ' The Precious Throne of Gan-den '. Mongolians, equally with Tibetans, are eligible for this high office, but they do not gain it very often, ' because ', as the Lord Chamberlain informed me, ' there is a Mongolian spirit (*lha*) which prevents them. One Mongolian did gain the post some time ago, but died almost immediately '. Tibetans from central Tibet do not often climb so high ; they freely admit the indolence generally prevailing among themselves. Eastern Tibetans often gain it ; the last two on the throne came from eastern Tibet.

It may well be imagined that the seven or eight hundred Mongolian monks who study and serve in the influential monasteries around Lhasa form a strong connexion between these two religious nations. When the Dalai Lama fled from the British expedition in 1904, it was to Mongolia that he naturally turned as his home in exile. On his return to Tibet five years later, he left an agent in Mongolia to look after the numerous gifts of property which his Mongol worshippers had showered upon him. With this agent the Tibetan Government maintain constant communication, and a slow but efficient news service is maintained also by the commercial agents of the leading Lhasa families, who come and go regularly between the two countries. It is through these agents also that Japanese and Russian rifles and am-munition—sometimes also machine-guns and bombs—are brought to the Tibetan capital.

During the Simla Conference in 1913–14, between British, Chinese, and Tibetan Plenipotentiaries, the atmosphere was clouded by a report that Tibet and Mongolia, through the agency of Dorjieff, had signed a treaty of alliance. Mongolia was at that time falling more and more under the power of

Russia, and the terms of the alleged treaty were such as seemed likely to establish an ever-increasing Russian influence in Tibet, an influence which could not fail to endanger British and Indian interests.

But such information as came to me rendered me sceptical as to whether any treaty was signed. I inquired of the Tibetan Prime Minister, who was his country's Plenipotentiary at this Conference, what were the facts. He referred to the Government at Lhasa, which replied to the following effect : ' The Dalai Lama never authorized Dorjieff to conclude any treaty with Mongolia. The letter given to Dorjieff was of a general nature, asking him merely to work for the benefit of the Buddhist religion.'

After giving me this reply the Prime Minister added, ' It is the custom of us Tibetans to write to everybody asking for help ; for instance, in the letters written to you yourself we frequently made requests similar to that which the Dalai Lama made to Dorjieff. Unfortunately, the draft of this letter cannot be traced now, and it is feared that it was destroyed when the Yuto house was burnt down (I saw the evidence of this fire in Lhasa in 1921), as the Yuto Chikyap Kempo was in charge of the records relating to the tour of the Dalai Lama in Mongolia and China.'

It was seldom that the Tibetan Government failed to show me the originals of letters and other documents. And in view of the devastation caused in Lhasa by the fighting with the Chinese, it may well be that this letter was one of the numerous records that were destroyed. As a proof of good faith the Tibetan Government forwarded to the Prime Minister, who passed them on to me, the original drafts of letters which they had written to the peoples of Tsaidam and Koko Nor and to the Chiefs and High Priests of Mongolia. These showed clearly the close relations subsisting between Tibet and Mongolia, treaty or no treaty.

Speaking some years later, a Tibetan nobleman in the confidence of his Government reviewed the matter as follows :

' I do not think that there is any treaty between Tibet and Mongolia. It is customary for the Dalai Lama to give

823140   Y

letters to persons, asking them to help the religion ; but
such letters would not be sufficient authority to warrant
their concluding a treaty on behalf of Tibet. If the Russians
said that there was such a treaty, they must either have
misunderstood the terms of the letter given by the Dalai
Lama to Dorjieff, or have wilfully misrepresented it.

' Tibet and Mongolia are closely related by race and are
of the same religion, so that either, if in trouble, would
receive perhaps a little help from the other. For instance,
when, during recent years, China was attacking Tibet, the
Mongolians are said to have made remonstrances in Peking.
But Lhasa is so far from Mongolia, that neither can Mongolia
help Tibet much, nor Tibet help Mongolia.'

It is true that the Mongols have invaded Tibet from time to
time during past centuries. But these contests were of the
same kind as frequently occurred between the tribes of
Tibet itself. When Gusri Khan invaded Tibet, his object
was to subdue the king of Tsang and to give to the young
Dalai Lama the sovereignty of Tibet. The later Dzungarian
invasion seems to have been directed mainly against the
Red Hats, the old, unreformed sect of Tibetan Buddhism.
The Yellow Hats appear to have profited by the invasion.
The Regent of Tibet, whose house near Ganden was pointed
out to me, is said by Tibetans who are acquainted with their
country's history to have lived on terms of amity with the
invaders. China indeed, then as always, was quick to
recognize that the Power which controls Lhasa will exercise
a compelling influence in Mongolia also. For the Mongols
are no less religious than the Tibetans, and the Dalai Lama is
the Head of their religion.

A traveller in Mongolia, during recent years, has testified
that, on account of the British connexion with Tibet,
Mongols have a high opinion of the British, although so far
they have themselves scarcely come into contact with the
latter. We have seen that a Japanese newspaper has
admitted that the prestige of the British name stands high in
Tibet. On the whole therefore it is perhaps not too much to
claim that both British policy and the way in which it has
been carried out have found justification in the land of the
Lamas.

XXV

NEPAL

NEPAL lies for five hundred miles along the Himalaya, to the north of Bihar and of the United Provinces of Agra and Oudh in the plains of India. Its area is fifty thousand square miles ; its population is estimated at four or five millions. It is inhabited by a number of tribes, nearly all of which are racially connected with the Tibetans, though hardly so closely as are the Mongols to the north. Each tribe speaks its own language or dialect in the home and in converse with fellow-tribesmen. The tribe to which the Gurkhas belong is of Indian, not Tibetan or Tartar, origin. Under their rule [1] their tribal language, Khaskura, which is of the same stock as Hindi, Bengali, &c., has become the *lingua franca* of Nepal, the means of communication between members of different tribes throughout the country. Except Khaskura, the other dialects of Nepal are related to Tibetan. It may be of interest to note that the Gurkha regiments of the Indian army, regiments whose valour and efficiency are household words throughout the British Empire and beyond, are recruited almost entirely from the tribes of Tartar stock.

The connexion between Tibet and Nepal, both socially and politically, is long and intimate. It was in large measure from Nepal that the early Tibetan kings received the Buddhist religion. For Nepal, though warmer than their own country, was habitable for Tibetans ; whereas the climate of the torrid plains of India exacted too heavy a toll of lives from the dwellers in the cold uplands, when these came down to study the new religion. Tibetan armies appear to have over-run the territory of Nepal from time to time, and, probably in concert with the Nepalese, to have invaded northern India. The victorious Tibetan king, Song-tsen Gam-po, took not only a Chinese, but also a Nepalese, princess as his wife.

[1] See page 41.

The Gurkha invasions of Tibet towards the close of the eighteenth century and their defeat by a Sino-Tibetan army have already been recorded.[1] I have also recorded how in 1855 hostilities broke out again, followed in 1856 by a treaty between Nepal and Tibet,[2] which is of importance to both countries, for on it is based the present position of the Nepalese in Tibet.

I was able to make a copy and translation of this treaty at first-hand, for, by the orders of His Holiness the Dalai Lama, the original itself was shown to me, together with the original of a subsidiary treaty that explained doubtful points in the main document. Two trustworthy and experienced members of my staff made copies of both the Tibetan and Gurkha texts, which lie side by side, in each treaty. Nepal received a payment of ten thousand rupees yearly, and her subjects gained the right of a trading factory at Lhasa exempt from all trade duties ; they gained also rights of extra-territoriality. In return Nepal undertook to come to the help of Tibet, if the latter were invaded. The Gurkha kingdom values highly the special position which it has gained, not only on account of national pride—for the Gurkhas are a high-spirited and patriotic people—but also from the influence that it gives the Nepal Government with its Buddhist subjects, and on account of the substantial trade advantages which the position confers.

Before the establishment of the Gurkha dynasty, Nepal was mainly under the rule of Buddhist kings of the Newar tribe, who are partly Buddhist, partly Hindu. Even now, when Hindu kings rule Nepal, a substantial minority of its inhabitants profess Tibetan Buddhism as their religion. The connexion between Tibet and Nepal, maintained by the large colony of Buddhist members of the Newar tribe—one of the Nepalese tribes—in Lhasa, is of advantage to the Nepalese Government in maintaining control over their Buddhist subjects in Nepal itself.

Again, the trade advantages are of especial importance to a country which finds itself in the position of Nepal. For it is

---

[1] Page 42.   [2] Appendix IV.

a small country with a full and rapidly increasing population, already approximating to that of the whole of Tibet, including the Tibetan territories under Chinese control, though Tibet with its cold, infertile expanses is sixteen times as large. Industrious and venturesome, the Nepalese have overflowed into Darjeeling and have even colonized in Assam, and in Manipur on the Assam-Burma border. The twenty thousand Nepalese who fill the Gurkha battalions in the Indian army are well known for their bravery and steadiness. The country is too small for its inhabitants ; they must find outlets both for emigration and for trade. As such an outlet Tibet is highly valued, and it follows accordingly that Nepal wishes to push her position in Tibet, or at any rate to maintain it.

There are some six or seven hundred Newars in Lhasa in addition to more than a thousand persons of mixed Nepalese and Tibetan parentage. Large numbers of this latter class are found also at Shigatse, Lha-tse, and Tse-tang, as well as in small scattered settlements in the province of Kong-po.

After the British military campaign on the Sikkim-Tibet border in 1888 a trade-route was constructed from Kalimpong, in the district of Darjeeling, through the south-eastern corner of Sikkim to the Tibetan frontier. Rough though it was, it was far better than any of the tracks across Nepal. Much of the traffic between Tibet and eastern Nepal was accordingly diverted along the new route ; and still more after the expedition of 1904, when the road was extended through the length of the Chumbi Valley to Phari and Gyantse. Nepal's trade with Tibet has thereby suffered great injury, a fact which we should appreciate all the more when we remember the large measure of assistance which she gave us in the latter expedition. In this the Nepalese Government furnished many thousands of highly efficient porters for carrying our supplies up the long line of communications. The 1904 expedition also opened up direct dealings between British and Tibetans, and this has reacted unfavourably on Nepal, which had at times played the part of an intermediary between the two, and had enjoyed the advantages with which such a position endowed her.

Nepal, in fact, on that occasion helped us towards a result which has worked to her own detriment. It need therefore cause no wonder that, when I took my Mission to Lhasa in 1920, the Nepalese there should have been uneasy and suspicious. A peaceful mission, not a military expedition, it made no appeal to the warlike valour of the Gurkhas, and they might well fear that some ill result would accrue from it as had actually accrued from the expedition which preceded it.

Those Newars who live in Tibet dress for the most part in Tibetan attire, especially during the winter, for their dwellings in Nepal are usually three to six thousand feet above sea-level, while their homes in Tibet are at an elevation of ten to thirteen thousand feet. They have adopted Tibetan pastimes, notably the national pastime of holding picnics. They worship in the Tibetan temples. Yet with them there is no feeling of brotherliness towards the Tibetans, as there is between the Tibetans and the Mongols from the far north. And indeed their relationship to the Tibetan is not the close relationship of the Mongol. They are neighbours but aliens. Thus has come into play that feeling of jealousy and dislike, which seems so often to divide neighbouring nations in Asia, and is no doubt one of the main reasons why the white man has played so prominent a part on the Asiatic stage.

The friction between the Tibetans and the Nepalese manifests itself both in domestic and in foreign affairs. As mentioned above,[1] there are strict laws against catching fish and killing the wild ducks and geese that frequent the river and the marshes surrounding Lhasa. But the Nepalese both shoot the birds and catch the fish. It is useless to prosecute the offenders, for under the treaty of 1856 they are tried by the Nepalese authorities, who refuse to convict in such cases. Some of the Nepalese are Hindus, and, as Hindus, they objected to the killing of cows. Let the Tibetan Government prohibit such slaughter; then they could consider the case

[1] Page 198.

of the other animals whose destruction was forbidden. A curious claim indeed for residents in a foreign country ! We of course neither shot nor fished, nor bought such birds or fish from the Nepalese.

Smoking is also forbidden in the streets of Lhasa, but I used to see Nepalese smoking there, even in the vicinity of the Temple. It is perhaps needless to add that, as soon as we heard of the rule, none of us in my Mission would have dreamt of smoking in the Lhasa streets.

When some mules were stolen from the Dalai Lama's stables, Nepalese, as I was informed, bought some of these mules at about ten ngü-sangs (equal to twenty-three shillings) each, this being from one-tenth to one-twentieth of their value. Far from being prosecuted for receiving stolen property, they even refused to restore the mules.

After learning of such illegalities and such unfair abuse of their extra-territorial status, it sounded somewhat incongruous to hear the Nepalese assert that the Tibetans had no sense of justice.

The mutual relations have also been embittered by personal discourtesy. When passing His Holiness in the street one day, a prominent member of the Nepalese community did not dismount from his pony, and thus, according to Oriental standards, was guilty of gross rudeness. Any discourtesy to the Dalai Lama is deeply resented by his subjects, who regard him as a god as well as a king.

Disputes between the Tibetan and Nepalese Governments are not uncommon, and sometimes reach an acute stage. A few months before we came to Lhasa, there was a shortage of yak-dung, the common fuel of the country. According to Tibetan accounts, Nepalese soldiers were utilized by Nepalese officials for collecting supplies of this by force from Tibetan villagers. The Tibetans naturally resented such action. The Nepalese found it increasingly difficult to obtain fuel. Their Government then, as the Tibetans assert, took up the matter and threatened a military expedition unless arrangements were made to enable their subjects in Lhasa to obtain a sufficient supply of this fuel.

A high Tibetan authority, discussing with me the diplomatic relations between the two countries, expressed himself as follows : ' For several years past frequent disputes have arisen between Nepal and Tibet, and many of these are still unsettled. Nepal adopts a high-handed line towards us. There have been cases in which Tibetans have killed Nepalese subjects. The Nepalese authorities demand that we shall put those Tibetans to death. So far we have not consented.'

I should mention here that capital punishment has been abolished in Tibet. Tibetans who murder their fellows are not executed, though some might say that the punishment which they receive is worse than death.

' There is also ', my informant continued, ' a frontier dispute at Nya-nam, in which the Nepalese claim Tibetan territory. The Nepalese Government threatened that they would send an army against us. In fear of this our representative there sealed an agreement making over the disputed territory to Nepal. But the Tibetan Government refused to ratify, and wrote to the Government of Nepal, suggesting that a British officer should be appointed to arbitrate. This was during last year' (i. e. between February 1919 and February 1920, for the Tibetan New Year commences in February). ' The Nepalese reply expressed deep chagrin at this suggestion, and proceeded to claim that Tibet and Nepal were on affectionate terms with each other, and could settle their dispute by themselves.'

Many Tibetans believe that Nepal wishes China to be strong in Tibet, in order to be able to play her off against Britain. Among those who held this belief was the late Prime Minister of Tibet, Lönchen Shatra, a man whose breadth of view and soundness of judgement in most cases are coming to be recognized more and more by his countrymen. He was confirmed in this view, as he informed me, by the attitude of the Nepalese in Lhasa, who, when Chao Erh Feng was advancing in Tibet, constantly advised the Tibetan Government to abstain from opposition. ' By this bad advice,' said the Prime Minister, ' Chinese troops were enabled to enter Lhasa.

'When the last Nepalese Mission visited Peking,' His Excellency continued, 'they were loaded with presents by the Chinese Government, and the Empress Dowager herself granted them a special interview. The Mission were delighted with the treatment that they received, and praised the Chinese Government highly on their return.'

Some of the Nepalese in Tibet do indeed wish for a certain measure of Chinese power in that country. Then if the Tibetan Government does not do what they wish, they can appeal to the Chinese Amban at Lhasa, and *vice versa*.

But the present Prime Minister of Nepal, a man of great ability, no doubt sees farther than this. It was under his administration some ten or eleven years ago—for then, as now, he was at the head of affairs—that the Government of Nepal discontinued their quinquennial Mission to Peking, which paid its last visit to the Chinese capital in 1908. And more particularly are the Nepalese Government afraid lest, if China increases her power in Tibet, she should curtail the privileges of the Nepalese in that country, as in effect she did during her brief ascendancy before the outbreak of the Chinese Revolution. The rights of extra-territoriality were being steadily curtailed and were well on the way to final abolition. The valuable concession of free trade would in time have followed suit.

From the above it will be evident that the relations of the Tibetan Government with that of Nepal are not friendly, for they feel that the latter has acted in an unjust and highhanded way towards them. Apart from the Gurkha invasions during the eighteenth and nineteenth centuries, which appear to have been dictated in the main by a consciousness of their own power and a desire for plunder, Tibet finds strong reason for complaint in the Nepalese attitude at the present day. Another Tibetan view which from time to time was put before me was as follows :

'We Tibetans realize that Nepal is too small for her population and that she might endeavour to seize Tibetan districts near the Nepal frontier on some pretext or other. But we do not think she will do so at present, as she has much to lose ; and we hope also that the British Government would prevent their ally from acting in that way.

'The Tibetan Government is not on good terms with Nepal. By the treaty [1] Nepal holds a very favourable position in Tibet at present. She has a trading colony with her own officers at Lhasa and elsewhere ; her subjects in our country are exempted from trade duties ; their magistrates adjudicate their quarrels and, when Tibetans are concerned, adjudicate jointly with Tibetan magistrates ; and we pay them ten thousand rupees a year. In return for these privileges the Nepalese undertook to come to our assistance whenever our territory was invaded, but this undertaking they have consistently ignored. They did not help us during the British military expedition to the Chumbi Valley in 1888, nor during that to Lhasa in 1904 ; they did not help us in our recent contests with China.

'We realized that it was difficult for them to fulfil their promise when the British came, for they appear to be in alliance with your people. But they were bound to help us against China. So far, however, from doing so, they stood aside, and then demanded from us compensation for the damage caused to Nepalese property in Tibet by the fighting between the Chinese and ourselves. And they threatened that they too would go to war with us if we did not pay. Being sore beset by China at the time, we had no option but to comply with their demands.

'Again, in boundary disputes and other lesser matters, such as the apprehension of thieves, they do not greatly bestir themselves to put matters right, when their own officers fail to act up to the treaty. But when our officers so fail, they make a terrible fuss. In this they are helped by the practice of our Government, which abstains from giving copies of treaties to its officers, in order that the latter may have to refer matters to the high officials at Lhasa, whose prestige and power are thereby enhanced. This practice often causes our officers to transgress treaties unwittingly, and renders them unable to remedy their mistake promptly.

'If Nepal should attack us at any time, she would not have matters all her own way. She has more soldiers and munitions than we have. But we should fight only in Tibet ; our country is difficult, the distances are great, and we too are learning a little how to fight. It is therefore doubtful whether Nepal would gain a lasting victory, even

[1] The treaty of 1856.

if the fighting were left to the two of us and neither Britain nor China intervened on our behalf.'

When in Lhasa I gave my Tibetan friends a theatrical entertainment lasting for three days. In one of the plays Shin-je Gyalpo, the Judge of the dead, holds his Court on the stage. Those who die are brought before him. With the sole exception of the heroine of the play, all, whether Chinese, Mongolians, Nepalese, or Tibetans, are condemned impartially to a sojourn in one of the various hells, the severest sentences being reserved for the Chinaman and the Mahomedan. To the Nepalese the Judge says, ' You have cheated many, charging exorbitantly for goods of small value.' This sentiment appears to reflect the opinion of Tibetans on many of the Nepalese traders in their country.

It is indeed a matter for regret that there should be such constant friction between the Nepalese and Tibetans. But— apart from other continents—Asia shows us everywhere instances of this bitterness between neighbouring nations. Japan and Korea, or China and Tibet, may be quoted among other cases. Perhaps one of the most conspicuous examples is that of China and the Lolos, whose small territories, which have been for many hundreds of years *enclaves* in the vast expanse of China, are still almost unknown, because the Chinese dare not even travel in them. As for the Gurkhas, having gained their present position in Tibet by forceful tactics, they perhaps hope to maintain and extend it by the same means.

While I am bound to represent the Tibetan aspect, in order to show a picture of things as they are in Tibet, I have no wish to prejudge the case between these two nations. No doubt the Nepalese Government have their own point of view on these and cognate subjects. In any case, we Britons are hardly entitled to sit in judgement on Nepal, for we too, whether under the protection of extra-territoriality or not, have not always gained the best of records when residing in the territories of others. And we, who have lived among the Nepalese in the district of Darjeeling or in Sikkim, cannot fail to recognize in them a brave, patriotic, practical, and law-abiding people ; in fact, one of the most steadfast and virile races in the world.

As mentioned above, the Nepalese were uneasy over my Mission to Lhasa. It is perhaps undesirable to quote full details in this connexion, but the signs were clear to all who could read them. The idea of a British official coming into personal and friendly contact with the Tibetan Government at Lhasa was naturally distasteful to them. I constantly visited the Dalai Lama and the Tibetan Ministers under conditions of privacy, which left no room for the Nepalese or for anybody else as an intermediary.

A prominent Tibetan more than once remarked to me, ' Your being here renders the Gurkhas less high-handed than they were. It is seen that you, the representative of a Great Power, observe our laws and customs, and thus it has become more difficult for the subjects of Nepal, a small State, to ignore them.' Other Tibetans echoed this view.

However, throughout the stay of my Mission in Lhasa, in in spite of difficulties, there was no friction of any kind between the Nepalese and ourselves. Our relations were friendly throughout. It is indeed important that the excellent relations which have been long maintained between the Governments of Britain and India on the one side, and that of Nepal on the other, should remain in the future also. For each is necessary to the other.

In an earlier chapter [1] mention has been made of the tribute Mission dispatched by the Gurkhas to Peking once in every five years. Wending its way overland across Tibet and China, it took many months to reach the Chinese capital, and many months again on its return journey. For several decades, however, Nepal has been virtually independent of China. The Mission was kept alive by the transport facilities and the trading opportunities which were accorded to it, no less than by the valuable presents which the Chinese Court showered on it in return for those that it offered. It is doubtful whether during latter years Nepal would have admitted that the Mission was one of tribute from a vassal to

[1] Chapter VI, page 42.

a suzerain. She could no doubt urge the cases of Burma and
of Hunza-Nagar, a small State to the north of Kashmir, both
of which sent periodical Missions to China after they had
admittedly come under British rule.

Nepal is nowadays a homogeneous State with a strong
army. She has the power of Britain and India behind her.
A vast land of mountains, occupied by a people themselves
hostile to Chinese domination, separates her from the land
of her former suzerain. Even after their victory in 1792, the
Chinese Government recognized that Nepal was too far away
to be held under Chinese rule. The inscription on the pillar
in Lhasa,[1] recording the victory, says :

' Even if all those territories had been obtained, as they
are more than a thousand distances from the frontiers of
Ü and Tsang, it would have been difficult to cultivate them
and to guard them. As for ordinary, simple people, even
if they obtain a thing, the end will not be gained.[2] Therefore orders were given, the respectful submission was noted,
and the army was withdrawn.'

If China could not then hold Nepal against the latter's will,
still less could she do so now. And in fact Nepal has cut the
Gordian knot ; for the last fifteen or sixteen years she has
discontinued the Mission, and thus openly renounced the
overlordship of China.

But Chinese power established in Tibet could do Nepal
great injury. Not only could it annul the highly-valued
privileges in Tibet, but it could foment disruptive influences
in Nepal itself.

The result to India would be no less disastrous. Nepal's
possession of the mountains overhanging five hundred miles
of the northern frontier, her growing influence in Darjeeling,
Sikkim, and Bhutan, the rapid increase of her virile population and the strength of her army—these are considerations
which closely concern the rulers of India. And, as India
takes upon herself the right of self-government which she

[1] For a translation of the entire inscription on this pillar see Appendix
III. As far as I am aware, this is the first time that the inscription has
been copied or translated.
[2] i.e. ' Even if Nepal be annexed to Tibet, the Tibetans will not be
able to hold it.'

claims, and takes upon herself also, as a natural corollary, the duty of self-defence, it will fall to responsible Indians to consider their attitude towards Nepal, Tibet, and China.

Meanwhile, it should be a cardinal object of British policy to work as far as possible for a good understanding between Tibet and Nepal. For the friendship of both is necessary to us and ours to them. Both depend on us to a greater or lesser degree for protection and for munitions of war. There is a large and valuable trade between Nepal and India ; to India this is valuable, to Nepal it is vital.

Nepal on the north and Afghanistan on the north-west are two nations with considerable military strength on the Indian frontier. But Nepal's attitude towards us has been by far the more friendly of the two. I have noted above how her friendliness has at times led to her own injury. Her trade-routes have suffered, her position as an intermediary is gone. Still she treats these matters as side-issues and remains our true friend and ally. She allows us to recruit twenty thousand soldiers for the Indian army, and that army knows no better soldiers than the twenty battalions of Gurkhas.

During the world war over two hundred thousand soldiers were taken out of Nepal to aid the British and Indian forces,[1] some twenty per cent. of the adult males between the ages of eighteen and fifty. This was indeed a generous contribution from an ally living in the heart of the Himalaya, far from the theatres of war. Their contribution was supplemented by gifts of machine-guns, money, tea, cardamoms, blankets, and timber.

In other ways also Nepal renders us from time to time military and other assistance of the utmost value. We should always bear these considerations in mind, when questions arise between Nepal and ourselves.

The chief colonies of foreigners or semi-foreigners in Lhasa are those of the Sino-Tibetan half-breeds—for of pure Chinese very few are now allowed in Lhasa—the Mongols, and the Nepalese. These communities, Chinese, Mongol, Nepalese, have each in their own degree—especially the two

[1] The *Pioneer Mail*, Allahabad, India, of the 28th December 1923.

Kashmiri Mission in Lhasa (p. 243)

former, the Nepalese less so—influenced Tibetan history and the daily life of the country.

There are also in Lhasa some two or three hundred Mahomedans from Ladakh, the north-eastern province of Kashmir. A few of these are descendants of the prisoners captured from Zorawar Singh's army. The latter were allowed to return to Ladakh, but some, of their own accord, remained in Lhasa. These Ladakhi Mahomedans are prosperous traders; an unaggressive community that goes quietly about its business and is amenable to the Tibetan jurisdiction. It was a common sight, when I was in Lhasa, to see them wending their way to a park, three miles west of the capital, where they often spent the day offering prayers, reading books, and enjoying themselves in the open air.

As is the case with the Nepalese, they wear Tibetan dress, and many of them have followed the example of both Chinese and Nepalese by marrying Tibetan wives.

The Bhutanese in Lhasa can hardly be classed as foreigners, for, though they live under a different government, they are predominantly of Tibetan stock and follow the Ka-gyü sect of Tibetan Buddhism. They come to Lhasa in the summer to sell rice and to buy tea, woollen cloth, &c. Not many come, and each party stays a few days only.

The only Bhutanese who remained in Lhasa throughout the year that I was there were the Agent to the Ruler of Bhutan, known as ' The Interpreter of Bhutan ',[1] and the commercial agents of the three leading Governors, namely, the Pa-ro Pen-lop and the Dzong-pöns of Tim-bu and Pu-na-ka. The ' Interpreter ' buys goods for his master and sends them to Bhutan either by Phari and the Tre-mo [2] Pass or via Nan-kar-tse and the Mŏn-la Ka-chung Pass. The latter route is shorter but very rough.

---

[1] *Druk Lo-cha-wa* in Tibetan.
[2] Entered as Pem-pa La in the Indian Government's maps, but called Tre-mo La by the people themselves.

XXVI

THE MAIN LINES OF BRITISH POLICY

IT may be that the British race will in the future withdraw from the task of administering Asiatic countries, whose peoples, both numerous and intellectual, are now too well educated in Western studies to permit, for long, the white man to order their forms of government. But a considerable time is likely to pass before the need for this withdrawal is fully recognized: recognition of the principle may long precede its translation into practice: and, even when she governs herself, India may well elect to enjoy the advantages with which membership of the British Commonwealth of nations endows her.

Until the advent of British power in India, the latter country exercised no political power in Tibet. Whenever she attempted to invade Tibet, she failed. A Tibetan, who has studied the question, expressed himself as follows on the relationship between Tibet and a self-governing India : ' Tibetans look on Indians as religious people, and should be able to be friendly with them. But India by itself will not be strong enough to help Tibet materially against China, unless India's support includes armed British assistance. If therefore Indian Home Rule should mean that British soldiers leave India, Tibet would throw in her lot with any strong Power that would treat her well, or would perforce gravitate back to a closer relationship with China.'

A very eminent Tibetan authority said, ' I do not think the grant of self-government to India should affect Tibet, provided always that British military power is fully maintained there. Otherwise, civil strife will break out in India, which will be powerless to aid Tibet. And indeed, without British troops, India could not materially help Tibet.' The same authority did not think Hindus would harm Tibet, but distrusted Mahomedans. Deep down in the minds of most Tibetans lies an instinctive dislike of the Mahomedan religion.

The people of Tibet have not been brought much into contact with those of India, for the Himalaya intervenes. The contact with India has been far closer in the Himalayan States of Nepal, Bhutan, and Sikkim, and in these there is a good deal of anti-Indian feeling. A leading man in Sikkim was of opinion that, ' If the Indians receive self-government, they will treat questions on this north-eastern frontier in such a way as to cause trouble. . . . By the treaty of 1910 Bhutan agreed to place her foreign relations under the British Government. She would not have agreed to put them under a Government controlled by Indians.'

On another occasion I was told :

' The British modify rules to suit the peoples of different countries. A Government of Indians will not be as considerate of the feelings of the Tibetans and others, as the British are. There will be friction between Indians and the frontier peoples. Besides, Tibetans look on the British as powerful, and will accept decisions from them which they will not accept from Indians.

' If the British soldiers leave India, every one on this frontier will wish to try his hand. The Gurkhas are always saying how fertile the plains of India are. They will find some pretext for invading them. The Bhutanese will set out to recover the Duars,[1] taken from them by the British in 1865. The Tibetan Government will see how weak the Indian Government is, and will know that it cannot help them against China. They will therefore throw in their lot with China or with any strong Power that will treat them well.'

The general conclusion would appear to be that unless British troops are retained in India and unless the politics of the Tibetan frontier remain under British control, Tibet will break away from the Indian environment. And Nepal, Bhutan, and Sikkim are not likely to continue, as now, in friendly partnership with India, but to become unfriendly and perhaps actively hostile.

It is therefore reasonable to assume that the British military strength in India will remain substantially un-

[1] A large sub-montane area, south of modern Bhutan, annexed after the Bhutan campaign of 1865, and now covered with tea gardens and forests.

changed and the politics of the frontier will remain under British control. Thus for many years the British Government will be concerned with the security of India, and especially with the chief danger to that security, the long land frontier on the north. Of this frontier Tibet forms no inconsiderable part, and one whose importance is likely to increase as the onward march of science reduces the obstacles presented by difficult mountainous countries. For it is in the first instance to the Himalayan ranges and the elevated plateaux of Tibet that we owe the comparative peace on the north-eastern frontier of India.

The countries that are territorially the most closely connected with Tibet are China, India, and Russia. Japan may be added later on, if she increases her influence in China. Nepal is not large enough to effect much ; she could not face the ulterior consequence of decided action in 1792 ; she could not face it now.

China is weak and is out of favour in Tibet ; Russia is almost powerless at present, though it would be unsafe to assume that she will not come again. With India, as a member of the British Commonwealth, the opportunity now rests, for we have been able to win the friendship of Tibet, and Tibet is convinced of British power. How then should India use her opportunity ?

We want Tibet as a buffer to India on the north. Now there are buffers and buffers ; and some of them are of very little use. But Tibet is ideal in this respect. With the large desolate area of the Northern Plains controlled by the Lhasa Government, central and southern Tibet governed by the same authority, and the Himalayan border States guided by, or in close alliance with, the British-Indian Government, Tibet forms a barrier equal, or superior, to anything that the world can show elsewhere.

Tibet desires freedom to manage her own affairs. Her people resent foreign interference. And it is well that it should be so, for thus is the barrier most efficient.

In 1910, when the Chinese were in power at Lhasa and the Dalai Lama a fugitive in India, the Tibetan Government

The road to India. On the Phari Plain

would have welcomed a British Protectorate, placing them in somewhat the same position as that in which our treaty of 1910 had placed Bhutan. At one of my many interviews with the Tibetan Ministers during this year, they remarked that the Indian States were in an ideal position, for each was safe from external aggression and free from interference as regards its internal administration. They sighed as they added, ' That is how we should like Tibet to be '.

Even two years later, when the Chinese authority in Lhasa was crumbling, the Ruler of Sikkim, Maharaja Sid-ke-ong, assured me, ' Tibet would be delighted to be under a British Protectorate controlling their external affairs and leaving them independence on the lines of the Bhutan Treaty of 1910. They are longing for it '.

An Indian merchant, who held a larger share of the Tibetan trade than any other, Indian or European, and was therefore brought into close touch with the commercial community of Tibet, was of the same opinion. Speaking in May 1912, when the Chinese menace had been almost removed, he informed me that, ' All the Tibetans, mostly traders, who come to see me, express their desire that the British would come into the country, that they may have peace and protection '.

Even now there are several influential Tibetans who desire a British Protectorate over their country. But it was recognized on our side from the first that this would have devolved far too heavy a burden upon us, the responsibility of protecting the distant and difficult expanses of Tibet. We made no advances in that direction, and this is now reckoned in some measure to our credit, as showing that we do not covet Tibetan territory.

Tibet has grown stronger during the last few years, and so the ambitions of most of her leading men are directed at the present time towards a relationship with India resembling that of Nepal. Her people do not desire the rapid opening up of their country by means of railways or roads, nor a large settlement of British or Indian or other foreign merchants in Tibet. The gradual development of the country

is, however, wanted ; especially on such lines as will increase
the revenue to the extent necessary to pay for the army and
for the improvements in the civil administration. Tibet, in
short, wishes to live her own life.

For the maintenance of her freedom, if not of her security,
Tibet wants, and has long wanted, a reasonable Agreement
with China. Such an Agreement China has so far denied to
her. In its absence Tibet must take action to defend herself,
great though the burden is on her scanty resources.

In some of the foregoing chapters [1] I have shown what in
my opinion are the lines on which action should be taken,
in fact, the main needs of Tibet and of Indian policy in Tibet.
As these lines are now being followed, Tibet should gradually
grow stronger. In due course China can hardly fail to realize
that, unless she concludes an Agreement with Tibet, she
cannot hope for the latter's adhesion to the Chinese Commonwealth. It is in this Commonwealth, as an autonomous
partner, that Tibet's natural destiny lies. There are still
many Tibetans who look towards China. They feel that
their country is not strong enough to stand alone, and fear
that, ' unless it joins the Chinese Commonwealth as one of
the Five United States,[2] it is likely in time to be overrun
by Indians ', as one expressed it to me. China may legiti-
mately make use of this feeling, but she should not push it
too far.

The Chinese tendency has been to treat the Tibetans as
a people far inferior to themselves, and to apply to them
methods of oppression at once brutal and stupid. The
Tibetans have shown themselves superior in many respects
to their would-be governors. If the Chinese persist in their
present attitude, there can be nothing but disaster before
them. Should Tibet break away, Mongolia is likely to follow,
and China will be a sorely shrunken China if she loses the
vast territories inhabited by these two nations.

Such being the present position of affairs, it would be well
for China to face the facts and conclude a reasonable settlement. That settlement should follow the lines of the Simla

[1] Chapter XX and elsewhere.
[2] Chinese, Mahomedans, Manchus, Mongols, and Tibetans.

Convention,[1] with such changes as the passage of time requires.

In 1914 the Chinese Government refused to ratify the action of their Representative at the Simla Conference. They explained that they had done this because the Convention prescribed boundaries between China and Tibet too favourable to the latter, but that this was the only point in the Convention which they were unable to accept.

Should negotiations be resumed, they would, in addition to the boundary and other matters, deal probably with the important question as to whether a Chinese Amban should be readmitted to Lhasa.

Since the Simla Conference Tibet has regained a large portion of her eastern territory and is stronger than she was. China, for the time at any rate, is weaker. The position has changed and is changing.

As regards the boundary, though it may seem a fantastic suggestion when applied to Tibetan lands, it is for consideration whether it could not be settled by a plebiscite of the districts in dispute. For this suggestion I am indebted to a member of my Lhasa Mission Staff. It was put to one of the most promising among the younger Tibetan officials and approved by him as a practical method of settling the dispute. The latter said :

' It should be done through the village councils, whose members are known as " the better masters ".[2] These councils have a large membership and form the body which in each rural unit—e.g. the Upper Chumbi Valley, the Lower Chumbi Valley or Phari—decides important village affairs. A large proportion of them can read and write a little, especially those in eastern Tibet, where the disputed boundary lies, for the percentage of literate persons there is higher than in central Tibet. A trio composed of one British, one Chinese, and one Tibetan official should collect the votes at different centres. The voting paper might contain a picture of the Dalai Lama or the Potala or other sign for Tibet on one line, and a sign for China on another line. The voter would affix his name or seal or a mark against one or the other, fold up the paper, and drop it into a box in the presence of the three officials.

---

[1] See Chapter XVI.   [2] *Tso-tra* in Tibetan.

' The people of the districts concerned are all Tibetans, and Tibetans are to some extent accustomed to voting in this way. For instance, every six years a new Manager [1] is elected for the Ne-chung Oracle Temple near Lhasa, his duty being to manage all its secular affairs. Each monk writes the name of his choice on a piece of paper, folds it and drops it into a basket. Thus the others do not know for whom he has voted. The one who receives most votes secures the appointment.'

I offer this suggestion merely for what it may be worth; it has not yet been considered sufficiently to warrant my putting it forward with any degree of assurance.

As regards the question of an Amban at Lhasa, I can find room only to quote the opinion of the Ruler of Tibet, which puts the Tibetan view clearly and succinctly. During one of our conversations the Dalai Lama said :

' In the Simla Convention provision was made for an Amban in Lhasa with an escort of three hundred soldiers, and so I have not been able to represent the matter to the British Government. But I am opposed to having an Amban in Lhasa. When the Chinese Government first sent an Amban with Chinese soldiers to Lhasa, they said that the soldiers were to be a bodyguard for the Dalai Lama, Ke-zang Gyatso. The bodyguard was gradually increased in size and transferred to the Amban. And, later on, a second Amban was introduced.

' Left to myself, I can control any disaffected elements in Tibet and hold the country together. But, if an Amban comes, those who are dissatisfied will turn to him and he will be able to foment opposition to the Tibetan Government and myself.

' If an Amban must come, I wish to have a British Representative also in Lhasa. But, until an Amban comes, it is sufficient that a British Representative should visit Lhasa occasionally, as necessity arises.

' The Chinese will make every effort to increase the number of their soldiers in Lhasa, by sending up a fresh escort to relieve the old one, and then not taking the old escort away ; and by whatever other means they can devise. If therefore the Chinese Amban is to have an escort, it should be composed of Tibetan, not Chinese, soldiers. And it should total a good deal less than three hundred.'

[1] *De-pa* in Tibetan.

In the above conversation the Dalai Lama was discussing the future of Tibet. He desired to see Tibet entirely independent of China and consulting the British Government whenever necessity arises.

It is possible also that a suggestion would be made to abolish the term ' Inner Tibet ', transferring part of this area to the autonomous territory under the Dalai Lama, and the remainder to China proper. But this would be unfair to Tibet and would perpetuate the strife between the two nations. In race, in religion, and in language, the men and women of Inner Tibet are one with their brothers and sisters in Outer Tibet. The Tibetan Government have real rights in Inner Tibet and real power there. A few examples may be quoted.

In the north of this country is the province of Go-lok, the land of robbers, where a Chinaman dare not venture. The Dalai Lama travelled through their country and was welcomed as their ruler and their divinity. Any people from Go-lok that we met on their visits to Lhasa emphatically asserted that their country was subordinate to the Tibetan Government, but in no way under the Government of China. In the south of Inner Tibet is the monastery of Cha-treng,[1] whose expeditions, marauding or other, are a terror to the Chinese garrisons. On one of these, as related above,[2] after cowing or subduing the Chinese garrisons in their vicinity, they arrived at the headquarters of the Chinese High Commissioner, with the intention of besieging it. But on the orders of the Dalai Lama they returned to their monastery.

The settlement of ecclesiastical questions in Inner Tibet rests with the Dalai Lama and his advisers, as does also the appointment of many of the secular Governors and their assistants. The power and responsibility of the Tibetan Government throughout this territory is greater than is generally supposed.

The above are likely subjects for discussion at the new Conference. Let us now consider where and how the Conference should be held.

---

[1] *Hsiangcheng* in Chinese.   [2] Page 201.

It is to be hoped that the British Government will not endeavour to conduct negotiations on the Tibetan question at Peking solely with the Chinese Government, no Tibetan Representative being present. This is a mistake which has from time to time been made in the past. But to such a procedure the Tibetan Government took a twofold objection. Firstly, that at any negotiations about Tibet, she herself must be represented. She had steadily refused to recognize any Agreement concluded without consulting her. And it must be admitted that she was entitled to refuse, all the more as she had been independent of China for several years. Secondly, the Tibetans were unwilling to negotiate at Peking. They felt that their Representative and the members of his staff there would be subjected to unfair pressure ; in view of past experiences they were not prepared to trust their Chinese hosts. The Dalai Lama and his Government desired that the negotiations should take place at Lhasa. If China objected to Lhasa, as he to Peking, then let the Conference be held in India. If it were a choice between London and Peking, they preferred London. But it was far away, and would involve them in heavy expense, if they followed their usual custom of sending a large staff with their Plenipotentiary, including a representative for each of the three great monasteries, Se-ra, Dre-pung, and Gan-den.

Whatever be the final form of the Peace Treaty between China and Tibet, it should, among other provisions, arrange for :

(a) Reasonable boundaries for Outer Tibet.

(b) The maintenance of existing Tibetan rights in Inner Tibet.

(c) The autonomy of Outer Tibet, and the exclusion from it of Chinese soldiers and any attempts at Chinese colonization.

(d) Direct dealings between the Tibetan Government and ourselves on matters of mutual concern.

(e) Reasonable facilities for our trade.

(f) The maintenance of the frontier between Tibet and north-eastern India, as arranged at the Simla Convention.

Meanwhile China is unwilling to negotiate. She had hoped that Tibet, finding British India apparently afraid to show friendliness, might grow weary of the strain and surrender to her again. Can Tibet continue to resist ?

The policy which we have now adopted shows Tibet that British India is a friendly neighbour, which is willing to accord her neighbourly facilities towards the establishment of her external and internal security. Her troops are now gradually increasing in number and improving in training and equipment. Eastern Tibet, through which the Chinese armies would have to pass, is full of narrow ravines, which a few riflemen can hold against greatly superior numbers. In 1910 their own Government forbade fighting, and therefore the Tibetan troops offered no serious opposition to the Chinese advance on Lhasa. Since 1914 the Tibetans have strengthened their little army. It is now trained and equipped far more efficiently than before.[1] From 1914 till the present day they have prevented any Chinese advance. In 1917, when their enemies did attack, the Tibetans defeated them everywhere and drove them out of districts which they had occupied for several years. And this they effected, though they then had but the merest rudiments of military training, and no machine-guns or mountain-guns, except such as they were able to capture from the Chinese. From a purely military point of view their achievement was no small one.

To the above must be added this consideration, that the people whose territory they have regained are of their own race, their own religion. Eastern Tibetans were no doubt accustomed to fall, though only to a limited extent, under the rule of Peking, when the Imperial City was to them the symbol of power. But the spirit of nationality is growing, and the influence of religion is as strong as ever. Peking, powerful no longer, represents not the Manchu, but the Chinaman. Lhasa now governs them fairly well. In these circumstances they may be trusted to help their Holy City against those who in recent years have oppressed and misgoverned them.

The Chinese whom the Tibetans have defeated are those

[1] See *Travels in Eastern Tibet*, by Eric Teichman, p. 51.

of southern China only. They have not yet had to face an
invasion of soldiers from the northern provinces, a much
tougher proposition. But they are growing in numbers and
efficiency. If such an attack should befall, they will be able
to offer solid opposition to it. And they may hope for a
measure of Mongol co-operation.

As for ourselves, we should continue the policy laid down
in 1921. We should continue also to prevent Chinese agents
from entering Tibet through India until their Government
comes to terms with the Government of Tibet. If ever a
Chinese invasion succeeds in penetrating Tibet, we should—
provided that diplomatic and other circumstances permit—
co-operate with Nepal, Bhutan, and Sikkim to prevent the
export of rice or other food grains to the Chinese troops. It
is on these countries, especially Bhutan, that the Chinese
rely for the rice which is, to the southern Chinaman at any
rate, an essential food. The three States might agree for
a time to prohibit the export out of friendliness towards
us ; Bhutan and Sikkim also, in order to help the Head of
their Faith in his hour of need.

The chief obstacle which confronts the Tibetan Government in their present circumstances is the difficulty of
raising additional revenue to support the new army. As in
other Asiatic countries, land would naturally be the sheet-
anchor of Tibetan finance. But large areas of this have been
alienated to the monasteries and to the nobles. The Government can resume these only in extreme cases, as in that of the
ill-fated monastery of Ten-gye-ling.

The expenditure by the State on monasteries, both by
these rent-free grants and by direct subsidies in money,
barley, butter, tea, &c., is enormous. Approximately one-
half of the entire revenues of the country, realized or
realizable, is spent on the priests. One-fourth is spent on the
nobles, though this is partly repaid by services rendered.
The result is that the State has to face the expense of
administration with its resources greatly diminished, for
some three-fourths of its revenue is alienated.

Speaking in 1914, the late Prime Minister hoped to reduce

the number of occasional services in the monasteries and chapels in order to obtain a small decrease in ecclesiastical expenditure. But the need of funds was so great that, during my stay in Lhasa in 1921, it was proposed to take the bold step of taxing the estates more recently acquired by the monasteries and other landed proprietors. The consent of the National Assembly, which is guided by the influence of the priests and the nobles, was gained. A Committee was appointed to work out the details. It may be that this new taxation is now in force. If so, it affords a clear instance of the willingness of those in power to make sacrifices for the sake of their country's freedom. They have done but a little of what the Daimyos of Japan, under far greater pressure, did in 1868, but at any rate it would seem that a beginning has been made.

In order still farther to meet the new requirements, a tax has been imposed on wool, the main product of Tibet, and on tea, which is imported in large quantities from China to satisfy the needs of this nation of tea-drinkers. The tax on wool works out at something like four per cent. of the value, the rate varying with the price of wool and the Tibetan exchange. It would seem that the Tibetan Government feared lest the Indian Government should object if a higher rate was fixed. The tax on tea is ten per cent., one brick of tea out of every ten being appropriated by the collectors of customs. Taxes were also imposed a few years ago on salt and on hides.

A mint, newly established in Lhasa, has brought in a good profit, though the Tibetan Government have had the fore-sight to confine the issue of currency notes within narrow limits, so that there has been hitherto no depreciation in the value of these. And a considerable increase of revenue, due to the late Lön-chen' Shatra, has resulted from letting out the grain in the Government granaries on loan. The farmers are thus benefited as well as the State, which gains the interest on the loans, totalling from twenty to thirty thousand *ke* [1] of barley yearly.

[1] A *ke* is a measure. One *ke* of barley weighs about thirty pounds.

The withdrawal of the contributions by the Chinese Government to the large monasteries at Lhasa and elsewhere will not decrease the revenue as a whole, for it is counterbalanced by money now received for transport, which formerly had to be given to the Chinese officials free of cost.

The new sources of revenue, which have been indicated above, will go some way towards meeting the expenses of the new army, but they will not go far enough. In the present condition of Tibet, ecclesiastical, political, and social, it would be unsafe to place heavy taxes on the monastic estates or on those of the nobility, tempting though these possessions might appear to the tax-gatherers of Western peoples. Tibet, deeply religious, is still in the feudal stage and cannot be judged by modern standards. Other means must be found.

The Convention of 1904, concluded at Lhasa, insisted on free trade between India and Tibet. Prior to this the Tibetan Government levied customs duties on goods and on persons passing both ways. Wool, the chief export from Tibet, paid at a rate which works out at one shilling and tenpence per hundredweight. Goods from India to Tibet paid the usual 'Ten tax', i. e. ten per cent. And every Tibetan passing through certain of the trade marts paid one penny.

Article IV of the Lhasa Convention bound the Tibetan Government ' to levy no dues of any kind other than those provided for in the tariff to be mutually agreed upon '. This loss of revenue has hampered the Tibetan Government sorely, more especially at the present time when the administrative needs are growing rapidly. The introduction of free trade causes friction also in various ways among the officials and among the people themselves, long accustomed to trade dues of different kinds.

The Article quoted above presupposes the arrangement of a customs tariff. The Tibetan Government have often asked for this. Moreover during recent years India has taken to imposing a substantial customs tariff on all goods imported overseas. This falls on merchandise imported to

Tibet from countries outside India. As India takes dues, why should not Tibet do so ?

In these circumstances it seems to me that we should in equity agree to the imposition by the Tibetan Government of a customs tariff on moderate and clearly-specified lines. In this way justice will be met, and money will be found for Tibetan needs, which are also the needs of India. For, when Tibet acquires the means of defending herself, she defends India also.

XXVII

SUBSIDIARY SUGGESTIONS

IN this concluding chapter I propose to indicate a few subsidiary, but not unimportant, considerations which should, I think, guide us in our relations with Tibet. I fear that these details are somewhat dull, but they treat of matters which are apt to make just the difference between success and failure in dealing with the Tibetan people. And I will be as brief as possible.

Firstly, it is essential that direct relations be maintained between the Tibetans and ourselves. For many years the Chinese strove to keep us apart. They knew perhaps that, if we came together, their power would be endangered. We have come together and their power has suffered eclipse. The more British officials and Tibetans come to see of each other in present conditions, the better do they understand and like each other. We must make no treaty with China or any other nation regarding Tibet, without associating the latter with us in the negotiations.

We should maintain a cordial friendship with the Tashi Lama also. He is our oldest friend in Tibet, for the British connexion with Tashi-lhünpo goes back to the eighteenth century and the time of Warren Hastings. On account of his great sanctity his influence is strong throughout Tibet and Mongolia. During the last twelve years of my service in Tibet the Tashi Lama frequently invited me to revisit him, but our Government permitted me to accept none of these invitations. The last invitation, which was of an especially pressing nature, reached me during my stay in Lhasa. The Tashi Lama pointed out that Tashi-lhünpo would be almost on my road as I returned from Lhasa to India. Having stayed eleven months in the city of the Dalai, a visit of a few days to Tashi-lhünpo would have followed as a natural corollary. It would have enabled me also to explain our dealings with the Tibetan Government at Lhasa, to promote confidence, and to renew the old friendship. Indeed, not to go was, according to Tibetan ideas, something of a rebuff.

While holding our friendship with the Tashi Lama, we must of course be careful to avoid encouraging Tashi-lhünpo in any aspirations towards independence of Lhasa. There have been such aspirations in the past, but they can work nothing but harm. We want a united Tibet.

The Indian Government should choose with care those officers whom they depute for service, whether permanent or temporary, in Tibet, sending only such as are likely to be sympathetic with the people. A man, efficient in administrative work in India, whether the work be that of a military officer, a magistrate, or an engineer, is not always the best for Tibet. We do not want the administration in these outlying diplomatic Agencies to be too bureaucratic, too much given to rules and regulations framed to meet—though they often do not meet—Indian conditions. Tibet is very different from India, different also from the border regions of Afghanistan. Rules framed for the latter countries must often be relaxed, or otherwise altered, when dealing with the Tartar populations living in and beyond the Himalaya. Tact and sympathy, and a capacity for getting on well with them, are the prime requisites for an officer serving among the people of Tibet.

As far as possible, such officers should learn the Tibetan language and preferably the Lhasan dialect. This is the *lingua franca* of Tibet, for it is more generally spoken than any other and commands respect for the speaker. The Chinese officials in Tibet made use of interpreters, and the abuses of Chinese rule were intensified by this screen between the two races. Tibetans maintain that these had to be bribed to induce them to translate truthfully. Apart from wilful errors the importance of speaking direct, without interpreters, is sufficiently obvious ; I have myself witnessed the mistakes that result from a contrary course. The dishonest interpreter is of course the worst, but the over-zealous one who puts in what he thinks one of the parties *meant* to say, is not much better.

The people of Tibet, Bhutan, and Sikkim, and indeed those of Nepal also, Hindus as well as Buddhists, do not as a rule live harmoniously with Mahomedans from India. Of this antipathy one sees frequent signs among all classes of the population. A friend of mine in Darjeeling had a Gurkha servant, a Hindu of the *Jimdar* tribe. In Darjeeling and Sikkim the word for a sweeper, the lowest of the castes, is *jemadar*. A Mahomedan passing by threw at this man the jeer, ' A Jimdar and a jemadar ; it is the same thing.' The Gurkha drew his kukri [1] on the instant, and it was not without difficulty that a serious quarrel was averted. Such incidents are of common occurrence.

Tibetans have often told me that they can worship in Hindu temples and in Christian churches—their religion is of a wide toleration—but they can have nothing to do with Mahomedan mosques. They find no excuse for the doctrine of Mahomedan Ghazis, who kill in cold blood persons of other Faiths, and believe that, in doing so, they have gained a passport for paradise. ' Buddhism, Christianity, and Hinduism ', said the Prime Minister of Tibet during one of our conversations, ' are all good religions. But Islam is not. It makes the killing of those who belong to other Faiths an act of merit. That is a horrible thing. The true spirit of religion cannot be present, where killing is regarded as an act of merit.'

The violence and desecration done to the Hindu religion by the Mahomedan conquerors of India are remembered by the people of Tibet. Their books of prophecy warn them against the Islamic nations, and the prophecies of olden times exercise always a potent influence over Tibetan feeling. Two high lamas of the Red Hat sect—the older sect, from which these inspirations chiefly emanate—quoted to a Tibetan friend of mine an old prophecy to the effect that the Turuka (Turks) would do their utmost to destroy the Tibetan religion and would very nearly succeed in destroying it, but the Chi-ling (Europeans) would not harm it. The prophecy of North Shamba-la on the same lines has already been alluded to.[2]

---

[1] The short curved sword used by the Gurkhas. [2] Page 63.

In fine, there is a strong antipathy between Mahomedans on the one side and Tibetans and Gurkhas on the other. In these circumstances the Indian Government should be doubly careful in posting Mahomedan officials to Tibet or otherwise associating them with Tibetan affairs. Tact and sympathy on the part of those selected will no doubt lessen the feeling against them in course of time.

We must avoid any tendency to Indianize or Anglicize Tibet. Let the country develop quietly on its own lines, taking from the outside only those things which will aid in such development. And we should not allow the administration of our Agencies in Tibet to become too rigid, too bureaucratic. If, for instance, a Tibetan gentleman of position and influence wishes once in a way to use the telephone attached to our telegraph offices in Tibet, he should be allowed to do so. This edifies him and promotes friendliness, while the loss to the Indian Government by potential telegrams is insignificant. And, after all, the Tibetans give something by permitting us to own and work telegraph lines in their country.

In the north-west of India, in Rajputana and the southern Punjab, live a people known as Marwaris. Among these is a large class of traders and money-lenders, many of whom have spread over a great part of India. They are keen and careful in business, but of a somewhat timid disposition. I had some good friends among them, especially one whose shrewd perspicacity, combined with a wide benevolence, gained the respect of all who were privileged to know him.

When I first came to Sikkim, I found that Marwaris had been permitted to establish themselves there during the preceding twenty years or so under the aegis of the British administration and the safety which this administration secured. They found Sikkim a profitable field, for the simple folk of these mountains were no match for them in rates and calculations, in matters of account. They lent money freely, the rate paid by farmers and others of average prosperity being two pice per rupee per mensem, which works out to a yearly rate of thirty-seven and a half per cent. Those less prosperous paid higher rates, frequently rising to over cent.

per cent. The loans were often left to fructify for long periods, and thus unconscionable profits were taken. ' Fruit grows on the tree of patience ' is a typical Marwari proverb ; in Sikkim it found fulfilment beyond the dreams of avarice. A large, and ever larger, part of the population was falling more and more into their clutches.

I was able to persuade the Council of the Sikkim State, without much difficulty, to introduce a law and to follow a line of action which succeeded in protecting the people of Sikkim in their unequal struggle. Before I left the country, some ten years later, the load of indebtedness was greatly lightened, and the farmers and others were reaping the results of their own labours, and were growing in prosperity.

It does not seem necessary to burden this book with an account of the measures thus initiated in Sikkim. The point which I desire to emphasize is that we should not encourage Indian money-lenders—or indeed British, if there be any so desirous—to settle in Tibet. As matters stand even now, many Tibetans feel that an undue proportion of the profits from their trade goes to Indian dealers living on the Tibetan borderland and elsewhere. But time should find its own remedy for this in the increase of Tibetan capital and business capacity ; as well as in the development of home industries by utilizing the wool, the hides, and other raw products that now so plentifully leave the country.

The States and districts on the northern frontier of India, being parts of the British Commonwealth, enjoy in Tibet an influence which they never gained by their own unaided efforts. We should prevent them from abusing that influence by acting in a high-handed manner towards their northern neighbour. There have indubitably been instances of this. Both equity and the maintenance of amicable relationship with Tibet require that the Indian Government should guard against their repetition.

In an earlier chapter [1] I have shown how suspicious Tibetans were of attempts by foreigners to explore their country, and how harmful these journeys had been to the

[1] Chapter VIII, p. 59.

Strolling players from Tibet, touring in Sikkim

By colour photography

relations between Tibet and India. Though not as strong as before, the feeling still survives and we should respect it. Tibetans cannot understand the idea of geographical or scientific explorations, and almost inevitably suspect that some sinister motive lies behind. They fear also that, whatever the explorer's motives may be, the spirits of places visited will be interfered with.

The British explorer himself is apt to be misled by the apparent welcome and the kindly treatment which nowadays he receives from Tibetans. The latter, with the courtesy that comes naturally to them, profess to welcome him, now that the British and Tibetan Governments have replaced the old hostility by a cordial friendship. But in their hearts they dislike his coming.

Some years ago the late Prime Minister remarked, ' We do not understand why —— and —— travelled in Tibet, exploring and gathering information about the country. If the British Government wanted any information, we would have given it to them gladly, now that the British and Tibetan Governments are on friendly terms with each other.'

In permitting the British mountaineering party, which essayed to climb Mount Everest, to travel in Tibet and live there for months at a time, the Tibetan Government showed a noteworthy friendliness Nepal still forbids British exploration, though we have had a Resident at her capital for over one hundred years.

If their own inclinations alone were to be considered, Tibetans would wish to be visited only by those who, as they think, can help them in their military or civil affairs—a political officer maybe who can advise them and remove obstacles, a military officer whom they can consult as to the equipment or the training of their troops, one who can help them in their engineering difficulties, and so on. But they must gradually come into contact with the outer world, and thus it was that I recommended that the restrictions placed on European travel should to some extent be removed.

The question of admitting Christian missionaries to Tibet

is one of difficulty. The Christian side of the case is well known ; I will content myself with presenting a few considerations from the Tibetan standpoint.

Tibetans do not try to push their creed in Christian countries ; they are opposed to Christian missionaries preaching religion in Tibet. This opposition, which is determined and of long standing, has been further intensified by recent events in eastern Tibet.

A Roman Catholic Mission has been established for many years in the portions of Tibet bordering on China. Its headquarters are at Tachienlu, with branches at Da-wu, Sha-ra-tong, Ba-tang, and Tsa-ka-lho (Yenching in Chinese). There is an American Protestant Mission at Ba-tang ; a missionary of the China Inland Mission at Tachienlu. These have all toiled devotedly ; the Protestant Missionaries in particular have added medical and educational work to their evangelical duties.

In the work of evangelization they have had hard struggles with the Tibetan priests and people, who are strongly devoted to their own religion. Conversions have been very few ; this is the case also with the Missions in the district of Darjeeling in the north-eastern Himalaya, where missionaries are free to work as they please. The nature-worshipping Lepchas are converted in large numbers, Nepalese Hindus also to some extent, but of Tibetans very few.

The Mission settlements mentioned above are in that portion of Tibet which is under Chinese occupation. China is bound by treaty to allow Christian missionaries to propagate their doctrines within her territories and to protect them in doing so. These Missions have relied on Chinese military protection, and have seemed to the Tibetans to preach their beliefs under cover of the Chinese rifles. Especially has this been the case with the Roman Catholics, who have been longer established in eastern Tibet. When Chinese troops have invaded and annexed fresh Tibetan territory, the missionaries can claim, and sometimes have claimed, to move forward after them. They have thus come to be identified by the Tibetans with Chinese interests.

Some missionaries have in published statements rejoiced over the destruction of Tibetan monasteries by Chinese troops, who were often under military adventurers of a low type. Such destruction was at times accompanied by acts of inhuman savagery. Yet in a missionary pamphlet of 1908 we read :

' I travelled to Drango in ten days. We found the road still open, though the huge Lamaseries, like sentinels on guard, are a constant obstacle and menace to Christian effort. But our God is a mighty God, and has already shown what He can do by destroying the chief monasteries on the Batang road.' [1]

The Chinese are by nature a kindly people, but their kindliness seems sometimes to take on a different colour when attempting to govern those whom they have conquered or half conquered. In 1916 an American missionary, of long frontier experience, wrote :

' There is no method of torture known that is not practised in here on these Tibetans, slicing, skinning, boiling, tearing asunder and all. . . . To sum up what China is doing here in eastern Tibet, the main things are collecting taxes, robbing, oppressing, confiscating, and allowing her representatives to burn and loot and steal.' [2]

In one of their Tibetan stations, the Roman Catholic Mission have founded a Chinese colony, making over a tract of Tibetan land to Chinese for agricultural purposes.

All this causes the missionaries, and more especially the Roman Catholics, to be associated in Tibetan minds with Chinese interests, if not with Chinese cruelty and oppression. Mr. Teichman, of the British Consular Service in China, spent a considerable period travelling in eastern Tibet, and has long been a close student of Sino-Tibetan relations. His opinion is on the above lines.[3] My own opinion, formed in conversation with members of the Tibetan Government and people from eastern Tibet, is to the same effect.

As missionaries are generally unwelcome in Tibet, so too

[1] *Travels in Eastern Tibet*, by Eric Teichman, p. 227.
[2] Idem, p. 228.
[3] Idem, pp. 226–8.

are sportsmen in search of game. The taking of life in this way is against the Tibetan religion, though in outlying districts we shall sometimes find Tibetans themselves who do so. Still, shooting and fishing have been prohibited of late years, and those who enter Tibet should conform with the Tibetan law.

From some of the foregoing paragraphs it may seem, no doubt, that life in Tibet is unduly hedged with restrictions. But we should remember that Tibet is still in the feudal age. Even so late as a hundred years ago a Buddhist missionary would have found scant welcome in Italy. We should remember how powerful the Tibetan priesthood is. Their leaders are self-made men who owe their positions to their own ability, and not, as is the case with the nobility, to a long line of ancestors. They are for the most part celibate, having no family liable to be injured, no landed property liable to be confiscated if they act against the Government. They can afford in large measure to be independent. And a religion-loving nation is in their hands and looks to them for guidance.

The China of two hundred years ago realized the power of the priests and shaped her policy accordingly, and with a fair measure of success. Modern China thought that she could override them, and to this is mainly due her present failure in Tibet. Any nation having dealings with Tibet must watch the priests and watch them carefully.

We should remember also what the Tibetan priesthood stand to lose in modern conditions. The Chinese Government cannot be expected to pay them subsidies, the growing Tibetan army curtails their power, and the advance of Western thought undermines the foundations of their temples and creeds.

Among those with whom the Tibetans do desire to maintain intercourse, none is more welcome than the British Consular Officer stationed at Tachienlu. They rely on him to hold the scales even in disputes between their country and China on the eastern frontier ; to report and, if possible, to restrain Chinese aggression from that side. But the present Prime Minister thinks—and others probably agree with him

—that this officer should be stationed at Ba-tang, where he would be in touch with the Tibetan authorities. Ba-tang being on the Chinese side of the boundary, he would still be in full touch with the Chinese. At Tachienlu he is so far within the Chinese sphere that he cannot well ascertain at first hand what is happening on the Tibetan side, nor hear the Tibetan point of view. He should of course visit various parts of the Sino-Tibetan frontier when need arises.

Nowadays the physician, and especially the surgeon, from the West are welcomed in Tibet. This was less so in the past, for illness and injury have been as a rule ascribed to the action of evil spirits, and have called for the services of the priest or of the professional exorcist rather than for those of the doctor. But hard facts, and the skill of our medical men who have worked at Gyantse and elsewhere, are modifying the old ideas. The Tibetans have indeed their own doctors, many of whom hold among them a high reputation as physicians, though not as surgeons, for of surgery they are almost entirely ignorant.

During one of our conversations in 1914 the late Prime Minister of Tibet expressed the wish that Tibetan doctors should be instructed in Western surgery as far as their limited capacity permitted, and especially in the treatment of sores and wounds. When we were in Lhasa, Colonel Kennedy found that his antiseptics aroused widespread admiration and that Tibetan doctors were particularly desirous of learning more about these. The uplands of Tibet are perhaps afflicted with noxious microbes less than are most other countries. But the winds are strong and carry dust and dirt from the heavily manured fields and from the insanitary towns and villages. The standard of cleanliness is very low.

Another matter in which Colonel Kennedy gave instruction was in vaccination and the preparation of vaccine lymph. Tibetans desire to learn all they can about vaccination. Smallpox is the most virulent of their epidemics. Vaccination has been carried on for many years in our Agency at Gyantse, and they have witnessed the protection that it confers.

Before the War we always had a British Medical Officer at
Gyantse. During the War he was of necessity removed.
After the War, up to the time of my departure from Tibet
in November 1921, he had not been replaced. But this
should be done now. On various grounds we need at least
one in central Tibet.

It will not be out of place to press two matters of procedure in which amendment seems desirable. Firstly, there
should be greater promptitude in dealing with Tibetan
affairs. Tibet is the Cinderella of the Indian Foreign
Department, but the patience of even a Cinderella may wear
out. Over and over again in the past our Government has
kept the Tibetan Government waiting too long for replies to
their communications.

Secondly, we should do more than is done at present
towards putting before the public the Tibetan side of
incidents that arise from time to time, especially when mis-
representations are published in the Chinese, the British, or
the Indian Press. People naturally become imbued with the
idea that the Tibetans are an aggressive or a savage people,
whereas the aggression and the savagery have proceeded in
almost every case from the Chinese.

As Tibet gradually develops under an autonomous regime,
India should benefit by an increase of trade and by Tibet's
dependence on her, partially at any rate, for military supplies.
Openings may arise for Indians and Britons who can aid
Tibet in her development and, in so doing, show themselves
friendly to Tibetan aspirations.

It is not impossible that later on it may be found desirable
to recruit Tibetan soldiers for the Indian army on somewhat
the same lines as Gurkhas are now recruited. A few have
already served in the Gurkha regiments, enlisting under
Nepalese names. One Tibetan of my acquaintance was
employed in the Remount Department in South Africa
during the Boer War, having enlisted previously in an
Indian cavalry regiment. A scheme of this kind, confined
within narrow limits, might prove advantageous to both
India and Tibet. But it is premature to consider it, until

it is seen how the political situation develops in both countries. Even if, after a complete balancing of the issues, it should be found desirable, it could hardly be tried till the Sino-Tibetan dispute is settled. Tibet has but a scattered population and at present requires her spare men as a reserve for the defence of her eastern frontier.

As the food-producing areas of the world are more and more exhausted by the growing populations, Tibet is likely to supply beef and mutton in larger quantities. The possibility too of finding gold, silver, and other minerals, whose value will pay for the cost of transportation, is not to be disregarded.

The present attitude of Tibet, unlike that of Afghanistan, is one of cordial friendship with Britain. But the effect of Home Rule in India, if this should entail the decrease of British military power there, and the substitution of Indian for British control of frontier affairs, would tend to turn her away. Among Tibetans who have been brought into contact with Indians, some fear that Indians may come to Tibet and endeavour to obtain influence there. For various reasons they do not desire too close a connexion with India. And they do not think that India, apart from Britain, has the power to help them against China.

Tibet's natural affinity is no doubt with the races of the Chinese Commonwealth. In religion and ethics, in social manners and customs, there is much common ground. Historically, the connexion is from the beginning of time.

This bond with China will presumably remain. It is not, however, likely to be one of Chinese domination. In the past, Chinese soldiers and officials have come to Lhasa from time to time, but they gained only a limited share in the government of the country, far less than the Chinese records claim. And their power was short-lived. Taken as a whole, Tibet has been a self-governing country and she intends to remain so. When she at length secures recognition of the integrity and autonomy of her territory, she may not unreasonably enter the Chinese Commonwealth ; but it seems likely that she will do so only on terms of equality.

As for ourselves, we cannot safely now revert to our former policy of aloofness. Tibet would turn to some foreign Power, and if none were available would fall again under Chinese leadership sufficiently to create hostile influences on the Indian frontier. She would feel that we had betrayed her. The old saying would be passed from mouth to mouth :

> Sheep that trusted in the pasture,
> O'er the precipice were hurled.

With these antagonistic influences at work, the long northern and north-eastern frontier of India would fall more and more into a state of turmoil. The lines that I have indicated in this and earlier chapters seem to me those along which we are most likely to find security, peace, and happiness.

APPENDIXES

THE first three Appendixes are translations of inscriptions on stone pillars in Lhasa. There are eight such inscriptions in Lhasa and one at Sam-ye. Through the kindness of the Tibetan Government the pillars were cleaned, to make the writing clearer. With the assistance of learned Tibetans, I was thus enabled to make a translation of all. But for the sake of space I include only three here.

APPENDIX I

TREATY BETWEEN CHINA AND TIBET DURING THE FIRST HALF OF THE EIGHTH CENTURY A.D.

Recorded on the western face of the stone pillar [1] *near the Temple in Lhasa.*

The Sovereign of Tibet, the Divine King of Miracles,[2] and the great King of China, Hwang Te, the Nephew and the Maternal Uncle, have agreed to unite their kingdoms. Having made this great Agreement, that it may be held faithfully and never be changed, all gods and men were invoked *to bear witness to the oath.*[3] That it may remain *from generation to generation, the sacred terms of the relationship have been duly inscribed* on the pillar.

The King of miracles *Ti*-de-tsen *and the Chinese King* Bun Pu He-u *Tig Hwang Te, Nephew* and Uncle, *united their kingdoms, considering the mutual* welfare *of Tibet and China*, and thus conferred great benefits upon the people of the inside and outside, making many and all happy and prosperous for a long time. They agreed to hold as sacred the respect of the old relationship and the happiness of *the neighbours.* Tibet and China shall guard the land and frontier, of which they have hitherto held possession. All to the east of the frontier is the country of Great China. All to the west is certainly the country of Great Tibet.

Henceforth there shall be no fighting as between enemies, and neither side will carry war into the other's country. Should there

---

[1] A four-sided monolith pillar, about fourteen feet high, standing behind a masonry wall and the wall of a house. Over it hang two weeping-willow trees, known to the people as Cho U-tra, i. e. ' The Lord's Hair '.

[2] These early kings are believed to have possessed miraculous powers, e. g. of flying through the air.

[3] Words in italics show the meanings which the Tibetan authorities assign to the blanks in the inscription.

be any suspected person, he can be arrested, questioned, and sent back. Thus the great Agreement has been made for uniting the kingdoms, and the Nephew and Uncle have become happy. In gratitude for this happiness it is necessary that travellers with good messages should go backwards and forwards. The messengers from both sides will also travel by the old road as before. According to the former custom ponies shall be exchanged at Chang-kün-yok, on the frontier between Tibet and China. At Che-shung-shek Chinese territory is met ; below this China will show respect.[1] At Tsen-shu-hwan Tibetan territory is met ; above this Tibet will show respect.

The Nephew and Uncle, having become intimate, will respect each other according to custom. No smoke or dust shall appear between the two countries. There shall be no sudden anger and the word ' enemy ' shall not even be mentioned. Not even those guarding the frontier shall feel apprehension or take fright. Land is land, and bed is bed ;[2] thus happiness will reign. Happiness will be established ; prosperity will be gained for ten thousand generations. The sound of praise shall cover all the places reached by the Sun and Moon.

This Agreement, that the Tibetans shall be happy in Tibet and the Chinese happy in China and the great kingdoms united, shall never be changed. The Three Precious Ones,[3] the Exalted Ones, the Sun and Moon, the Planets and Stars have been invoked to bear witness. Solemn words were also uttered. Animals were sacrificed and oaths taken, and the Agreement was made.

Is this Agreement held to be binding ? If this Agreement be violated, whether Tibet or China violates it first, that one has committed the sin. Whatever revenge is taken in retaliation shall not be considered a breach of the Agreement. In this way the Kings and Ministers of Tibet and China took oath and wrote this inscription of the Agreement in detail. The two great Kings affixed their seals. The Ministers, considered as holding the Agreement, wrote with their hands. This *inscribed* Agreement shall be observed by both sides.

[1] i.e. supply transport and other necessary assistance.
[2] An old Tibetan saying, which means that a man's land will remain unharmed, and he can sleep freely in his bed, without having to be constantly on the watch for enemies.
[3] Buddha, the Buddhist scriptures, and the Buddhist priesthood.
[4] The Celestial Buddhas, Chen-re-zi, &c.

A Pillar of Record. Award by King Ti-song De-tsen inscribed
on the northern face of the monolith below the Potala

'Recorded on the southern face of the stone pillar
below the Potala'

APPENDIX II

TIBETAN CONQUESTS IN WESTERN CHINA
DURING A.D. 763

Recorded on the southern face of the stone pillar [1]
below the Potala.

During the time of King Ti-de Tsuk-tsen, Ngen-lam Lu-kong, being in the confidence of the King, became the Chief Minister. Bal-dong-tsap and Lang-mi . zik, though they were Ministers of high rank, became estranged from the Father King, Ti-de Tsuk-tsen, and did injury to him, so that he went to Heaven.

They were near to doing injury also to the Son King Ti-song De-tsen. Dissension was caused in the kingdom of the black-headed [2] Tibetans. Lu-kong brought to the notice of the Son King, Ti-song De-tsen, the circumstances regarding the estrangement of Bal and Lang. The estrangement of Bal and Lang was proved. Rebuke fell on them. Lu-kong was brought into the confidence of the King.

During the time of King Ti-song De-tsen, Ngen-lam Lu-kong was in the King's confidence, and was great in counsel. The King, being of unchanging mind, made him the Inner Minister.[3] He considered and ascertained the affairs of the kingdom of China.[4] He gave instructions to the military Commander, who first led the troops to Kar-tsen. Being skilful in military matters, he went by degrees. He subdued Ha-sha, which is in the kingdom of China. Those useful to China . . . . . . '. China shivered with fear. Yar-mo-tang . . . . of China. . . . . Towards Chong-ka . . . . . etcetera. Lu-kong . . . . . enemy . . . . . great kingdom . . . . . . represented to the Great Councillor. . . being friendly . the officer . . endured hardships . . the kingdom.[5]

[1] A four-sided monolith pillar, about twenty-three feet high, raised on three stone steps, two of which are bound round with iron bands. On the top is a small pyramidal finial.

[2] This epithet is still used, but only with reference to laymen, not priests ; e. g. in the popular refrain about the Dalai Lama, which runs :

> The Lama of the Yellow Hats ;
> The Ruler of the Black Heads.

[3] i.e. the minister nearest the king. The present Prime Minister is often known as the ' Inner Minister '.

[4] This king had a Chinese mother, who would have a large retinue of Chinese with her.

[5] The inscription in the blanks above is greatly broken, as though with hammers and other such weapons. The Tibetans state that the injury was done by the Chinese, when in power at Lhasa, to obliterate the names of the places in China which Tibet conquered.

This portion of the inscription is high above the ground and could not

King Ti-song De-tsen, being of profound intellect and broad-minded in counsel, whatever he did for the kingdom turned out well in every way. He conquered and held under his control many districts and forts in the kingdom of China.

The Chinese King, He Hu Hik Wang Te, and his Ministers, were terrified. They offered a perpetual yearly tribute of fifty thousand rolls of silk. China was made to pay tribute.

After this, He Hu Hik Wang Te, the Father King of China, died. The Prince, Wang Peng Wang, became King of China. He considered it unfitting to pay tribute to Tibet. The King of Tibet became uneasy in his mind. Then Ngen-lam Lu-kong assumed the leadership of the Council, in order that Tibet might carry war to the Chinese King's palace of Keng-shi, which is in the very heart of China.

Zhang Chim Gyal Gyal Zik Shu Teng and Minister Ta-dra Lu-kong, the two great Commanders, were ordered to carry war to Keng-shi. On the bank by the ford of Chi-hu Chir a great battle was fought with the Chinese. Tibet put them to flight. Many Chinese were killed. The Chinese King, Kwang Peng Wang,[1] also fled from the fort of Keng-shi to Shem Chi-hu. Keng-shi was captured. The Inner Minister Gye-hu . . Keng . . life . Tong-kwan and Po Kan . . . . of the Tibetan King . . . . . Tibet . . . .

Being devoted to . . . . Kem Shing Kong Cho's name . . . . Minister . . . . Kings, great and small, ... kingdom in the end . . . . . . made famous . Lu-kong, being in the confidence of the King, ... underwent hardships.[2]

have been injured by the casual mischief of street urchins and others. A leading Tibetan official, over sixty years old, informed me that, when he was a young man, the Chinese said that they were going to take a copy of one of the inscriptions on the pillar near the Temple. But what they did was to scratch out several of the letters with stones, &c.

[1] Written ' Wang Peng Wang ' higher up.

[2] A Tibetan official told me, ' The Chinese not only rubbed out parts of the inscriptions adverse to China, but used also to tell the Tibetans that the powder, scraped from these pillars and taken internally, was good for chest diseases. Thus, some Tibetans were persuaded to help in the work of destruction '.

APPENDIX III

DEFEAT OF THE GURKHAS IN A.D. 1792

Recorded on a stone slab below the Potala.

Written
by
the
King.

The monument of the deeds fully accomplished ten times.

Now that the Gurkhas have submitted to me, the Imperial army has been withdrawn, and the completion of this brilliant tenth achievement has been set out in the Letter. Though the fame of this matter was great, it has not been fully manifested. Therefore the proclamation has been inscribed on this monument, that the monument may serve as a moral for the minds of men.

It comes to my mind that my mind was formerly attached to the Yü-kur writing. According to the writing of Che-u-kur the acts of the respectful and sympathetic Amban, and of the Owner of the country, able to perform all things, are set down here. It is written in a chapter of the Lü A-u that, when the mind is in a good state, the mind and the deeds are joined together. However, he who acts in accordance with the above precepts will obtain the approval of the Heavenly Protector [1] and will gain reward. As my conduct was on those lines, I gained all the merits necessary for carrying out the ten wars to a successful conclusion. It is fitting that they should be carved on this monument.

The merits of the ten times are as follow :

Two victories over the Chung-kar.[2]
One victory over Hu-i Se.
Two victories over Tsa-la and Chu-chen.
One victory over Ta-i Wan.
Two victories over Mi-han-tan and An-tan.

Now I have fought twice with the Gurkhas. I have made an end of them, and they have tendered their submission to me. This completes the ten times. Three of the internal victories are of lesser importance.

Now as regards the submission of the Gurkhas in the Female Earth-Bird year.[3] Although they brought troops for looting Ü and

---

[1] i. e. the Emperor of China.
[2] Apparently the Oëlot Mongols.
[3] In the Tibetan system of chronology five elements are joined to twelve

Tsang,[1] the A-u Hu-i not daring, Pa-chung did not go into the matter thoroughly, but arranged it in a hurry. So the Gurkhas were not frightened.

Again, having obtained loot last year, they came back. The wicked Minister was degraded, and the famous Chang-chun was sent. The latter arranged on a large scale for provisions and wages. Fu-kang men appreciated my gifts highly, and did not consider fatigue or fear.

During the winter of last year additional soldiers of So-lon [2] and Szechuan came quickly, batch by batch, along the Si-ning road, and arrived in the country of the thieves [3] during the fifth month of this year. Immediately on their arrival they retook the country of Ü and Tsang, and captured the territory of the thieves. They traversed the mountains, so difficult to push through, as though they were moving over a level plain. They crossed rivers with great waves and narrow gorges as though they were small streams. They climbed up the peaks of mountains and descended again in the pursuit. They captured the important places and at the same time captured the roads in the gorges. Not considering injuries to hands or feet, they fought seven battles and gained seven victories. The thieves were panic-stricken.

After that, when the troops arrived close to Yam-bu,[4] the chief leaders of the thieves were sent. They submitted respectfully and represented that they would conduct themselves according to our orders. Although they carried out the orders of the great Commander-in-Chief, they were not allowed to enter our encampment. The reason for this was that last year they seized Ten-dzin Pal-jor [5]

animals. Each element is repeated once to indicate male and female. Thus :

1924. Male Wood Rat year.
1925. Female Wood Bull year.
1926. Male Fire Tiger year.
1927. Female Fire Hare year.

The first round of elements ends at the tenth (Female Water Bird) year, and is recommenced immediately, so that the eleventh year is the Male Wood Dog, and the twelfth the Female Wood Pig. At sixty years the two series end together, the animals having run five times and the elements six times. We then get the Male Wood Rat year again and the series runs through as before.

[1] The two main provinces of Central Tibet. Lhasa is in Ü ; Shigaʦse in Tsang.

[2] A district in the upper part of the Tibetan province of Gya-rong, annexed by China in 1863. It is therefore evident that there were Tibetan troops in this army that conquered the Gurkhas.

It appears also that several Tibetan officers took part, including Do-ring Shap-pe, Yu-to Shap-pe, and Chang-lo-chen De-pön (Colonel).

[3] i. e. the Gurkhas.   [4] i. e. Khatmandu, the capital of Nepal.

[5] The Do-ring Shap-pe. It is said that the Chinese sent him with the

and those with him by means of a falsehood ; and so they were not allowed to enter.

Owing to the great heroism of the mighty army the thieves were helpless. He could have had them removed from his presence, and could have made an end of them, letting not even one of them escape. However, that was not the wish of the Heavenly Protector. Even if all those territories had been obtained, as they are more than a thousand distances from the frontiers of Ü and Tsang, it would have been difficult to cultivate them and to guard them. As for ordinary, simple people, even if they obtain a thing, the end will not be gained.[1] Therefore orders were given, the respectful submission was noted, and the army was withdrawn. Thereby the work was completed.[2]

Formerly, in the time of King Thang Tha-ï Tsung, there was a conference with the Chi-li.[3] As it was shown that they (the Gurkhas) were conquered and powerless, he (the Chi-li) said [4] that they would always remain on good terms (with China). It is not fitting to take the Chi-li as an example.[5] The frontiers of Ü and Tsang are not near to China. They (the Gurkhas), fearing to lose their lives, were compelled to submit respectfully. A pretended submission, made in order to obtain peace, will not suffice. A great victory has now been obtained. The thieves have offered a heart-felt submission, and this is believed and accepted. Affairs have been arranged in accordance with the three points of King Tha-ï Tsung of Thang-gur.

Need I write the former affairs of the Tor-gö,[6] how they became afraid of us and followed us ? How they came to agree with us and to follow us, this has all been written already. Now the Gurkhas having admitted their fault, and wishing to save their lives, fear us and follow us. Thus agreeing with us and following, the two qualities are complete. The failing was theirs, and they have admitted their fault : that is how the matter stands.

If this matter be considered, it will be seen that the people of

Yu-to Shap-pe and Chang-lo-chen De-pön as peace envoys to the Gurkhas, and that the Gurkhas seized them and carried them off to Nepal.

[1] i. e. ' Even if Nepal be annexed to Tibet, the Tibetans will not be able to hold it.'

[2] European writers, following Chinese authorities, put the Gurkha army at 18,000 men and the Chinese at 70,000. Tibetans in general put the Gurkha army at about 4,000, and the Chinese army at about 9,000, of whom half or rather more were Tibetan.

[3] Apparently the British. The Tibetan word for foreigners of European extraction is ' Chi-ling '.

[4] The non-honorific word for ' said ' is used here—the word applied to the common people—to indicate contempt for the representative of the Chi-li.

[5] Semble, in keeping Indian territory for themselves, after conquering it.

[6] A Mongolian tribe conquered by the Chinese.

Ü, abandoning military pursuits, devote themselves solely to literature. Thus they have become like a body bereft of vigour. This
is unfitting. If a people abandon military pursuits and make literature their chief object, they become unable to safeguard their former
position. This should be known.

The manner of going and the manner of returning [1] are clearly
written in the book entitled *The Planets and Stars.* Now understand this and do not forget it.[2] It is to be considered again and
again at the time of making war, that it may be of advantage.

Owing to the knowledge gained during fifty-seven years of warfare
these ten deeds have been fully completed. This is the gift of the
Heavenly Protector. Thus the kindness of the Heavenly Protector
is exceedingly deep. I also have faith in it. They (the Gurkhas)
thought they could achieve a great deal by violence, but the favour
of the Heavenly Protector remained. It is hoped that this will tend
to turn people into men of complete justice. Besides this, there is
nothing to be said.

This has been written by the King on an upper date [3] in the first
month of winter in the fifty-seventh year of the reign of the Heavenly
Protector, that is to say, in the Male Water Rat year.

APPENDIX IV

TREATY BETWEEN TIBET AND NEPAL, 1856
Translation of the Tibetan text.

The undermentioned gentlemen, monks and laymen, of the Gurkha
and Tibetan Governments held a conference and mutually agreed
upon and concluded a Treaty of ten Articles, and invoked the
Supreme Being as their witness, and affixed their seals to it. They
have agreed to regard the Chinese Emperor as heretofore with
respect, in accordance with what has been written, and to keep
both the States in agreement and to treat each other like brothers.
If either of them violate the Treaty, may the Precious Ones not
allow that State to prosper. Should either State violate the terms
of the Treaty, the other State shall be exempt from all sin in making
war upon it.

(Here follow the names of the signatories and their seals.)

List of Articles of the Treaty.
1. The Tibetan Government shall pay the sum of ten thousand
rupees annually as a present to the Gurkha Government.

[1] i. e. the rules of human conduct.
[2] As a matter of fact the Tibetans, with but few exceptions, do not
even know that this inscription relates to the campaign against the
Gurkhas. They know only that it was erected by a former Amban.
[3] i. e. during the first half of the month.

2. Gurkha and Tibet have been regarding the Great Emperor with respect. Tibet being the country of monasteries, hermits and celibates, devoted to religion, the Gurkha Government have agreed henceforth to afford help and protection to it as far as they can, if any foreign country attacks it.

3. Henceforth Tibet shall not levy taxes on trade or taxes on roads or taxes of any other kind on the merchants or other subjects of the Gurkha Government.

4. The Government of Tibet agrees to return to the Gurkha Government the Sikh soldiers captured by Tibet, and all the Gurkha soldiers, officers, servants, women, and cannon captured in the war. The Gurkha Government agrees to return to the Tibetan Government the Tibetan troops, weapons, yaks, and whatever articles may have been left behind by the Tibetan subjects residing at Kyi-rong, Nya-nang, Dzong-ga, Pu-rang, and Rong-shar. And on the completion of the Treaty all the Gurkha troops in Pu-rang, Rong-shar, Kyi-rong, Dzong-ga, Nya-nang, Tar-ling, and La-tse will be withdrawn and the country evacuated.

5. Henceforth the Gurkha Government will keep a high officer, and not a Newar, to hold charge at Lhasa.

6. The Gurkha Government will open shops at Lhasa, where they can freely trade in gems, jewellery, clothing, food, and different articles.

7. The Gurkha officer is not allowed to try any case arising from quarrels amongst Lhasa subjects and merchants, and the Tibetan Government is not allowed to try any case arising from quarrels amongst the Gurkha subjects and traders and the Mahomedans of Khatmandu who may be residing in the jurisdiction of Lhasa. In the event of quarrels between Tibetan and Gurkha subjects the high officials of the two Governments will sit together and will jointly try the cases; the fines imposed upon the Tibetan subjects as punishments will be taken by the Tibetan official, and the fines imposed upon Gurkha subjects, merchants, and Mahomedans as punishments will be taken by the Gurkha official.

8. Should any Gurkha subject, after committing a murder, go to the country of Tibet, he shall be surrendered by Tibet to Gurkha; and should any Tibetan subject, after committing a murder, go to the country of Gurkha, he shall be surrendered by Gurkha to Tibet.

9. If the property of a Gurkha merchant or other subject be plundered by a Tibetan subject, the Tibetan officials after inquiry will compel the restoration of such property to the owner. Should the plunderer not be able to restore such property, he shall be compelled by the Tibetan official to draw up an agreement to make good such property within an extended time. If the property of a Tibetan merchant or other subject be plundered by a Gurkha

subject, the Gurkha official after inquiry will compel the restoration of such property to the owner.   Should the plunderer not be able to restore such property, he shall be compelled by the Gurkha official to draw up an agreement to make good such property within an extended time.

10. After the completion of the Treaty neither Government will take vengeance [1] on the persons or property of Tibetan subjects who may have joined the Gurkha Government during the recent war, or on the persons or property of Gurkha subjects who may have so joined the Tibetan Government.

Dated the 18th day of the 2nd month of the Fire-Dragon Year.[2]

APPENDIX V

CONVENTION BETWEEN GREAT BRITAIN AND CHINA RELATING TO SIKKIM AND TIBET, 1890

Signed at Calcutta on the 17th March 1890.
Ratified at London on the 27th August 1890.

Whereas Her Majesty the Queen of the United Kingdom of Great Britain and Ireland, Empress of India, and His Majesty the Emperor of China, are sincerely desirous to maintain and perpetuate the relations of friendship and good understanding which now exist between their respective Empires ; and whereas recent occurrences have tended towards a disturbance of the said relations, and it is desirable to clearly define and permanently settle certain matters connected with the boundary between Sikkim and Tibet, Her Britannic Majesty and His Majesty the Emperor of China have resolved to conclude a Convention on this subject, and have, for this purpose, named Plenipotentiaries, that is to say :

Her Majesty the Queen of Great Britain and Ireland, His Excellency the Most Honourable Henry Charles Keith Petty Fitzmaurice, G.M.S.I., G.C.M.G., G.M.I.E., Marquess of Lansdowne, Viceroy and Governor-General of India,

And His Majesty the Emperor of China, His Excellency Shêng Tai, Imperial Associate Resident in Tibet, Military Deputy Lieutenant-Governor ;

Who, having met and communicated to each other their full powers, and finding these to be in proper form, have agreed upon the following Convention in eight Articles :—

ARTICLE I.

The boundary of Sikkim and Tibet shall be the crest of the mountain range separating the waters flowing into the Sikkim Teesta and

---

[1] *Lit.* ' be angry with '.   [2] 1856.

its affluents from the waters flowing into the Tibetan Mochu and northwards into other rivers of Tibet. The line commences at Mount Gipmochi on the Bhutan frontier, and follows the above-mentioned water-parting to the point where it meets Nipal territory.

ARTICLE II.

It is admitted that the British Government, whose Protectorate over the Sikkim State is hereby recognized, has direct and exclusive control over the internal administration and foreign relations of that State, and except through and with the permission of the British Government, neither the Ruler of the State nor any of its officers shall have official relations of any kind, formal or informal, with any other country.

ARTICLE III.

The Government of Great Britain and Ireland and the Government of China engage reciprocally to respect the boundary as defined in Article I, and to prevent acts of aggression from their respective sides of the frontier.

ARTICLE IV.

The question of providing increased facilities for trade across the Sikkim-Tibet frontier will hereafter be discussed with a view to a mutually satisfactory arrangement by the High Contracting Powers.

ARTICLE V.

The question of pasturage on the Sikkim side of the frontier is reserved for further examination and future adjustment.

ARTICLE VI.

The High Contracting Powers reserve for discussion and arrangement the method in which official communications between the British authorities in India and the authorities in Tibet shall be conducted.

ARTICLE VII.

Two joint Commissioners shall, within six months from the ratification of this Convention, be appointed, one by the British Government in India, the other by the Chinese Resident in Tibet. The said Commissioners shall meet and discuss the questions which, by the last three preceding Articles, have been reserved.

ARTICLE VIII.

The present Convention shall be ratified, and the ratifications shall be exchanged in London as soon as possible after the date of the signature thereof.

In witness whereof the respective negotiators have signed the same, and affixed thereunto the seals of their arms.

Done in quadruplicate at Calcutta, this 17th day of March, in the year of our Lord 1890, corresponding with the Chinese date, the 27th day of the second moon of this 16th year of Kuang Hsü.

APPENDIX VI

REGULATIONS OF 1893 REGARDING TRADE, COMMUNICA-
TION, AND PASTURAGE TO BE APPENDED TO THE
SIKKIM-TIBET CONVENTION OF 1890

Signed at Darjeeling, India, on the 5th December 1893.

I.—A trade-mart shall be established at Yatung on the Tibetan
side of the frontier, and shall be open to all
British subjects for purposes of trade from the
first day of May 1894. The Government of India shall be free to
send officers to reside at Yatung to watch the conditions of British
trade at that mart.

Trade.

II.—British subjects trading at Yatung shall be at liberty to travel
freely to and fro between the frontier and Yatung, to reside at
Yatung, and to rent houses and godowns for their own accommodation and the storage of their goods. The Chinese Government
undertake that suitable buildings for the above purposes shall be
provided for British subjects, and also that a special and fitting
residence shall be provided for the officer or officers appointed by
the Government of India under Regulation I to reside at Yatung.
British subjects shall be at liberty to sell their goods to whomsoever
they please, to purchase native commodities in kind or in money,
to hire transport of any kind, and in general to conduct their business transactions in conformity with local usage, and without any
vexatious restrictions. Such British subjects shall receive efficient
protection for their persons and property. At Lang-jo and Ta-chun,
between the frontier and Yatung, where rest-houses have been built
by the Tibetan authorities, British subjects can break their journey
in consideration of a daily rent.

III.—Import and export trade in the following articles—

   arms, ammunition, military stores, salt, liquors, and intoxi-
   cating or narcotic drugs,

may at the option of either Government be entirely prohibited,
   or permitted only on such conditions as either Government
   on their own side may think fit to impose.

IV.—Goods, other than goods of the description enumerated in
Regulation III, entering Tibet from British India, across the Sikkim-
Tibet frontier, or *vice versâ*, whatever their origin, shall be exempt
from duty for a period of five years commencing from the date of
the opening of Yatung to trade ; but after the expiration of this
term, if found desirable, a tariff may be mutually agreed upon and
enforced.

Indian tea may be imported into Tibet at a rate of duty not
exceeding that at which Chinese tea is imported into England, but

trade in Indian tea shall not be engaged in during the five years for which other commodities are exempt.

V.—All goods on arrival at Yatung, whether from British India or from Tibet, must be reported at the Customs Station there for examination, and the report must give full particulars of the description, quantity, and value of the goods.

VI.—In the event of trade disputes arising between British and Chinese or Tibetan subjects in Tibet, they shall be inquired into and settled in personal conference by the Political Officer for Sikkim and the Chinese Frontier Officer. The object of personal conference being to ascertain facts and do justice, where there is a divergence of views the law of the country to which the defendant belongs shall guide.

VII.—Dispatches from the Government of India to the Chinese Imperial Resident in Tibet shall be handed over Communication. by the Political Officer for Sikkim to the Chinese Frontier Officer, who will forward them by special courier.

Dispatches from the Chinese Imperial Resident in Tibet to the Government of India will be handed over by the Chinese Frontier Officer to the Political Officer for Sikkim, who will forward them as quickly as possible.

VIII.—Dispatches between the Chinese and Indian officials must be treated with due respect, and couriers will be assisted in passing to and fro by the officers of each Government.

IX.—After the expiration of one year from the date of the opening of Yatung, such Tibetans as continue to graze Pasturage. their cattle in Sikkim will be subject to such Regulations as the British Government may from time to time enact for the general conduct of grazing in Sikkim. Due notice will be given of such Regulations.

GENERAL ARTICLES.

I.—In the event of disagreement between the Political Officer for Sikkim and the Chinese Frontier Officer, each official shall report the matter to his immediate superior, who, in turn, if a settlement is not arrived at between them, shall refer such matter to their respective Governments for disposal.

II.—After the lapse of five years from the date on which these Regulations shall come into force, and on six months' notice given by either party, these Regulations shall be subject to revision by Commissioners appointed on both sides for this purpose who shall be empowered to decide on and adopt such amendments and extensions as experience shall prove to be desirable.

III.—It having been stipulated that Joint Commissioners should be appointed by the British and Chinese Governments under the seventh article of the Sikkim-Tibet Convention to meet and discuss, with a view to the final settlement of the questions reserved under articles 4, 5 and 6 of the said Convention ; and the Commissioners thus appointed having met and discussed the questions referred to, namely, Trade, Communication, and Pasturage, have been further appointed to sign the agreement in nine Regulations and three General Articles now arrived at, and to declare that the said nine Regulations and the three General Articles form part of the Convention itself.

In witness whereof the respective Commissioners have hereto subscribed their names.

Done in quadruplicate at Darjeeling this 5th day of December, in the year one thousand eight hundred and ninety-three, corresponding with the Chinese date the 28th day of the 10th moon of the 19th year of Kuang Hsü.

APPENDIX VII

CONVENTION BETWEEN GREAT BRITAIN AND TIBET, 1904

Signed at Lhasa on the 7th September 1904.
Ratified at Simla on the 11th November 1904.

Whereas doubts and difficulties have arisen as to the meaning and validity of the Anglo-Chinese Convention of 1890, and the Trade Regulations of 1893, and as to the liabilities of the Tibetan Government under these agreements ; and whereas recent occurrences have tended towards a disturbance of the relations of friendship and good understanding which have existed between the British Government and the Government of Tibet ; and whereas it is desirable to restore peace and amicable relations, and to resolve and determine the doubts and difficulties as aforesaid, the said Governments have resolved to conclude a Convention with these objects, and the following articles have been agreed upon by Colonel F. E. Younghusband, C.I.E., in virtue of full powers vested in him by His Britannic Majesty's Government and on behalf of that said Government, and Lo-Sang Gyal-Tsen, the Ga-den Ti-Rimpoche, and the representatives of the Council, of the three monasteries Se-ra, Dre-pung and Ga-den, and of the ecclesiastical and lay officials of the National Assembly on behalf of the Government of Tibet :—

I.

The Government of Tibet engages to respect the Anglo-Chinese Convention of 1890 and to recognize the frontier between Sikkim and Tibet, as defined in Article I of the said Convention, and to erect boundary pillars accordingly.

II.

The Tibetan Government undertakes to open forthwith trade marts to which all British and Tibetan subjects shall have free right of access at Gyantse and Gartók, as well as at Yatung.

The Regulations applicable to the trade mart at Yatung, under the Anglo-Chinese Agreement of 1893, shall, subject to such amendments as may hereafter be agreed upon by common consent between the British and Tibetan Governments, apply to the marts above mentioned.

In addition to establishing trade marts at the places mentioned, the Tibetan Government undertakes to place no restrictions on the trade by existing routes, and to consider the question of establishing fresh trade marts under similar conditions if development of trade requires it.

III.

The question of the amendment of the Regulations of 1893 is reserved for separate consideration, and the Tibetan Government undertakes to appoint fully authorized delegates to negotiate with representatives of the British Government as to the details of the amendments required.

IV.

The Tibetan Government undertakes to levy no dues of any kind other than those provided for in the tariff to be mutually agreed upon.

V.

The Tibetan Government undertakes to keep the roads to Gyantse and Gartok from the frontier clear of all obstruction and in a state of repair suited to the needs of the trade, and to establish at Yatung, Gyantse, and Gartok, and at each of the other trade marts that may hereafter be established, a Tibetan Agent who shall receive from the British Agent appointed to watch over British trade at the marts in question any letter which the latter may desire to send to the Tibetan or to the Chinese authorities. The Tibetan Agent shall also be responsible for the due delivery of such communications and for the transmission of replies.

VI.

As an indemnity to the British Government for the expense incurred in the dispatch of armed troops to Lhasa, to exact reparation for breaches of treaty obligations, and for the insults offered to and attacks upon the British Commissioner and his following and escort, the Tibetan Government engages to pay a sum of pounds five hundred thousand—equivalent to rupees seventy-five lakhs— to the British Government.

The indemnity shall be payable at such place as the British

Government may from time to time, after due notice, indicate whether in Tibet or in the British districts of Darjeeling or Jalpaiguri, in seventy-five annual instalments of rupees one lakh each on the 1st January in each year, beginning from the 1st January 1906.

VII.

As security for the payment of the above-mentioned indemnity, and for the fulfilment of the provisions relative to trade marts specified in Articles II, III, IV, and V, the British Government shall continue to occupy the Chumbi Valley until the indemnity has been paid and until the trade marts have been effectively opened for three years, whichever date may be the later.

VIII.

The Tibetan Government agrees to raze all forts and fortifications and remove all armaments which might impede the course of free communication between the British frontier and the towns of Gyantse and Lhasa.

IX.

The Government of Tibet engages that, without the previous consent of the British Government,—

(a) no portion of Tibetan territory shall be ceded, sold, leased, mortgaged or otherwise given for occupation, to any Foreign Power ;

(b) no such Power shall be permitted to intervene in Tibetan affairs ;

(c) no Representatives or Agents of any Foreign Power shall be admitted to Tibet ;

(d) no concessions for railways, roads, telegraphs, mining or other rights, shall be granted to any Foreign Power, or to the subject of any Foreign Power. In the event of consent to such concessions being granted, similar or equivalent concessions shall be granted to the British Government ;

(e) no Tibetan revenues, whether in kind or in cash, shall be pledged or assigned to any Foreign Power, or to the subject of any Foreign Power.

X.

In witness whereof the negotiators have signed the same, and affixed hereunto the seals of their arms.

Done in quintuplicate at Lhasa, this 7th day of September in the year of our Lord one thousand nine hundred and four, corresponding with the Tibetan date, the 27th day of the seventh month of the Wood Dragon year.

DECLARATION SIGNED BY THE VICEROY OF INDIA ON THE 11TH NOVEMBER 1904, AND APPENDED TO THE RATIFIED CONVENTION OF 7TH SEPTEMBER 1904

His Excellency the Viceroy and Governor-General of India, having ratified the Convention which was concluded at Lhasa on 7th September 1904 by Colonel Younghusband, C.I.E., British Commissioner for Tibet Frontier Matters, on behalf of His Britannic Majesty's Government ; and by Losang Gyal-Tsen, the Ga-den Ti-Rimpoche, and the representatives of the Council, of the three monasteries Sera, Dre-pung, and Ga-den, and of the ecclesiastical and lay officials of the National Assembly, on behalf of the Government of Tibet, is pleased to direct as an act of grace that the sum of money which the Tibetan Government have bound themselves under the terms of Article VI of the said Convention to pay to His Majesty's Government as an indemnity for the expenses incurred by th· latter in connection with the dispatch of armed for·es to Lhasa, be reduced from Rs. 75,00,000 to Rs. 25,00,000 ; and to declare that the British occupation of the Chumbi valley shall cease after the due payment of three annual instalments of the said indemnity as fixed by the said Article, provided, however, that the trade marts as stipulated in Article II of the Convention shall have been effectively opened for three years as provided in Article VI of the Convention : and that, in the meantime, the Tibetans shall have faithfully complied with the terms of the said Convention in all other respects.

APPENDIX VIII

CONVENTION BETWEEN GREAT BRITAIN AND CHINA, 1906

Signed at Peking on the 27th April 1906. Ratified at London on the 23rd July 1906.

Whereas His Majesty the King of Great Britain and Ireland and of the British Dominions beyond the seas, Emperor of India, and His Majesty the Emperor of China are sincerely desirous to maintain and perpetuate the relations of friendship and good understanding which now exist between their respective Empires ;

And whereas the refusal of Tibet to recognize the validity of or to carry into full effect the provisions of the Anglo-Chinese Convention of 17th March 1890, and Regulations of 5th December 1893, placed the British Government under the necessity of taking steps to secure their rights and interests under the said Convention and Regulations ;

And whereas a Convention of ten articles was signed at Lhasa on

7th September, 1904, on behalf of Great Britain and Tibet, and was ratified by the Viceroy and Governor-General of India on behalf of Great Britain on 11th November, 1904, a declaration on behalf of Great Britain modifying its terms under certain conditions being appended thereto ;

His Britannic Majesty and His Majesty the Emperor of China have resolved to conclude a Convention on this subject and have for this purpose named Plenipotentiaries, that is to say :—

HIS MAJESTY THE KING OF GREAT BRITAIN AND IRELAND :

Sir Ernest Mason Satow, Knight Grand Cross of the Most Distinguished Order of St. Michael and St. George, His said Majesty's Envoy Extraordinary and Minister Plenipotentiary to His Majesty the Emperor of China ;

AND HIS MAJESTY THE EMPEROR OF CHINA :

His Excellency Tong Shoa-yi, His said Majesty's High Commissioner Plenipotentiary and a Vice-President of the Board of Foreign Affairs,

who having communicated to each other their respective full powers and finding them to be in good and due form have agreed upon and concluded the following Convention in six articles :—

ARTICLE I.

The Convention concluded on 7th September, 1904, by Great Britain and Tibet, the texts of which in English and Chinese are attached to the present Convention as an annexe, is hereby confirmed, subject to the modification stated in the declaration appended thereto, and both of the High Contracting Parties engage to take at all times such steps as may be necessary to secure the due fulfilment of the terms specified therein.

ARTICLE II.

The Government of Great Britain engages not to annex Tibetan territory or to interfere in the administration of Tibet. The Government of China also undertakes not to permit any other foreign state to interfere with the territory or internal administration of Tibet.

ARTICLE III.

The concessions which are mentioned in Article 9 (d) of the Convention concluded on 7th September, 1904, by Great Britain and Tibet are denied to any state or to the subject of any state other than China, but it has been arranged with China that at the trade marts specified in Article 2 of the aforesaid Convention Great Britain shall be entitled to lay down telegraph lines connecting with India.

ARTICLE IV.

The provisions of the Anglo-Chinese Convention of 1890 and Regulations of 1893 shall, subject to the terms of this present Convention and annexe thereto, remain in full force.

ARTICLE V.

The English and Chinese texts of the present Convention have been carefully compared and found to correspond, but in the event of there being any difference of meaning between them the English text shall be authoritative.

ARTICLE VI.

This Convention shall be ratified by the Sovereigns of both countries and ratifications shall be exchanged at London within three months after the date of signature by the Plenipotentiaries of both Powers.

In token whereof the respective Plenipotentiaries have signed and sealed this Convention, four copies in English and four in Chinese.

Done at Peking this twenty-seventh day of April, one thousand nine hundred and six, being the fourth day of the fourth month of the thirty-second year of the reign of Kuang-hsü.

APPENDIX IX

CONVENTION BETWEEN GREAT BRITAIN AND RUSSIA, 1907

Signed at St. Petersburg on the 18th (31st) August 1907.

His Majesty the King of the United Kingdom of Great Britain and Ireland and of the British Dominions beyond the Seas, Emperor of India, and His Majesty the Emperor of All the Russias, animated by the sincere desire to settle by mutual agreement different questions concerning the interests of their States on the Continent of Asia, have determined to conclude Agreements destined to prevent all cause of misunderstanding between Great Britain and Russia in regard to the questions referred to, and have nominated for this purpose their respective Plenipotentiaries, to wit :

His Majesty the King of the United Kingdom of Great Britain and Ireland and of the British Dominions beyond the Seas, Emperor of India, the Right Honourable Sir Arthur Nicolson, His Majesty's Ambassador Extraordinary and Plenipotentiary to His Majesty the Emperor of All the Russias ;

His Majesty the Emperor of All the Russias, the Master of his Court Alexander Iswolsky, Minister for Foreign Affairs ;

Who, having communicated to each other their full powers, found in good and due form, have agreed on the following :—

* * * * * * * * * * *

Arrangement concerning Thibet.

The Governments of Great Britain and Russia recognizing the suzerain rights of China in Thibet, and considering the fact that Great Britain, by reason of her geographical position, has a special interest in the maintenance of the *status quo* in the external relations of Thibet, have made the following arrangement :—

ARTICLE I.

The two High Contracting Parties engage to respect the territorial integrity of Thibet and to abstain from all interference in the internal administration.

ARTICLE II.

In conformity with the admitted principle of the suzerainty of China over Thibet, Great Britain and Russia engage not to enter into negotiations with Thibet except through the intermediary of the Chinese Government. This engagement does not exclude the direct relations between British Commercial Agents and the Thibetan authorities provided for in Article V of the Convention between Great Britain and Thibet of the 7th September 1904, and confirmed by the Convention between Great Britain and China of the 27th April 1906 ; nor does it modify the engagements entered into by Great Britain and China in Article I of the said Convention of 1906.

It is clearly understood that Buddhists, subjects of Great Britain or of Russia, may enter into direct relations on strictly religious matters with the Dalai Lama and the other representatives of Buddhism in Thibet ; the Governments of Great Britain and Russia engage, as far as they are concerned, not to allow those relations to infringe the stipulations of the present arrangement.

ARTICLE III.

The British and Russian Governments respectively engage not to send Representatives to Lhassa.

ARTICLE IV.

The two High Contracting Parties engage neither to seek nor to obtain, whether for themselves or their subjects, any Concessions for railways, roads, telegraphs, and mines, or other rights in Thibet.

ARTICLE V.

The two Governments agree that no part of the revenues of Thibet, whether in kind or in cash, shall be pledged or assigned to Great Britain or Russia or to any of their subjects.

Annex to the arrangement between Great Britain and
Russia concerning Thibet.

Great Britain reaffirms the declaration, signed by His Excellency
the Viceroy and Governor-General of India and appended to the
ratification of the Convention of the 7th September 1904, to the
effect that the occupation of the Chumbi Valley by British forces
shall cease after the payment of three annual instalments of the
indemnity of 25,00,000 rupees, provided that the trade marts mentioned in Article II of that Convention have been effectively opened
for three years, and that in the meantime the Thibetan authorities
have faithfully complied in all respects with the terms of the said
Convention of 1904. It is clearly understood that if the occupation
of the Chumbi Valley by the British forces has, for any reason, not
been terminated at the time anticipated in the above Declaration,
the British and Russian Governments will enter upon a friendly
exchange of views on this subject.

The present Convention shall be ratified, and the ratifications
exchanged at St. Petersburgh as soon as possible.

In witness whereof the respective Plenipotentiaries have signed
the present Convention and affixed thereto their seals.

Done in duplicate at St. Petersburgh, the 18th (31st) August 1907.

APPENDIX X

TIBET TRADE REGULATIONS, 1908.

Signed at Calcutta on the 20th April 1908.

Preamble.—Whereas by Article I of the Convention between Great
Britain and China on the 27th April 1906, that is the 4th day of
the 4th moon of the 32nd year of Kwang Hsü, it was provided that
both the High Contracting Parties should engage to take at all
times such steps as might be necessary to secure the due fulfilment
of the terms specified in the Lhasa Convention of 7th September
1904 between Great Britain and Tibet, the text of which in English
and Chinese was attached as an Annexe to the above-mentioned
Convention ;

And whereas it was stipulated in Article III of the said Lhasa
Convention that the question of the amendment of the Tibet Trade
Regulations which were signed by the British and Chinese Com-
missioners on the 5th day of December 1893 should be reserved
for separate consideration, and whereas the amendment of these
Regulations is now necessary ;

His Majesty the King of the United Kingdom of Great Britain
and Ireland, and of the British Dominions beyond the Seas, Emperor

of India, and His Majesty the Emperor of the Chinese Empire have for this purpose named as their Plenipotentiaries, that is to say :

His Majesty the King of Great Britain and Ireland and of the British Dominions beyond the Seas, Emperor of India,—Mr. E. C. Wilton, C.M.G. ;

His Majesty the Emperor of the Chinese Empire—His Majesty's Special Commissioner Chang Yin Tang ;

And the High Authorities of Tibet have named as their fully authorized Representative to act under the directions of Chang Tachen and take part in the negotiations—The Tsarong Shape, Wang Chuk Gyalpo.

And whereas Mr. E. C. Wilton and Chang Tachen have communicated to each other since their respective full powers and have found them to be in good and true form and have found the authorization of the Tibetan Delegate to be also in good and true form, the following amended Regulations have been agreed upon :—

I.—The Trade Regulations of 1893 shall remain in force in so far as they are not inconsistent with these Regulations.

II.—The following places shall form, and be included within, the boundaries of the Gyantse mart :—

(a) The line begins at the Chumig Dangsang (Chhu-Mig-Dangs-Sangs) north-east of the Gyantse Fort, and thence it runs in a curved line, passing behind the Pekor-Chode (Dpal-Hkhor-Chos-Sde), down to Chag-Dong-Gang (Phyag-Gdong-Sgang) ; thence, passing straight over the Nyan Chu, it reaches the Zamsa (Zam-Srag). (b) From the Zamsa the line continues to run, in a south-eastern direction, round to Lachi-To (Gla-Dkyii-Stod), embracing all the farms on its way, viz., The Lahong ; The Hogtso (Hog-Mtsho) ; The Tong-Chung-Shi (Grong-Chhung-Gshis) , and the Rabgang (Rab-Sgang), &c. ; (c) From Lachi-To the line runs to the Yutog (Gyu-Thog), and thence runs straight, passing through the whole area of Gamkar-Shi (Ragal-Mkhar-Gshis), to Chumig Dangsang.

As difficulty is experienced in obtaining suitable houses and godowns at some of the marts, it is agreed that British subjects may also lease lands for the building of houses and godowns at the marts, the locality for such building sites to be marked out specially at each mart by the Chinese and Tibetan Authorities in consultation with the British Trade Agent. The British Trade Agents and British subjects shall not build houses and godowns except in such localities, and this arrangement shall not be held to prejudice in any way the administration of the Chinese and Tibetan Local Authorities over such localities, or the right of British subjects to rent houses and godowns outside such localities for their own accommodation and the storage of their goods.

British subjects desiring to lease building sites shall apply through the British Trade Agent to the Municipal Office at the mart for a permit to lease. The amount of rent, or the period or conditions of the lease, shall then be settled in a friendly way by the lessee and the owner themselves. In the event of a disagreement between the owner and lessee as to the amount of rent or the period or conditions of the lease the case will be settled by the Chinese and Tibetan Authorities in consultation with the British Trade Agent. After the lease is settled, the sites shall be verified by the Chinese and Tibetan Officers of the Municipal Office conjointly with the British Trade Agent. No building is to be commenced by the lessee on a site before the Municipal Office has issued him a permit to build, but it is agreed that there shall be no vexatious delays in the issue of such permit.

III.—The administration of the trade marts shall remain with the Tibetan Officers, under the Chinese Officers' supervision and directions.

The Trade Agents at the marts and Frontier Officers shall be of suitable rank, and shall hold personal intercourse and correspondence one with another on terms of mutual respect and friendly treatment.

Questions which cannot be decided by agreement between the Trade Agents and the Local Authorities shall be referred for settlement to the Government of India and the Tibetan High Authorities at Lhasa. The purport of a reference by the Government of India will be communicated to the Chinese Imperial Resident at Lhasa. Questions which cannot be decided by agreement between the Government of India and the Tibetan High Authorities at Lhasa shall, in accordance with the terms of Article I of the Peking Convention of 1906, be referred for settlement to the Governments of Great Britain and China.

IV.—In the event of disputes arising at the marts between British subjects and persons of Chinese and Tibetan nationalities, they shall be inquired into and settled in personal conference between the British Trade Agent at the nearest mart and the Chinese and Tibetan Authorities of the Judicial Court at the mart, the object of personal conference being to ascertain facts and to do justice. Where there is a divergence of view the law of the country to which the defendant belongs shall guide. In any of such mixed cases, the Officer, or Officers of the defendant's nationality shall preside at the trial ; the Officer, or Officers of the plaintiff's country merely attending to watch the course of the trial.

All questions in regard to rights, whether of property or person, arising between British subjects, shall be subject to the jurisdiction of the British Authorities.

British subjects, who may commit any crime at the marts or on the routes to the marts, shall be handed over by the Local Authorities to the British Trade Agent at the mart nearest to the scene of offence, to be tried and punished according to the laws of India, but such British subjects shall not be subjected by the Local Authorities to any ill-usage in excess of necessary restraint.

Chinese and Tibetan subjects, who may be guilty of any criminal act towards British subjects at the marts or on the routes thereto, shall be arrested and punished by the Chinese and Tibetan Authorities according to law.

Justice shall be equitably and impartially administered on both sides.

Should it happen that Chinese or Tibetan subjects bring a criminal complaint against a British subject before the British Trade Agent, the Chinese or Tibetan Authorities shall have the right to send a representative, or representatives, to watch the course of trial in the British Trade Agent's Court. Similarly, in cases in which a British subject has reason to complain of a Chinese or Tibetan subject in the Judicial Court at the mart, the British Trade Agent shall have the right to send a representative to the Judicial Court to watch the course of trial.

V.—The Tibetan Authorities, in obedience to the instructions of the Peking Government, having a strong desire to reform the judicial system of Tibet, and to bring it into accord with that of Western nations, Great Britain agrees to relinquish her rights of extra-territoriality in Tibet, whenever such rights are relinquished in China, and when she is satisfied that the state of the Tibetan laws and the arrangements for their administration and oth r considerations warrant her in so doing.

VI.—After the withdrawal of the British troops, all the rest-houses, eleven in number, built by Great Britain upon the routes leading from the Indian frontier to Gyantse, shall be taken over at original cost by China and rented to the Government of India at a fair rate. One-half of each rest-house will be reserved for the use of the British officials employed on the inspection and maintenance of the telegraph lines from the marts to the Indian frontier and for the storage of their materials, but the rest-houses shall otherwise be available for occupation by British, Chinese, and Tibetan officers of respectability who may proceed to and from the marts.

Great Britain is prepared to consider the transfer to China of the telegraph lines from the Indian frontier to Gyantse when the telegraph lines from China reach that mart and in the meantime Chinese and Tibetan messages will be duly received and transmitted by the line constructed by the Government of India.

In the meantime China shall be responsible for the due protection of the telegraph lines from the marts to the Indian frontier and it is agreed that all persons damaging the lines or interfering in any way with them or with the officials engaged in the inspection or maintenance thereof shall at once be severely punished by the Local Authorities.

VII.—In law suits involving cases of debt on account of loans, commercial failure, and bankruptcy, the authorities concerned shall grant a hearing and take steps necessary to enforce payment ; but, if the debtor plead poverty and be without means, the authorities concerned shall not be held responsible for the said debts, nor shall any public or official property be distrained upon in order to satisfy these debts.

VIII.—The British Trade Agents at the various trade marts now or hereafter to be established in Tibet may make arrangements for the carriage and transmission of their posts to and from the frontier of India. The couriers employed in conveying these posts shall receive all possible assistance from the Local Authorities whose districts they traverse and shall be accorded the same protection as the persons employed in carrying the dispatches of the Tibetan Authorities. When efficient arrangements have been made by China in Tibet for a Postal Service, the question of the abolition of the Trade Agents' couriers will be taken into consideration by Great Britain and China. No restrictions whatever shall be placed on the employment by British officers and traders of Chinese and Tibetan subjects in any lawful capacity. The persons so employed shall not be exposed to any kind of molestation or suffer any loss of civil rights to which they may be entitled as Tibetan subjects, but they shall not be exempted from all lawful taxation. If they be guilty of any criminal act, they shall be dealt with by the Local Authorities according to law without any attempt on the part of their employer to screen or conceal them.

IX.—British officers and subjects, as well as goods, proceeding to the trade marts, must adhere to the trade routes from the frontier of India. They shall not, without permission, proceed beyond the marts, or to Gartok from Yatung and Gyantse, or from Gartok to Yatung and Gyantse, by any route through the interior of Tibet, but natives of the Indian frontier, who have already by usage traded and resided in Tibet, elsewhere than at the marts shall be at liberty to continue their trade, in accordance with the existing practice, but when so trading or residing they shall remain, as heretofore, amenable to the local jurisdiction.

X.—In cases where officials or traders, *en route* to and from India or Tibet are robbed of treasure or merchandise, public or private, they shall forthwith report to the Police officers, who shall take immediate measures to arrest the robbers, and hand them to the Local Authorities. The Local Authorities shall bring them to instant trial, and shall also recover and restore the stolen property. But, if the robbers flee to places out of the jurisdiction and influence of Tibet, and cannot be arrested, the Police and the Local Authorities shall not be held responsible for such losses.

XI.—For public safety tanks or stores of kerosene oil or any other combustible or dangerous articles in bulk must be placed far away from inhabited places at the marts.

British or Indian merchants, wishing to build such tanks or stores, may not do so until, as provided in Regulation II, they have made application for a suitable site.

XII.—British subjects shall be at liberty to deal in kind or in money, to sell their goods to whomsoever they please, to purchase native commodities from whomsoever they please, to hire transport of any kind, and to conduct in general their business transactions in conformity with local usage and without any vexatious restrictions or oppressive exactions whatever.

It being the duty of the Police and Local Authorities to afford efficient protection at all times to the persons and property of the British subjects at the marts, and along the routes to the marts, China engages to arrange effective police measures at the marts and along the routes to the marts. On due fulfilment of these arrangements, Great Britain undertakes to withdraw the Trade Agents' guards at the marts and to station no troops in Tibet so as to remove all cause for suspicion and disturbance among the inhabitants. The Chinese Authorities will not prevent the British Trade Agents holding personal intercourse and correspondence with the Tibetan officers and people.

Tibetan subjects trading, travelling or residing in India shall receive equal advantages to those accorded by this Regulation to British subjects in Tibet.

XIII.—The present Regulations shall be in force for a period of ten years reckoned from the date of signature by the two Plenipotentiaries as well as by the Tibetan Delegate ; but if no demand for revision be made on either side within six months after the end of the first ten years, then the Regulations shall remain in force for another ten years, from the end of the first ten years ; and so it shall be at the end of each successive ten years.

XIV.—The English, Chinese, and Tibetan texts of the present Regulations have been carefully compared, and, in the event of any question arising as to the interpretation of these Regulations, the sense as expressed in the English text shall be held to be the correct sense.

XV.—The Ratifications of the present Regulations under the hand of His Majesty the King of Great Britain and Ireland, and of His Majesty the Emperor of the Chinese Empire, respectively, shall be exchanged at London and Peking within six months from the date of signature.

In witness whereof the two Plenipotentiaries and the Tibetan Delegate have signed and sealed the present Regulations.

Done in quadruplicate at Calcutta, this twentieth day of April, in the year of our Lord nineteen hundred and eight, corresponding with the Chinese date, the twentieth day of the third moon of the thirty-fourth year of Kuang Hsü.

APPENDIX XI

TREATY BETWEEN GREAT BRITAIN AND BHUTAN, 1910.

Signed at Punaka, Bhutan, on the 8th January 1910.
Ratified at Calcutta on the 24th March 1910.

Whereas it is desirable to amend Articles IV and VIII of the Treaty concluded at Sinchula on the 11th day of November 1865, corresponding with the Bhutia year Shing Lang, 24th day of the 9th month, between the British Government and the Government of Bhutan, the undermentioned amendments are agreed to on the one part by Mr. C. A. Bell, Political Officer in Sikkim, in virtue of full powers to that effect vested in him by the Right Honourable Sir Gilbert John Elliot-Murray-Kynynmound, P.C., G.M.S.I., G.M.I.E., G.C.M.G., Earl of Minto, Viceroy and Governor-General of India in Council, and on the other part by His Highness Sir Ugyen Wangchuk, K.C.I.E., Maharaja of Bhutan.

The following addition has been made to Article IV of the Sinchula Treaty of 1865.

'The British Government has increased the annual allowance to the Government of Bhutan from fifty thousand rupees (Rs. 50,000) to one hundred thousand rupees (Rs. 100,000) with effect from the 10th January 1910.'

Article VIII of the Sinchula Treaty of 1865 has been revised and the revised Article runs as follows :—

' 'The British Government undertakes to exercise no interference in the internal administration of Bhutan. On its part, the Bhutanese Government agrees to be guided by the advice of the British Government in regard to its external relations. In the event of disputes with or causes of complaint against the Maharajas of Sikkim and Cooch Behar, such matters will be referred for arbitration to the British Government, which will settle them in such manner as justice may require, and insist upon the observance of its decision by the Maharajas named.'

Done in quadruplicate at Punaka, Bhutan, this eighth day of January in the year of our Lord one thousand nine hundred and ten, corresponding with the Bhutia date, the 27th day of the 11th month of the Earth-Bird (Sa-ja) year.

APPENDIX XII

RUSSO-MONGOLIAN AGREEMENT AND PROTOCOL [1]

Signed at Urga on the 21st [2] October (3rd November) 1912.

AGREEMENT.

In accordance with the desire unanimously expressed by the Mongolians to maintain the national and historic constitution of their country, the Chinese troops and authorities were obliged to evacuate Mongolian territory, and Djebzoun Damba-Khutukhta was proclaimed Ruler of the Mongolian people. The old relations between Mongolia and China thus came to an end.

At the present moment, taking into consideration the facts stated above, as well as the mutual friendship which has always existed between the Russian and Mongolian nations, and in view of the necessity of defining exactly the system regulating trade between Russia and Mongolia ;

The actual State Councillor Ivan Korostovetz, duly authorized for the purpose by the Imperial Russian Government ; and

The protector of the ten thousand doctrines Sain-noin Khan Namnan-Souroun, President of the Council of Ministers of Mongolia ;

The plenipotentiary Tchin-souzouktou Tzin-van Lama Tzerin-Tchimet, Minister of the Interior ;

The plenipotentiary Daitzin-van Handa-dorji, of the rank of Khan-erdeni, Minister for Foreign Affairs ;

The plenipotentiary Erdeni Dalai Tzun-van Gombo-Souroun, Minister of War ;

The plenipotentiary Touchetou Tzun-van Tchakdorjab, Minister of Finance ; and

The plenipotentiary Erdeni Tzun-van Namsarai, Minister of Justice ;

Duly authorized by the Ruler of the Mongolian nation, by the Mongolian Government and by the ruling Princes, have agreed a follows :—

ARTICLE 1.

The Imperial Russian Government shall assist Mongolia to maintain the autonomous régime which she has established, as also the right to have her national army, and to admit neither the presence of Chinese troops on her territory nor the colonization of her land by the Chinese.

ARTICLE 2.

The Ruler of Mongolia and the Mongolian Government shall grant, as in the past, to Russian subjects and trade the enjoyment

---

[1] Official copy [Cd. 6604].   [2] According to the Russian calendar.

in their possessions of the rights and privileges enumerated in the protocol annexed hereto.

It is well understood that there shall not be granted to other foreign subjects in Mongolia rights not enjoyed there by Russian subjects.

ARTICLE 3.

If the Mongolian Government finds it necessary to conclude a separate treaty with China or another foreign Power, the new treaty shall in no case either infringe the clauses of the present agreement and of the protocol annexed thereto, or modify them without the consent of the Imperial Russian Government.

ARTICLE 4.

The present amicable agreement shall come into force from the date of its signature.

In witness whereof the respective plenipotentiaries, having compared the two texts, Russian and Mongolian, of the present agreement, made in duplicate, and having found t e two texts to correspond, have signed them, have affixed thereto their seals, and have exchanged texts.

Done at Urga on the 21st October 1912, corresponding to the 24th day of the last autumn month of the 2nd year of the reign of the Unanimously Proclaimed, according to the Mongolian calendar.

Protocol annexed to Russo-Mongolian Agreement of the 21st October (3rd November) 1912.

By virtue of the enactment of the second article of the agreement, signed on this date between Actual State Councillor, Ivan Korostovetz, Plenipotentiary of the Imperial Russian Government, and the President of the Council of Ministers of Mongolia, Sain-noin Khan Namnan-Souroun, the Protector of ten thousand doctrines ; the Plenipotentiary and Minister of the Interior, Tchin-souzouktou Tzin-van Lama Tzerin-Tchimet ; the Plenipotentiary and Minister for Foreign Affairs, Daitzin-van Handa-dorji of the rank of Khanerdeni ; the Plenipotentiary and Minister of War, Erdeni Dalai Tzun-van Gombo-Souroun ; the Plenipotentiary and Minister of Finance, Touchetou Tzun-van Tchakdorjab ; and the Plenipotentiary and Minister of Justice, Erdeni Tzun-van Namsarai, on the authority of the Ruler of Mongolia, the Mongolian Government, and the Ruling Princes ; the above-named Plenipotentiaries have come to an agreement respecting the following articles, in which are set forth the rights and privileges of Russian subjects in Mongolia, some of which they already enjoy, and the rights and privileges of Mongolian subjects in Russia :—

ARTICLE 1.

Russian subjects, as formerly, shall enjoy the right to reside and move freely from one place to another throughout Mongolia ; to engage there in every kind of commercial, industrial, and other business ; and to enter into agreements of various kinds, whether with individuals, or firms, or institutions, official or private, Russian, Mongolian, Chinese, or foreign.

ARTICLE 2.

Russian subjects, as formerly, shall enjoy the right at all times to import and export, without payment of import and export dues, every kind of product of the soil and industry of Russia, Mongolia, and China, and other countries, and to trade freely in it without payment of any duties, taxes, or other dues.

The enactments of this (2nd) article shall not extend to combined Russo-Chinese undertakings, or to Russian subjects falsely declaring themselves to be owners of wares not their property.

ARTICLE 3.

Russian credit institutions shall have the right to open branches in Mongolia, and to transact all kinds of financial and other business, whether with individuals, institutions, or companies.

ARTICLE 4.

Russian subjects may conclude purchases and sales in cash or by an exchange of wares (barter), and they may conclude agreements on credit. Neither ' khoshuns ' nor the Mongolian Treasury shall be held responsible for the debts of private individuals.

ARTICLE 5.

The Mongolian authorities shall not preclude Mongolians or Chinese from completing any kind of commercial agreement with Russian subjects, from entering into their personal service, or into commercial and industrial undertakings formed by them. No rights of monopoly as regards commerce or industry shall be granted to any official or private companies, institutions, or individuals in Mongolia. It is, of course, understood that companies and individuals who have already received such monopolies from the Mongolian Government previous to the conclusion of this agreement shall retain their rights and privileges until the expiry of the period fixed.

ARTICLE 6.

Russian subjects shall be everywhere granted the right, whether in towns or ' khoshuns ', to hold allotments on lease, or to acquire them as their own property for the purpose of organizing commercial industrial establishments, and also for the purpose of constructing houses, shops, and stores. In addition, Russian subjects shall have the right to lease vacant lands for cultivation. It is, of course, understood that these allotments shall be obtained and leased for the above-specified purposes, and not for speculative aims. These allotments shall be assigned by agreement with the Mongolian Government in accordance with existing laws of Mongolia, everywhere excepting in sacred places and pasture lands.

ARTICLE 7.

Russian subjects shall be empowered to enter into agreements with the Mongolian Government respecting the working of minerals and timber, fisheries, &c.

ARTICLE 8.

The Russian Government shall have the right, in agreement with the Government of Mongolia, to appoint consuls in those parts of Mongolia it shall deem necessary.

Similarly, the Mongolian Government shall be empowered to have Government agents at those frontier parts of the Empire where, by mutual agreement, it shall be found necessary.

ARTICLE 9.

At points where there are Russian consulates, as also in other localities of importance for Russian trade, there shall be allotted, by mutual agreement between Russian consuls and the Mongolian Government, special ' factories ' for various branches of industry and the residence of Russian subjects. These ' factories ' shall be under the exclusive control of the above-mentioned consuls, or of the heads of Russian commercial companies if there be no Russian consul.

ARTICLE 10.

Russian subjects, in agreement with the Mongolian Government, shall retain the right to institute, at their own cost, a postal service for the dispatch of letters and the transit of wares between various localities in Mongolia and also between specified localities and points on the Russian frontier. In the event of the construction of ' stages ' and other necessary buildings, the regulations set forth in article 6 of this protocol must be duly observed.

ARTICLE 11.

Russian consuls in Mongolia, in case of need, shall avail themselves of Mongolian Government postal establishments and messengers for the dispatch of official correspondence, and for other official requirements, provided that the gratuitous requisition for this purpose shall not exceed one hundred horses and thirty camels per month. On every occasion, a courier's passport must be obtained from the Government of Mongolia. When travelling, Russian consuls, and Russian officials in general, shall avail themselves of the same establishments upon payment. The right to avail themselves of Mongolian Government ' stages ' shall be extended to private individuals, who are Russian subjects, upon payment for the use of such ' stages ' of amounts which shall be determined in agreement with the Mongolian Government.

ARTICLE 12.

Russian subjects shall be granted the right to sail their own merchant-vessels on, and to trade with the inhabitants along the banks of, those rivers and their tributaries which, running first through Mongolia, subsequently enter Russian territory. The Russian Government shall afford the Government of Mongolia assistance in the improvement of navigation on these rivers, the establishment of the necessary beacons, &c. The Mongolian Government authorities shall assign on these rivers places for the berthing of vessels, for the construction of wharves and warehouses, for the preparation of fuel, &c., being guided on these occasions by the enactments of article 6 of the present protocol.

ARTICLE 13.

Russian subjects shall have the right to avail themselves of all land and water routes for the carriage of wares and the droving of cattle, and, upon agreement with the Mongolian authorities, they may construct, at their own cost, bridges, ferries, &c., with the right to exact a special due from persons crossing over.

ARTICLE 14.

Travelling cattle, the property of Russian subjects, may stop for the purpose of resting and feeding. In the event of prolonged halts being necessary, the local authorities shall assign proper pasturage areas along travelling cattle routes, and at cattle markets. Fees shall be exacted for the use of these pasturing areas for periods exceeding three months.

ARTICLE 15.

The established usage of the Russian frontier population harvesting (hay), as also hunting and fishing, across the Mongolian border shall remain in force in the future without any alteration.

ARTICLE 16.

Agreements between Russian subjects and institutions on the one side and Mongolians and Chinese on the other may be concluded verbally or in writing, and the contracting parties may present the agreement concluded to the local Government authorities for certification. Should the latter see any objection to certifying the contract, they must immediately notify the fact to a Russian consul, and the misunderstanding which has arisen shall be settled in agreement with him.

It is hereby laid down that contracts respecting real estate must be in written form, and presented for certification and confirmation to the proper Mongolian Government authorities and a Russian consul. Documents bestowing rights to exploit natural resources require the confirmation of the Government of Mongolia.

In the event of disputes arising over agreements concluded verbally or in writing, the parties may settle the matter amicably with the assistance of arbitrators selected by each party. Should no settlement be reached by this method, the matter shall be decided by a mixed legal commission.

There shall be both permanent and temporary mixed legal commissions. Permanent commissions shall be instituted at the places of residence of Russian consuls, and shall consist of the consul, or his representative, and a delegate of the Mongolian authorities of corresponding rank. Temporary commissions shall be instituted at places other than those already specified, as cases arise, and shall consist of representatives of a Russian consul and the prince of that ' khoshun ' to which the defendant belongs or in which he resides. Mixed commissions shall be empowered to call in as experts persons with a knowledge of the case from among Russian subjects, Mongolians, and Chinese. The decisions of mixed legal commissions shall be put into execution without delay, in the case of Russian subjects through a Russian consul, and in the case of Mongolians and Chinese through the prince of the ' khoshun ' to which the defendant belongs or in which he is resident.

ARTICLE 17.

The present protocol shall come into force from the date of its signature.

In witness whereof, the respective plenipotentiaries, finding, upon comparison of the two parallel texts of the present protocol—Russian and Mongol—drawn up in duplicate, that the texts correspond, have signed each of them, affixed their seals, and exchanged texts.

Executed at Urga, the 21st October 1912 (o.s.), and by the Mongolian calendar, on the twenty-fourth day of the last autumn moon, in the second year of the administration of the ' Unanimously Proclaimed '.

In the original follow the signature of M. Korostovetz, Minister Plenipotentiary ; and in the Mongol language the signatures of the President of the Mongolian Council of Ministers, and the Plenipotentiaries, the Ministers of the Interior, Foreign Affairs, War, Finance, and of Justice.

APPENDIX XIII[1]

ALLEGED MONGOL-TIBETAN TREATY, 1913.

Said to have been signed at Urga in January 1913.

Whereas Mongolia and Tibet, having freed themselves from the Manchu dynasty and separated themselves from China, have become independent States, and whereas the two States have always professed one and the same religion, and to the end that their ancient mutual friendships may be strengthened : on the part of the Government of the Sovereign of the Mongolian people—Nikta Biliktu da Lama Rabdan, acting Minister of Foreign Affairs and Assistant Minister-General and Manlai Caatyr Bei-Tzu Damdinsurun ; on the part of the Dalai Lama, ruler of Tibet—Gujir tsanshib Kanchen Lubsan-Agwan, donir Agwan Choinzin, Tshichamtso, manager of the bank, and Gendun-Galsan, secretary, have agreed on the following :—

ARTICLE 1.

The Dalai Lama, Sovereign of Tibet, approves of and acknowledges the formation of an independent Mongolian State, and the proclamation on the 9th day of the 11th month of the year of the Swine, of the master of the Yellow Faith Je-tsun Dampa Lama as the Sovereign of the land.

ARTICLE 2.

The Sovereign of the Mongolian people Je-tsun Dampa Lama approves and acknowledges the formation of an independent State and the proclamation of the Dalai Lama as Sovereign of Tibet.

ARTICLE 3.

Both States shall take measures, after mutual consideration, for the prosperity of the Buddhist faith.

ARTICLE 4.

Both States, the Mongolian and the Tibetan, shall henceforth, for all time, afford each other aid against dangers from without and from within.

ARTICLE 5.

Both States, each on its own territory, shall afford mutual aid to their subjects, travelling officially and privately on religious or on State business.

ARTICLE 6.

Both States, the Mongolian and the Tibetan, shall, as formerly, carry on mutual trade in the produce of their lands—in goods, cattle, &c., and likewise open industrial institutions.

[1] pp. 10–13 of *With the Russians in Mongolia*, by Perry-Ayscough and Otter-Barry (John Lane).

ARTICLE 7.

Henceforth transactions on credit shall be allowed only with the knowledge and permission of official institutions; without such permission no claims shall be examined by Government Institutions.

Should such agreements have been entered into before the conclusion of the present treaty, and should the parties thereto be unable to settle matters amicably, while the loss suffered is great, the payment of such debts may be enforced by the said institutions, but in no case shall the debts concern the *Shabinars* and *Hoshuns*.

(*Shabinars*—people who depend from the Court of Hu-tuk-tu and pay taxes to the Court Department.)

(*Hoshun*—principality.)

ARTICLE 8.

Should it be necessary to supplement the articles of this treaty, the Mongolian and Tibetan Governments shall appoint special Plenipotentiaries, who shall come to an Agreement according to the circumstances then existing.

ARTICLE 9.

The present treaty shall come into force on the date of the signature thereof.

Plenipotentiaries of the Mongolian Government : Acting Ministers of Foreign Affairs Biliktu da-Lama Rabdan and Assistant Minister-General and Manlai Caatyr Bei-Tzu Damdinsurun.

Plenipotentiaries of the Dalai Lama, Sovereign of Tibet : Gujir tsanshib Kanchen Lubsan-Agwan Choinzin, Tshichamtso, manager of the Bank of Tibet, and Gendun-Galsan, secretary.

According to the Mongolian chronology, on the 4th day of the 12th month of the second year of ' Him who is exalted by all '.[1]

According to the chronology of Tibet, in the year of the Water-mouse, on the same month and day.

APPENDIX XIV [2]

RUSSO-CHINESE AGREEMENT, 1913.

Signed at Peking on the 5th (18th) November 1913.

The Russian Government having formulated the principles constituting the basis of its relations with China regarding Outer Mongolia, and the Chinese Government having signified its approval thereof, the two Powers agree as follows :—

1. Russia recognizes Outer Mongolia as being under the suzerainty of China.

[1] Or ' The Unanimously Proclaimed '. See Appendix XII.
[2] pp. 40–2 of *With the Russians in Mongolia*, by Perry-Ayscough and Otter-Barry (John Lane).

2. China recognizes the autonomy of Outer Mongolia.

3. Recognizing the exclusive right of the Mongols of Outer Mongolia to administer their internal affairs and to settle all commercial and industrial questions concerning autonomous Mongolia, China will not maintain there either civil or military officials, and will abstain from all colonization,—it being understood, however, that a dignitary sent by the Chinese Government can reside in Urga, accompanied by the requisite subordinate staff and an escort. Also China may station in certain localities of Outer Mongolia, to be arranged subsequently, agents for the protection of the interests of her subjects. Russia, in turn, undertakes not to maintain troops in Outer Mongolia, with the exception of Consular guards, nor to interfere with the administration, and to refrain from colonization.

4. China will accept the good offices of Russia to establish her relations with Outer Mongolia conformably with the above principles and the stipulations of the Convention of Urga concluded between Russia and Mongolia on November 3rd, 1912.

5. Questions regarding the interests of China and Russia in Outer Mongolia arising from the new conditions will form the subject of subsequent negotiations.

The Notes exchanged are to the following effect :—

1. Russia recognizes that the territory of Outer Mongolia forms part of Chinese territory.

2. In any negotiations regarding political and territorial questions between the Chinese and Russian Governments, the authorities of Outer Mongolia will participate.

3. All three parties will participate in the negotiations referred to in Article 5 of the Declaration and designate the place of meeting.

4. Autonomous Outer Mongolia will comprise the regions formerly under the jurisdiction of the Chinese Amban at Urga, the Tartar General at Uliassutai, and the Chinese Amban at Kobdo ; but since no detailed maps exist and the boundaries are uncertain, it is agreed that the frontier of Outer Mongolia, together with the boundaries between Kobdo and the Altai Mountains, shall be the subject of negotiations as provided in Article 5 of the Declaration.

INDEX

Abbots, character and intelligence of, 136, 137 ; rule of, 142.
Abors, 7, 107.
A-chuk Tse-ring, 177 ; ability of, 94 ; death of, 184.
Administration, orderly nature of Tibet, 189.
Afghanistan, compared with Nepal, 242 ; subsidy to, 110.
Almora, 7.
Altan Khan, 34.
Altyn-tagh, 6.
Amban, 60, 62, 68, 106, 124, 215, 216, 249 ; contest of, with Dalai Lama, 139 ; contest of, with Tibetan Minister, 117, 118 ; Dalai Lama on escort of, 250 ; on origin of, 250 ; on readmission of, 250 ; infringes treaty, 116 ; letter to Bhutanese Chiefs, 100, 101 ; Tibetan Government's reports to, 55.
Ambans murder Tibetan Regent, 40 ; powers of, 44, 45.
Am-do, 6, 33, 226.
America, Tibetan opinion regarding, 223.
Amitabha, 35.
Anglicization of Tibet, 261.
Anglo-Chinese Convention of 1906, 88 ; terms of, 287–9 ; Tibetan Government repudiates, 111.
Anglo-Russian Agreement, 90 ; Arrangement concerning Tibet, terms of, 290, 291.
Anti-British reports in Lhasa, 199.
Antiseptics, appreciation of, by Tibetans, 267.
Antonio de Andrada, 36.
Appointments made by Dalai Lama, 136.
Arka Tagh, 10.
Armies in Tibet, how fed, 43 ; strength exaggerated, 277.
Army, Tibetan : see Tibetan army.
Arun river, 19.
Asia, future of British in, 244.
Asiatic nations, friction between, 239.
Assembly National : see National Assembly.
Astrology, 25.

Astronomy, 25.
Atisha, 31.
Atmosphere, clearness of, 17.
Avalokitesvara, 35.

' Bag of Lies, the ', 139.
Bailey, Capt. (now Major), 94.
Baltistan, 28.
Bank of Dalai Lama, in Mongolia, 130.
Barley that never ripens, 78.
Barley-flour, 159.
Barons, rule of, 142.
Barrier formed by Tibet and Himalaya, 190, 191.
Bashahr, 7.
Ba-tang, 6, 60, 93, 94, 105, 157 ; overpowered by Chinese, 95.
Baths imported into Tibet, 164, 165.
Bell Mission, 177–207 ; house provided for, 180, 181 ; rumoured massacre of, 187 ; abstains from shooting and fishing, 198 ; opposition of Indians to, 198 ; courtesy of Tibetans to, 204, 205 ; effect of, on Nepalese, 240 ; receives congratulations of Viceroy and Secretary of State, 203 ; departure of, from Lhasa, 206 ; economy of, 207.
Bell, Mr. (now Sir Charles), study of Tibetan language, &c. by, 2 ; work of, 2–4 ; dispatched through Bhutan, 67 ; posted to Sikkim and Chumbi Valley, 73 ; transferred from Tibet to India, 74 ; appealed to as regards Buddhist oracle, 79, 80 ; returns to Sikkim and Tibet, 82 ; arrival of, at Shigatse, 82 ; public reception of, by Tashi Lama, 83 ; private visits of, to Tashi Lama, 83 ; relations of, with Mr. Chang Yin Tang, 89 ; advocates investigation of north-east frontier, 108 ; signs Bhutan Treaty, 297 ; first interview of, with Dalai Lama, 111 ; mediation of, contemplated by Dalai Lama, 121 ; numerous interviews of, with Dalai Lama, 123, 124 ; correspondence of, with Dalai Lama, 145 ; invited

INDEX

315

of Tibet to, 91 ; interests of, in
Tibet, 193 ; invaded by Tibetans,
28 ; little known to Tibetan
Government, 131 ; needs Tibet
as a barrier, 246 ; security of,
116 ; Tibetan frontier with, 29.
Indian agitators deported by Tibetan
Government, 199.
— army, Tibetan soldiers for, 268,
269.
— climate, health of Tibetan Ministers in, 159.
— frontier politics, future of, 246.
— frontier States, 262.
— Government, treatment of Tashi
Lama by, 258, 259.
— Home Rule, 199, 200 ; effect on
Tibet, 244, 245.
— merchants on Tibetan border,
262.
— money-lending to be discouraged
in Tibet, 262.
— pandits and priests visit Tibet,
31.
— sorcery, 26.
— teachers, 27.
Indianization of Tibet, 261.
Indians in Lhasa, 199.
— opposition of, to Bell Mission,
198.
— travel of, in Tibet, restricted, 91.
Indus river, 7, 11.
Influenza, 178.
Inner Minister, 273.
Inner Tibet, 154, 155 ; Tibetan
authority in, 251 ; Tibetan Prime
Minister's views regarding, 155.
Insurrection, both sides in, approach
Mr. Bell, 188, 189 ; quelled, 189.
Internal administration, 57.
— order, preservation of, 193.
' Interpreter of Bhutan, The ', 243.
Interpreters, 259.
Invasions of Tibet : by Mirza
Haidar, 34 ; by Dogras, 46 ; by
Gurkhas, 41-4, 46, 47 ; by
British, 66-71 ; by Chinese, 95-8.
Irawadi river, 13.
Irrigation first established, 23.
Ivan Chen, Mr., 157, 158.

Jam-pe-yang, 131.
Japan, 192, 220-2 ; Daimyos of,
255 ; Tibetan feeling towards,
220, 221 ; visited by Tibetans,
221.
Japan-China war, 61.
Japanese, 173, 174 ; drill for Tibetan
troops, 163 ; influence in Mongolia, 225 ; interest in Tibet

taken by, 221, 222 ; munitions
for Tibet, 221 ; power of, in
Mongolia, 220.
Japanese in Lhasa, 220.
Japanese newspaper on increased
British prestige in Tibet, 221.
Jelf, Mr., 112.
Jenghiz Khan, 30.
' Jewel Park ' : see Nor-pu Ling-ka.
Jimdar, 260.
Joint investigators must be unani-
mous, 136.
Jordan, Sir John, 92, 96.
Judge of the dead, 239.
Judicial cases : Chumbi Valley, 75 ;
decision by Dalai Lama can be
claimed, 136.
— inquiries, method of, 136.
Judiciary transferred to monks, 141.
Justice in Sikkim, 171.

Kailas, Mt., 11.
Kalimpong, 19, 78 ; rumour in,
that Bell Mission had been
massacred, 187 ; settlement work
in, 171.
Kampa Dzong, British Mission to,
in 1903, 66.
Kampu, hot springs at, 77.
— Valley, 74, 78.
Kang-hsi, 40.
Kan-gyur, 77, 86.
Kansu, 224.
Karak, 7.
Karma, doctrine of, 27.
Kashgar, 28.
Kashmir, 63.
Katmandu, 37, 41.
Kawaguchi, Mr. Ekai, 63, 220.
Kazi U-gyen, 62, 67, 102, 104.
Kennedy, Capt. (now Lt. Col.),
94, 102, 104, 177, 187, 220, 226,
267.
Kennion, Capt. (now Lt. Col.), 62.
Kerosene oil, 296.
Khublai Khan converted by High
Priest of Sakya, 31.
' King of Love ', image of, 169.
King, The, answers letter from Dalai
Lama, 115 ; interview with Maha-
raja of Bhutan, 119 ; receives
congratulations from Dalai Lama,
168.
Kings, early, 271.
Kiria river, 10.
Kirong, 19.
Koko Nor, 6, 15, 29, 37, 226 ;
fixed as north-eastern boundary
of Tibet, 29.
Kong-po, 107.

INDEX

Tibetan civilization, whence derived, 25.
— Conference, mistakes to be avoided in, 252 ; where to be held, 252.
— conquests, 25, 28, 29.
— Council urges Mr. Bell to remain at work, 176.
— crowds, 183.
— doctors, 76, 267, 268.
— friendship for Britain, how gained, 111, 146.
— geography, 11.
— Government, Anglo-Chinese (Sikkim) Convention of 1890 accepted by, in 1904, 284 ; anxiety of, during World War, 166, 167 ; army increased by, 185 ; brings seals of office to India, 109 ; British distrusted by, 84 ; changes from enmity to friendship, 129, 161, 162 ; Chinese connexion pleaded by, 56 ; Chinese unable to control, 66 ; deports anti-British Indians, 199 ; desire of, to develop mines, 158, 159 ; difficulties of, 160, 254, 255 ; disavows Chinese suzerainty, 56 ; discontinues Mission to China, 175 ; foreign exploration disliked by, 262, 263 ; good faith of, 229 ; granaries of, 164 ; invites Mr. Bell to Lhasa, 145 ; knows but little of India, 131 ; party factions in, 120 ; predicts Chinese intervention in States on Indian frontier, 111 ; receives arms from Russian Government, 64 ; regains power in Central Tibet, 121 ; rejects Chinese proposals, 173 ; replies to, should not be delayed, 268 ; repudiates Chinese suzerainty and Anglo - Chinese Convention of 1906, 111 ; result of good relations with, 84 ; revenue and expenditure of, 144, 254-7 ; 'sick but not dead', 117 ; verbal message to Mr. Bell from, 160, 161 ; visits of foreigners, 263 ; withholds information from frontier officials, 238.
— hardihood, 127.
— histories, 22–35 ; monks forbidden to read, 22 ; teachings of, 116.
— independence, 217.
— insurrection, both sides in, approach Mr. Bell, 188, 189 ; quelled, 189.
— ladies, care of complexions, 17 ; love of dress and jewellery, 17.

Tibetan language, need for learning, 259.
— medicinal herbs, 219.
— Minister, contest of wits with Amban, 117 ; dismissal of, 187, 188 ; feeling of, towards British Government, 191, 192.
— Ministers, 112 ; blessing of, by Dalai Lama, 138 ; bored with antiquities, 159 ; change of attitude in, 129, 161, 162 ; choosing of, 137 ; distressed surprise of, 115 ; health of, in Indian climate, 159 ; imprisoned, 66 ; protection of, in India, 110 ; quick to show their feelings, 129 ; responsible for the acts of their rulers, 85 ; urge Mr. Bell to remain in Lhasa, 186 ; wish to see factories, 159.
— momo (pastry puff), 133, 134.
— New Year, 186.
— nobility, agents of, in Mongolia, 228.
— officials : compared with Chinese, 213, 214 ; copies of treaties not given to, 238.
— opinion on relations with Nepal, 237–9.
— postal service, 177, 201, 202.
— power influences British policy, 122.
— priesthood, power of the, 266.
— prophecies : British, 114 ; Chang Shambala, 132 ; Great War, 168 ; Mr. Bell, 186 ; Tibet the 'root' of China, 212, 213.
— Regent, 124, 191.
— Representative, need for, at Tibetan Conference, 252.
— revenue, 290.
— rule, extent of country under, 5.
— sayings : see Sayings.
— settlements in Peking, 208.
— soldier in Boer War, 268.
— soldiers, drilling of, 163, 164 ; fined for losing rifles, 162 ; in Indian army, 268, 269.
— tea, etiquette regarding, 180.
— territory, integrity of, 288, 290.
— trade with China, 219.
— troops forbidden to fight Chinese, 97.
— verses : see Verses.
— writing, introduction of, 23.
Tibetans : aid Sikkim, 46 ; blame ministers rather than rulers, 85 ; capture Chinese capital in eighth century, 28 ; Chinese treatment of, 248 ; demand modern rifles,